About the editors

Radhika Balakrishnan is Professor, Women's ar
and executive director of the Center for Womer
Rutgers University, in New Brunswick, NJ. She has a PhD in economics
from Rutgers University. Previously, she was Professor of Economics
and International Studies at Marymount Manhattan College. She
has worked at the Ford Foundation as a programme officer in the
Asia Regional Programme. She is currently the chair of the board of
the US Human Rights Network and on the board of the Center for
Constitutional Rights. She has published in the field of gender and
development and economic policy and human rights. Her publications
include: 'Financial regulation, capabilities and human rights in the US
financial crisis: the case of housing', co-authored with Diane Elson and
James Heintz (*Journal of Human Development and Capabilities*, 12(1):
153–68, 2011); *Rethinking Macro-economic Strategies from a Human Rights
Perspective* (Why MES with Human Rights II), 2009; *Why MES with
Human Rights: Integrating Macro-economic Strategies with Human Rights*,
2005. She has also authored numerous articles that have appeared in
books and journals.

Diane Elson holds a chair in sociology at the University of Essex, UK,
and is a member of the Essex Human Rights Centre. She has acted as
adviser to UNIFEM, UNDP, Oxfam and other development agencies
and is a past vice-president of the International Association for Feminist
Economics. She has published widely on gender and development. Her
recent publications include: 'Financial regulation, capabilities and human rights in the US financial crisis: the case of housing', co-authored
with Radhika Balakrishnan and James Heintz (*Journal of Human
Development and Capabilities*, 12(1): 153–68, 2011); *Budgeting for Women's
Rights; Monitoring Government Budgets for Compliance with CEDAW*,
UNIFEM, New York, 2006; '"Women's rights are human rights": campaigns and concepts', in L. Morris (ed.), *Rights: Sociological Perspectives*,
Routledge, 2006; 'Auditing economic policy in the light of obligations
on economic and social rights' (*Essex Human Rights Review*, 5(1), 2008);
and 'Gender equality and economic growth in the World Bank' (*World
Development Report*, 2006, *Feminist Economics*, 15(3), 2009). Her academic degrees include a BA in philosophy, politics and economics from
the University of Oxford and a PhD in economics from the University
of Manchester.

ECONOMIC POLICY AND HUMAN RIGHTS

HOLDING GOVERNMENTS TO ACCOUNT

edited by Radhika Balakrishnan and Diane Elson

Zed Books

LONDON | NEW YORK

Economic Policy and Human Rights: Holding Governments to Account was first published in 2011 by Zed Books Ltd, 7 Cynthia Street, London N1 9JF, UK and Room 400, 175 Fifth Avenue, New York, NY 10010, USA

www.zedbooks.co.uk

Set in Monotype Plantin and FontFont Kievit by Ewan Smith, London
Index: ed.emery@thefreeuniversity.net
Cover designed by Rogue Four Design
Printed and bound in Great Britain by CPI Group (UK) Ltd, Croydon, CR0 4YY

Distributed in the USA exclusively by Palgrave Macmillan, a division of St Martin's Press, LLC, 175 Fifth Avenue, New York, NY 10010, USA

A catalogue record for this book is available from the British Library
Library of Congress Cataloging in Publication Data available

ISBN 978 1 84813 875 9 hb
ISBN 978 1 84813 874 2 pb

CONTENTS

FIGURES, TABLES AND BOX

Tables

Box

ABBREVIATIONS

AFORE	Administradora de Fondos para el Retiro
ASF	Auditoría Superior de la Federación
CEDAW	Convention on the Elimination of All Forms of Discrimination Against Women
CERD	Convention on the Elimination of All Forms of Racial Discrimination
CESCR	Committee on Economic, Social and Cultural Rights
CONSAR	Comisión Nacional del Sistema de Ahorro para el Retiro Inicio
CPI	Consumer Price Index
DB	defined benefit
DC	defined contribution
ERISA	Employee's Retirement Income Security Act
ESCR	Economic, Social and Cultural Rights
FOIA	Freedom of Information Act
GDP	gross domestic product
GNP	gross national product
HCTC	Health Care Tax Credit
ICCPR	International Covenant on Civil and Political Rights
ICESCR	International Covenant on Economic, Social and Cultural Rights
ICSID	International Centre for the Settlement of Investment Disputes
IFAI	Federal Institute for Access to Public Information
ILO	International Labour Organization
IMF	International Monetary Fund
IMSS	Mexican Social Security Institute/Instituto Mexicano del Seguro Social
IRE	Investigative Reporters and Editors
IRS	Internal Revenue Service
ISR	revenue from income tax
ISSSTE	The State Employees' Social Security and Social Services Institute
ITAM	Instituto Tecnológico Autónomo de México
ITEP	Institute on Taxation and Economic Policy
LFTAIPG	Federal Law for Access to Public and Governmental Information
Mexican CAIP	Programa Complementario de Apoyo a Comunidades y Empresas
NAALC	North American Agreement on Labour Cooperation

NADB   North American Development Bank
NAFTA   North American Free Trade Agreement
NAFTA-TAA   North American Free Trade Agreement – Transitional
            Adjustment Assistance
OECD   Organisation for Economic Co-operation and Development
PBGC   Pension Benefit Guaranty Corporation
SAT   Tax Administration Service
SHCP   Secretary of the Treasury and Public Credit/Ministry of Finance
SIEFORE   Sociedad de Inversión Especializada en Fondos para el Retiro
SSI   Supplemental Security Income
TAA   Trade Adjustment Assistance
UDHR   Universal Declaration of Human Rights
UNCITRAL   United Nations Commission on International Trade Law
UNDP   United Nations Development Programme
UPR   Universal Periodic Review
USDA   US Department of Agriculture
USITC   US International Trade Commission
VAT   value added tax

ACKNOWLEDGEMENTS

This book draws on four years of collaborative work undertaken in the United States and Mexico. Many people and organizations have been involved in this project and this book is one of the final products to emerge from the efforts of this diverse group.

The Ford Foundation has provided invaluable support at multiple levels since the inception of this project in 2006. We are indebted to Mario Bronfman and David Myhre, who facilitated the identification and selection of Mexico-based partners, and provided financial assistance as well as substantive input. Jael Silliman and Monette Zard at Ford in New York have been champions of this work, committing both resources and important advice for several years.

We would like to thank Fundar, the Center for Analysis and Investigation, who have been the primary partners in Mexico, as well as the UN Economic Commission for Latin America and the Caribbean in Mexico, who provided us with advice and important substantive support.

The project had an advisory committee of progressive economist and human rights advocates. They were: Cathy Albisa, National Economic and Social Rights Initiative; Alejandro Alvarez, Universidad Nacional Autónoma de México; Ajamu Baraka, US Human Rights Network; Ann Blyberg, International Institute of Education; Jerry Epstein, Political Economy Research Institute; Sakiko Fakudo-Parr, New School University; Alicia Giron, Universidad Nacional Autónoma de México; Shalmali Guttal, Focus on the Global South; James Heintz, Political Economy Research Institute; Margaret Huang, Right Working Group; Clara Jusidman, Iniciativa Ciudadana y Desarrollo Social, INCIDE Social; Patrick Mason, Florida State University; Aubrey McCutcheon, Global Rights; David Mhyre, Mastercard Foundation; Manuel Montes, United Nations Department of Economic and Social Affairs; Juan Carlos Moreno, Comisión Económica para América Latina y el Caribe; Lucia Fragoso Perez, Equidad; Blanca Rico, Semillas; Areli Sandoval, Equipo Pueblo. They have provided valuable insight and counsel at many stages of the project. Their input helped clarify the conceptualization and direction of the work. In particular we would like to acknowledge the contributions of Clara Jusidman. Caren Grown, William Milberg and Christian Weller gave advice on various chapters and we thank them for their insight and suggestions. Savi Bisnath provided editorial help in early drafts of select chapters.

Mehilka Hoodbhoy was the rapporteur at the first project meeting and

Rajeev Patel was the rapporteur and co-authored the report from the second meeting. Several students from Marymount Manhattan College helped as research assistants: Ryan Francis, Alexis Krauss, Daniel Mathews, Chris Perre and Audrey Thweatt.

We would also like to thank the staff at the Center for Women's Global Leadership at Rutgers University for all the help they provided as this book was being written: Margot Baruch, Natalia Cardona, Jewel Daney, Mika Kinose, Keely Swan and Lucy Vidal. Sarah Weirich and Nadine Banu Olcay were our primary research assistants and helped in the final editing of this book. We would not have been able to complete this without their help.

We would like to thank David Gillcrist, who has always provided valuable intellectual advice and, when we needed it the most, great company and good food and drink to keep us going.

Finally we would like to thank all the authors of the chapters in this book. They have been an outstanding team, able to work collaboratively over many changes, and we thank everyone for their hard work as well as their humour and friendship.

Radhika Balakrishnan and Diane Elson

INTRODUCTION: ECONOMIC POLICIES AND HUMAN RIGHTS OBLIGATIONS

Radhika Balakrishnan and Diane Elson

The current global economic crisis is evidence that the neoliberal economic policies that have been followed for almost three decades have not worked. The devastation that the crisis has already wrought on the most vulnerable households in the global North and global South is a reminder that the formulation of economic policy and the realization of human rights (economic and social rights, as well as political, civil and cultural rights) have, for too long, been divorced from one another. Over the past three decades, economic policy has been geared towards achieving economic growth, underwritten by assumptions about the virtues of the market. Efficiency rather than ethics has been the focus of concern. When attention has been paid to human rights, economic policy-making has proceeded with the assertion that economic growth, no matter how skewed in favour of a few, will ultimately benefit all by providing resources for the realization of human rights. Yet the means adopted to achieve economic growth may be responsible for undermining goals in the domain of human rights. It is clearly time to assess economic policy using the ethical lens of the human rights standards that all governments have agreed upon. This book contributes to such an assessment by presenting a framework for the assessment of macroeconomic policies in the light of the human rights obligations of government on economic and social rights; and applying it to the conduct of the macroeconomic policies of Mexico and the USA, including fiscal, monetary, trade and regulatory policies; and related achievements in economic and social rights.

We focused on these two countries because we wanted to test out our approach by examining two countries of comparable size, but different levels of economic development, and different levels of legislative commitment to economic and social rights. The fact that these two countries border one another and are closely linked by trade and migration also meant that we could highlight issues of the obligations of governments to people who are not their citizens and/or do not live in their jurisdiction. Our aim was not so much to compare the economic and social rights achievements in the two countries, as to examine how each had been living up to its human rights obligations. On a variety of the indicators we consider, we compare the USA with other high-income countries that are members of the Organisation for

Economic Co-operation and Development (OECD); and Mexico with other middle-income countries in Latin America. The study pays particular attention to gender, class, race, ethnicity and citizenship status. The important question of cultural rights is beyond the scope of this book, but we do examine as far as possible the obligation to ensure non-discrimination in the enjoyment of economic and social rights by different ethnic groups. Our entry point is the conduct of macroeconomic policy, and so this book is organized in terms of policy instruments, with a chapter on how the policy has been used in Mexico, followed by a chapter on how the policy has been used in the USA.

The analysis we present of Mexico and the USA shows how our framework can be applied in practice; and we believe it can be a guide to its application to other countries. The book demonstrates the kinds of statistical and documentary evidence required to examine how far a government is conducting its macroeconomic policy in line with its human rights obligations; and whether there is cause for concern as to whether these policies are supporting or undermining the realization of economic and social rights. We hope it will inspire others to try out our framework to analyse other countries.

Dialogue between human rights advocates and progressive economists

The analysis presented here is the outcome of a dialogue between a group of human rights advocates and progressive economists, who share similar goals of promoting social justice.[1]

In the human rights community, there has been an increasing interest in economic and social rights, including the equal enjoyment of such rights; and growing concern that neoliberal policies, based on mainstream, neoclassical economics, are not helping to support the realization of these rights. However, neoclassical economics is not the only kind of economics; there have always been progressive, critical economists, committed to the creation of social justice, analysing economies using different conceptual approaches. These economists present diverse alternatives to the neoliberal orthodoxy, drawing upon Keynesian, structuralist, Marxist, ecological and feminist thinking. (Amartya Sen has called this group of economists 'non-conformist economists', because they do not conform to the currently dominant forms of economic analysis and policy prescription.)[2] Some heterodox economists have received acclaim: for example, Paul Krugman, Amartya Sen and Joe Stiglitz have won the Nobel Prize for economics. The United Nations has provided a venue for progressive economics in publications like the annual UNDP *Human Development Report*.

The default position of heterodox economists is an empirically based scepticism about competitive markets' ability to use resources efficiently, and an appreciation that competition can sometimes be wasteful. These debates have gained currency lately; discussions about the causes of the ongoing global economic crisis, for example, have centred on the weaknesses of poorly regulated financial markets, and the consequences for society when markets systematically fail.

- Keynesian economists stress that competitive markets cannot be relied upon to achieve full employment, in the form of decent jobs for all who want them. There is waste of human capacities, reflected in unemployment, underemployment and exploitative employment.
- Feminist economists stress that competitive markets cannot be relied upon to achieve sufficient provision of good-quality care for all who need it; nor for an appropriate balance between paid work, unpaid work, and leisure for care providers. The result is a waste of human capacities, reflected in both neglect of some who need care, and over-work for some who provide it.
- Ecological economists stress that competitive markets cannot be relied upon to achieve sustainable economies. There is waste of natural resources, reflected in environmental degradation.

Heterodox economists and human rights advocates share an ultimate goal: to promote human flourishing, and to protect human beings from the vulnerabilities and insecurities to which the current global economy has exposed them. Human rights have significant economic implications, since promoting, protecting and fulfilling them require resources and involve costs. In turn, economic policies have significant impacts on human rights; they shape the extent to which the economic and social rights of different groups of people are realized. Both progressive economists and human rights advocates challenge a vision of economic development that claims that remaining internationally competitive must be the key objective, despite growing inequality and increasing risk.

Human rights activism and advocacy typically focus on the violations and deprivations suffered by individuals and social groups, but have little to say about ways in which economic analysis and policies may contribute to these problems. Heterodox economists have provided alternative analysis and policy advice, but have typically not linked this to an explicit ethical framework. The norms and standards of human rights offer progressive economists a widely accepted ethical language in which to pose economic questions without reducing them to simple questions of economic calculus. The ethical appeal of human rights offers a framework for social mobilization for economic justice in a way that potentially transcends sectional interests. The legal and quasi-legal processes of international human rights reporting and monitoring offer other arenas in which to contest the hegemony of neoliberal economic policies.

Clarification of human rights obligations

The Universal Declaration of Human Rights (UDHR) includes economic and social rights, as well as civil and political rights, and makes no arbitrary distinction between them. It states in its Preamble that 'Member States have pledged themselves to achieve, in co-operation with the United Nations, the promotion of universal respect for and observance of human rights and fundamental freedoms'. It proclaims the Declaration to be 'a common standard of achievement for all peoples and all nations'. Article 28 of the Declaration states that 'Everyone is entitled to a social and international order in which the rights and freedoms set forth in this Declaration can be fully realized.' All states that are party to the UDHR (which include the USA and Mexico) have a moral obligation to realize this pledge and to realize the rights specified in the UDHR.

The UDHR has been followed by a series of international treaties which legally bind the states that have ratified[3] them (and are described as being 'party' to them) to realize the rights contained therein. In 1965 came the Convention on the Elimination of All Forms of Racial Discrimination (CERD); followed in 1966 by the International Covenant on Civil and Political Rights (ICCPR) and the International Covenant on Economic, Social and Cultural Rights (ICESCR); and in 1979 by the Convention on the Elimination of All Forms of Discrimination Against Women (CEDAW).[4]

Mexico is party to all of these treaties. The USA is party to CERD and ICCPR but not to ICESCR and CEDAW. However, this does not mean that the USA has no legally binding obligations with respect to economic and social rights. As pointed out by the Center for Economic and Social Rights:

> Even states that have not ratified international treaties on ESCR are bound to respect human rights principles that are part of 'customary law', law that has gained universal acceptance in the international community. The Universal Declaration is widely considered to be part of customary law and therefore binding on all states, whether or not they have ratified subsequent human rights treaties. (Center for Economic and Social Rights 2000: 7)

The US government has accepted that it is subject to the Universal Periodic Review (UPR) process, which involves a review of the human rights records of each of the 192 UN member states once every four years. In November 2010 the USA was reviewed by the Human Rights Council under the UPR process. The report that the USA submitted to the Council referred to economic and social rights, though not in explicit terms of particular obligations.[5] However, in the US response to the recommendations made to them by other member states, the State Department agreed to recommendations concerning economic, social and cultural rights: 'We have continued to establish programs that empower our citizens to live what FDR called a "healthy peacetime life." The recent landmark healthcare reform is the latest major example, and we are committed to continue pursuing policies that will build an economy and society that lifts us all.'[6] Many of the recommendations that were made during the process referred to economic and social rights and over twenty countries urged the USA to ratify ICESCR. The final response from the US government was due in March 2011. The US government did not ratify the ICESCR.

The Universal Declaration of Human Rights includes the following economic and social rights: Right to work (Article 23); Right to rest and leisure (Article 24); Right to an adequate standard of living, including food, clothing, housing, medical care and necessary social services, and right to security in the event of unemployment, sickness, disability, widowhood, old age or other lack of livelihood in circumstances beyond their control (Article 25); and Right to education (Article 26). These are spelled out in more detail in the International Covenant on Economic, Social and Cultural Rights and other treaties.[7]

Economic and social rights need to be considered in the context of the principle of the indivisibility of human rights. The human rights framework sees a human as a whole person whose rights are indivisible and interdependent and intrinsic to the status of being human. Therefore it is not permissible for a state to ignore some rights and focus only on others; or to seek to discharge its obligations with respect to some rights in ways that violate other rights. So while focusing on economic and social rights, it is also important to keep in mind the International Covenant on Civil and Political Rights (ICCPR), which provides for important checks and balances on the power of the state. ICCPR has some important implications for the conduct of economic policy, including, for instance, the right 'to seek, receive and impart information' (Article 19).

In addition to the UN human rights instruments, there are also a series of Conventions of the International Labour Organization. Particularly important is the ILO Declaration on Fundamental Principles and Rights at Work (1998), which reaffirms, as fundamental rights, freedom of association, the effective recognition of the right to collective bargaining, the elimination of all forms of forced or compulsory labour, the effective abolition of child labour, and the elimination of discrimination with respect to employment and occupation (Valticos 1998). As well as the international human rights system, some regions also have a regional human rights system. The inter-American human rights system is based on the American Convention on Human Rights (which entered into force in 1978). Mexico both signed and ratified the Convention. The USA signed the Convention but Congress has not ratified it. Nevertheless, the USA is considered a member of the inter-American human rights system, and provides financial support to the Inter-American Commission on Human Rights. The Convention's provisions on economic and social rights have been expanded by the Additional Protocol in the Area of Economic, Social and Cultural Rights (the Protocol of San Salvador), which has been ratified by Mexico but not the USA.

The obligations implied by international human rights instruments have been spelled out more fully through a number of mechanisms, including General Comments and General Recommendations issued from time to time by UN treaty monitoring bodies such as the Committee on Economic, Social and Cultural Rights (CESCR); and by experts in international law, such as the groups of experts who produced the Limburg Principles on the Implementation of the International Covenant on Economic, Social and Cultural Rights (1986) and the Maastricht Guidelines on Violations of Economic, Social and Cultural Rights (1997).[8]

The CESCR has stated (in General Comment 12, 'The Right to Adequate Food', and in other subsequent General Comments) that human rights treaties give states duties to respect, protect and fulfil human rights. These duties have been spelt out in the following way in the Maastricht Guidelines on Violations of Economic, Social and Cultural Rights:

> The obligation to *respect* requires states to refrain from interfering with the enjoyment of economic, social and cultural rights. Thus the right to housing is violated if the State engages in arbitrary forced evictions.
>
> The obligation to *protect* requires States to prevent violations of such rights by third parties. Thus the failure to ensure that private employers comply with basic labour standards may amount to a violation of the right to work or the right to just and favourable conditions of work.
>
> The obligation to *fulfil* requires States to take appropriate legislative, administrative, budgetary, judicial and other measures towards the full realization of such rights. Thus, the failure of States to provide essential primary health care to those in need may amount to a violation.

Each of these obligations contains elements of obligations of *conduct*, and obligations of *result* (see CESCR, General Comment 3, 'The Nature of States Parties' Obligations', 1999). The Maastricht Guidelines explain these obligations thus:

> The obligation of *conduct* requires action reasonably calculated to realize the enjoyment of a particular right ... The obligation of *result* requires States to achieve specific targets to satisfy a detailed substantive standard.

The obligations of states extend beyond their own borders, as is made clear in the UN Charter Articles 55 and 56. Obligations with respect to international development cooperation between governments are explicitly referred to in Article 2 of ICESCR, and underlined in specific provisions in Article 11 (right to an adequate standard of living). Articles 22 and 23 specifically refer to the need for international measures. CESCR General Comment 3, 'The Nature of States Parties' Obligations', explicitly states that: 'international co-operation for development ... is an obligation of all States'.

Obligations with respect to international trade and investment have been clarified further in the period since 2000, when a report of the UN secretary-general stated that: 'The norms and standards of international human rights law have an important role in providing principles for globalization' (UN Secretary-General 2000). The UN High Commissioner for Human Rights has subsequently produced a number of reports on trade and investment clarifying that international trade and investment agreements must be consistent with the human rights obligations of states (see, for instance, Report E/CN.4/2002/54, which focuses on trade in agriculture, and Report E/CN.4/Sub.2/2003/9, which focuses on investment).

Key principles in meeting obligations regarding economic and social rights

States enjoy a margin of discretion in selecting the means to carry out their obligations, but in discharging their obligations regarding realization of economic and social rights, states must pay regard to the following key points: the requirement for progressive realization; the use of maximum available resources; the avoidance of retrogression; the satisfaction of minimum essential levels of economic and social rights; non-discrimination and equality; and participation, transparency and accountability.

Progressive realization The ICESCR specifies that states parties have the obligation of 'achieving progressively the full realization of the rights recognized in the present Covenant' 'to the maximum of available resources'. This obligation does recognize that the resources at the disposition of a government are not unlimited, and that fulfilling economic and social rights will take time. At the same time, the concept of 'progressive realization' is not intended to take away all 'meaningful content' of a state's obligation to realize economic, social and cultural rights (CESCR, General Comment 3, para. 9). Progressive realization imposes a 'specific and continuing' (CESCR General Comment 12, para. 44) or 'constant and continuing' (CESCR, General Comment 15, para. 18) duty to move as 'expeditiously and effectively as possible' (CESCR, General Comment 3, para. 9; CESCR, General Comment 12, para. 44; CESCR, General Comment 15, para. 18) towards full realization of rights. These steps towards full realization of rights must be 'taken within a reasonable short time after the Covenant's entry into force for the States concerned' and such steps should be 'deliberate, concrete and targeted as clearly as possible' in order to meet the obligations of states (CESCR, General Comment 3, para. 2; CESCR, General Comment 12, para. 43; CESCR, General Comment 15, para. 17).

Maximum available resources The definition of the 'maximum available resources', which the government should utilize for 'progressive realization' of human rights, has not yet been fully elaborated. CESCR made a statement in 2007 entitled 'An Evaluation of the Obligation to Take Steps to the "Maximum of Available Resources" Under an Optional Protocol to the Covenant'. However, the statement did not define what constitutes 'available resources', beyond stating that it refers to 'both the resources existing within a state as well as those available from the international community through international cooperation and assistance' (E/C.12/2007/1).

It seems reasonable to argue that 'maximum available resources' does not just depend on the level of output of an economy, its rate of growth, and the level and growth of inflows of resources from other economies. It also depends on how the state mobilizes resources from the people living under its jurisdiction to fund its obligation to fulfil human rights. For instance, if it generates very little revenue, it will be able to provide only limited public services. The key role of taxation has been noted by some of the UN Special Rapporteurs on human rights. For instance, the Special Rapporteur on the right to education has noted that 'It is hard to imagine how any state would raise the revenue to finance health, education, water, and sanitation, or assistance for those too young or too old to work, were it not for taxation' (Tomasevski 2005: 5). Another Special Rapporteur who has commented on taxation is Philip Alston, Special Rapporteur on extrajudicial, summary or arbitrary executions. In a statement of the Human Rights Council in March 2007, he comments that in Guatemala

> The reason the executive branch of the Guatemalan State has so little money to spend on the criminal justice system is that the Congress resist the imposition of all but the most perfunctory taxes. To put this in perspective, as a percentage of GDP, Guatemala's total tax revenue in 2005 was 9.6 percent of GDP. By regional comparison, its percentage tax revenue is lower than that of Belize, Costa Rica, El Salvador, Honduras, or Nicaragua, and radically lower than that of the countries of South America.

Of course, the system of taxation must be organized so as to comply with human rights standards. Tomasevski (2005) notes that the European Court of Human Rights has legitimized the power of states to levy taxes, provided that judicial remedies exist to prevent taxation amounting to arbitrary confiscation. She further notes that 'The human rights jurisprudence regarding taxation has affirmed the principle of ability to contribute.' Taxation must also be non-discriminatory as between different social groups, such as women and men (Elson 2006).

Non-retrogression There is a strong presumption that retrogressive measures on the part of a state are not permitted. An example of a potentially retrogressive measure would be cuts to expenditures on public services that are critical for realization of economic and social rights; or cuts to taxes that are critical for funding such services. CESCR has stated that:

> ... any deliberately retrogressive measures ... would require the most careful consideration and would need to be fully justified by reference to totality of rights provided for in the Covenant and in context of the full use of the maximum of available resources. (CESCR General Comment 3, para. 9)

Minimum essential levels/minimum core obligations States that are parties to the ICESCR are also under a 'minimum core' obligation to ensure the satisfaction of, at the very least, 'minimum essential levels of each of the rights' in the ICESCR. This means that a state party in which any 'significant number' of persons is 'deprived of essential foodstuffs, of essential primary healthcare, etc. is prima facie failing to meet obligations' under the Covenant (CESCR, General Comment 3, para. 10). The Committee on Economic, Social and Cultural Rights has clarified that this is a continuing obligation, requiring states with inadequate resources to strive to ensure enjoyment of rights (General Comment 3, para. 11). However, even in times of severe resource constraints, states must ensure that rights are fulfilled for vulnerable members of society through the adoption of relatively low-cost targeted programmes (General Comment 3, para. 12; General Comment 12, para. 28; General Comment 14, para. 18). The Committee on Economic, Social and Cultural Rights has begun to identify the content of the minimum core obligations with respect to the rights to food, education, health and water (General Comments 11, 13, 14 and 15 respectively), though it has not specified this in quantitative terms. The provision of minimum essential levels is an immediate obligation. This means that it is the duty of the state to prioritize the rights of the poorest and most vulnerable people. Nevertheless, this does not imply that states must adopt a very narrowly targeted approach, using special programmes which are only for the very poor. The Committee on Economic, Social and Cultural Rights has emphasized that 'the obligation remains for a State party to strive to ensure the widest possible enjoyment of the relevant rights' (General Comment 3, para. 11). Several UN Special Rapporteurs have highlighted the importance of broad-based systems as the best way to meet minimum core obligations.

Non-discrimination and equality A fundamental aspect of states' human rights obligations is that of non-discrimination and equality. The UDHR Article 2 states that:

> Everyone is entitled to all the rights and freedoms set forth in this Declaration without distinction of any kind, such as race, colour, sex, language, religion, political or other opinion, national or social origin, property, birth or other status.

It is widely recognized that the term 'property' in this article refers to economic status. MacNaughton (2009) points out that the official Spanish version of the UDHR translates 'property' as '*posición económica*' rather than '*propiedad*' or '*patrimonio*'. She notes that a study of the drafting of the UDHR (Morsink 1999) suggests that the drafters understood the non-discrimination provision as calling for far-reaching egalitarianism. ICCPR (Article 2) and ICESCR (Article 2) use comparable language to UDHR. The CESCR has clarified this further in General Comment 20, 'Nondiscrimination in Economic, Social and Cultural Rights', which explicitly specifies that 'other status' includes 'economic status'.

Several human rights treaties specifically deal with non-discrimination in relation to particular categories of people. For instance, CEDAW (Article 2) prohibits discrimination against women in all its forms and obligates states to condemn this discrimination and take steps 'by all appropriate means and without delay' to pursue a policy of eliminating this discrimination. Article 2 also sets out steps that a state party must take to eliminate this discrimination, including adopting appropriate legislative and other measures. Article 4(1) recognizes the legitimacy of 'temporary special measures aimed at accelerating *de facto* equality between men and women'. It is clear that CEDAW means not only the absence of a discriminatory legal framework, but also that policies must not be discriminatory in effect. CEDAW requires that states achieve both substantive and formal equality and recognizes that formal equality alone is insufficient for a state to meet its affirmative obligation to achieve substantive equality between men and women (CEDAW 2004, General Recommendation 25, para. 8).

In the same vein the International Convention for the Elimination of All Forms of Racial Discrimination (CERD, Article 2) requires that states parties condemn racial discrimination and pursue by all appropriate means and without delay a policy of eliminating racial discrimination in all its forms. The state is also obliged to take special and concrete measures to ensure the adequate development and protection of certain racial groups or individuals belonging to them, for the purpose of guaranteeing them the full and equal enjoyment of human rights and fundamental freedoms. These measures cannot maintain unequal or separate rights for different racial groups (CERD, Article 2, para. 2). CERD (Article 5, para. e) further elaborates that in compliance with the fundamental obligations laid down in Article 5 of this Convention, states parties undertake to prohibit and to eliminate racial discrimination in all its forms and to guarantee the right of everyone, without distinction as to race, colour or national or ethnic origin, to equality before the law, notably in the enjoyment of economic social and cultural rights.

The Committee on Economic, Social and Cultural Rights has made it clear that the recognition that realization of economic, social and cultural rights will be progressive does not provide states with an excuse for the persistence of discrimination. States have an immediate obligation to guarantee that there will be no discrimination in the exercise of rights (CESCR, General Comment 3, para. 2; CESCR, General Comment 12, para. 43; CESCR, General Comment 14, para. 31; CESCR, General Comment 15, para. 17). This means that non-discrimination must always be a priority in the progressive realization of economic and social rights and that any steps that a state takes to progressively realize such rights must be non-discriminatory in both policy and effect. Like provision of minimum essential levels, non-discrimination is an immediate obligation.

Accountability, participation and transparency The importance of accountability and participation is emphasized in the Limburg Principles on the implementation of ICESCR, which state that:

> States parties are accountable both to the international community and to their own people for their compliance with the obligations under the Covenant. A concerted national effort to invoke the full participation of all sectors of society is, therefore, indispensable to achieving progress in realizing economic, social and cultural rights. Popular participation is required at all stages, including the formulation, application and review of national policies. (Limburg Principles 1986)

The Committee on Economic, Social and Cultural Rights has indicated that the right of individuals to participate must be an 'integral component' of any policy or practice that seeks to meet the state obligation to ensure the equal right of men and women to the enjoyment of all human rights (General Comment 16, para. 37. See further General Comment 14, para. 54; General Comment 15, paras 16(a) and 48).

In a statement on poverty and the ICESCR, the Committee has stated that: 'the international human rights normative framework includes the right of those affected by key decisions to participate in the relevant decision-making processes' (CESCR 2001: para. 12). It has also emphasized that: 'rights and obligation demand accountability ... whatever the mechanisms of accountability, they must be accessible, transparent and effective' (ibid.: para. 14).

Accountability, participation and transparency require information. Article 19 of the Universal Declaration of Human Rights refers to the right to receive and impart information. This is further elaborated in Article 19 of ICCPR. The Inter-American Commission on Human Rights has recently noted that:

> Adequate access to public information is a key tool for citizen participation in public policies that implement the rights enshrined in the Protocol [of San Salvador]. (IACHR 2007)

Evaluating economic policies in the light of human rights obligations[9]

Governments do not usually explicitly bear human rights in mind when designing and implementing their economic policies, but they did recognize, at the UN World Conference on Human Rights in Vienna in 1993, that human rights are 'the first responsibility of Governments' (Vienna Declaration, Part I, para. 1). A focus on human rights obligations provides a framework for evaluating economic policy that is different from that used in neoclassical economics. In the latter, policy is judged in terms of a utilitarian framework, in which the best policies are judged to be those that are likely to maximize utility. This is operationalized in terms of maximizing the level and rate of growth of the country's gross national product (GNP). It is assumed that once the output is produced, it can then be redistributed via taxation and public expenditure to achieve the social goals of the country. This might be described as a strategy of first maximize the size of the pie and then slice it up. The default presumption of neoclassical economics is that private owner-ship and market forces are likely to be the best mechanisms for maximizing GNP, though it is acknowledged that there are various cases of failure of private enterprise and market forces that require government action; and that redistribution of output to achieve social goals requires government action.

Progressive, critical economists outside the mainstream challenge these views. They point to the inherent riskiness and uncertainty of market competi-tion; and argue that most successful cases of rapid economic growth have in fact been achieved with leadership from the state, to provide the appropriate incentives and infrastructure and security. They also question whether it is possible to separate production and distribution. The process of production produces 'winners' who tend to resist any redistribution of their gains to those who are losers. The way in which the pie is produced constrains the way in which it can be sliced.

Clearly, the level and growth of GNP have implications for the progressive realization of economic and social rights. For instance, they are important influences on the resources that states have available. But the goal of economic growth cannot be substituted for the goal of realizing human rights. Human rights obligations prescribe priority to human rights, not economic growth, which must be seen as a potential means for realizing human rights, not an end in itself. Episodes of rapid economic growth have often been achieved in ways that violate human rights, such as rights at work and the right to adequate food. Economic growth has frequently destroyed the livelihoods of some people while improving the livelihoods of others. There are a variety of ways to achieve economic growth, and states have the duty to pursue growth strategies that are compliant with their human rights obligations. Moreover, human rights do entail some immediate obligations in relation to economic and social rights, notably minimum core obligations regarding minimum essential levels; and non-discrimination and equality. States have an obligation to prioritize these irrespective of the level and rate of growth of GNP.

The human rights obligations set out above do not directly prescribe a particular mix of private and public responsibilities (as noted in para. 8 of the CESCR General Comment 3 on the nature of states parties' obligations). But it is clear that they do require states to adopt that mix of public policies, and regulation of the private sector, that will best address both immediate obligations and progressive realization. The realization of economic and social rights requires more than a minimalist state. Indeed, as the UN Special Rap-porteur on the right to education has noted: 'The *raison d'être* of economic and social rights is to act as correctives to the free market' (Tomasevski 1998).

In providing this corrective, a state must, of course, also respect, protect and fulfil civil and political rights.

States do have other obligations besides human rights obligations. For instance, they have obligations to other states with which they have made international trade and investment agreements, through the mechanisms of the World Trade Organization, or regional mechanisms. They also have obligations to their creditors, from whom they have borrowed money, including their own citizens, and international private and public financial institutions, including the IMF and the World Bank. These obligations may constrain the economic policies that states can pursue. But these obligations should not take precedence over human rights obligations: in the Vienna Declaration (1993), states have undertaken to make human rights their first responsibility. This implies that they should not seek to bind themselves or other states to international agreements that may weaken the capacity of the latter to realize economic and social rights. This applies not only to intergovernmental agreements but also to the agreements that a state approves by virtue of its position on the board of international institutions such as the IMF and the World Bank. In evaluating economic policies in the light of human rights obligations, it is important to consider the extent to which such policies are being constrained by obligations to trading partners and creditors, and the extent to which these obligations are consistent with their human rights obligations. It is also important to consider the extent to which a state has bound other states, directly or indirectly, to agreements that may not be consistent with human rights obligations. Here there are important issues of asymmetrical power between different states, with some having much more power than others to set the rules for international trade, investment and finance.

It is important to recognize that attention to human rights obligations does not provide the answers to all economic policy questions (Gauri 2004). What such attention can help us do is define the set of policies that are consistent with human rights obligations, and rule out policies that are not consistent. In choosing among the policies that are consistent with human rights obligations, human rights analysis can also provide some guidance on sequencing of policies (attention to the most deprived should have priority) and on procedures (which must be transparent, participatory and accountable). But it cannot provide definitive answers to questions such as: should priority in investment in public services be given to the urban poorest people or the rural poorest people, bearing in mind that a given expenditure can reach more of the poorest urban people than the poorest rural people, because the latter are more spatially dispersed? An economic analysis of any particular human-rights-consistent policy provides important quantitative information that should also be taken into account.

However, it is equally important to recognize that the economic analysis cannot provide a definitive answer either. Many abstractions and simplifications (often referred to as 'models') have to be made in order to produce economic analysis; and weights often have to be given to competing policy objectives. The abstractions, simplifications and weights used in heterodox economics are different from those used in mainstream economics. Greater priority is given to equality and provision of an adequate standard of living to all. The room for policy discretion is judged to be broader. More attention is paid to the inherent uncertainty and inequality of market processes. Because of such factors, the analysis produced by heterodox economics is likely to be more congruent with human rights norms and standards.

However, no matter how progressive the economic analysis, the quantitative information it produces does not eliminate the role of social and political judgement. Judgement among competing human-rights-consistent policies should therefore not only be informed by a progressive economic analysis but also be reached through a participatory, transparent and accountable process. However, the first step is to conduct analysis of whether current economic policies are consistent with human rights obligations. We do not aim to identify the best possible set of policies to realize human rights. There are far too many uncertainties to be able to do that. Our aim is rather to move policy in a better direction. In this book we seek to do that by examining the use of some key economic policy instruments in two countries, Mexico and the USA: overall fiscal and monetary policy; more detailed examinations of public expenditure, and taxation; international trade with a focus on the North American Free Trade Agreement (NAFTA); and the regulation of the private sector, using the case of pension reform. Two chapters are devoted to each policy, the first examining its use in relation to economic and social rights in Mexico, the second its use in relation to economic and social rights in the USA. This is done so that the conceptual tools that are being used can be seen in operation in two different contexts. Our hope is that this framework will be applied in other countries, so that human rights norms can be used to question and challenge the neoliberal policies that have dominated the world for the last three decades.

The policy instruments that we consider affect the whole, or large sectors of, the economy, and have implications for all economic and social rights, though any specific instrument may have a more direct relation with some rights than others. In choosing policy instruments as our entry point, rather than the enjoyment of specific rights, we are in agreement with those who have argued that the assessment of states' compliance with obligations regarding economic and social rights should pay particular attention to obligations of conduct (Rowarth 2001). But we think it is also important to cross-check evidence on conduct with evidence on relevant aspects of the enjoyment of economic and social rights. This book does not aim to provide studies of the full impact of the selected economic policies on the enjoyment of economic and social rights. In any case, no such study can definitely establish causation, but only establish correlation. Rather, the method adopted is to examine how policy has been conducted – has it consisted of action 'reasonably calculated to realize the enjoyment of a particular right', selecting rights that might reasonably be thought to have a strong relation to the policy instrument. The method uses both quantitative indicators and a qualitative examination of relevant legislation and policy processes. Where appropriate, the analysis of conduct is then cross-checked with a quantitative and qualitative analysis of relevant 'results' for the relevant rights.

The data on results may reinforce or challenge the conclusions about the conduct of policy. For example, spending public money on healthcare might be considered to be 'action reasonably calculated to realize' the right to health, but it may not be organized in a way that complies with obligations regarding non-discrimination and equality. If we find that public expenditure is very unequally distributed between different social groups, this suggests a prima facie case of violation of obligation of conduct. We can cross-check this with data on the health status of different social groups (which measure some dimension of how far they enjoy particular levels of the rights to health). If we find the health status of the group with the lowest share of expenditure is worse than that of those with higher shares of expenditure, this suggests that the government is not in compliance with its obligations of conduct. But if the social group with the lowest share of public expenditure has the highest health status, then this suggests that the needs for public health services of this group are lower, and thus the government may be justified in its conduct of health expenditure.

In choosing indicators and making judgements, we are mindful of the need to take into account differences of context. As Rowarth (ibid.) points out, when examining compliance with obligations regarding progressive realization of economic and social rights, it is not appropriate to compare countries with different levels of wealth against the same set of 'results' using some absolute standard (e.g. full enrolment of all children in school). We have selected our indicators with this issue in mind, focusing on benchmarking with comparable countries; benchmarking in the same country over time; and benchmarking between social groups in the same country. In cross-checking conduct and results, the analysis pays attention, where appropriate, to qualitative indicators of the institutional system that links economic policy to enjoyment of economic and social rights. For instance, is there a relatively secure link, such as is provided by a system of universal citizen entitlements to public provision, specified in legislation, possibly in the constitution? Or a less secure link, based on targeted entitlements, available only on a means-tested basis to the poorer groups? Or a reliance on families, communities, charities and churches to provide a minimum essential level of the rights? The empirical evidence across a wide range of countries suggests that the most effective way of reducing poverty is through 'targeting within universalism' in which there are strong universal entitlements, plus extra benefits directed to low-income groups (Mkandawire 2007).

In making judgements, this book is sceptical of the view that 'there is no alternative' to neoliberal policies. But we have also kept in mind the possibility of a variable range of alternatives. The main point we wish to establish is both the necessity and the feasibility of taking human rights obligations into account in economic policy. This book does not discuss issues of justiciability of economic and social rights. Rather, the approach is in line with the 'policy approach' to economic and social rights, identified by Paul Hunt, the UN Special Rapporteur on the right to health (Hunt 2006). The contributors consider empirical evidence relevant to the question of whether economic policies are in compliance with human rights obligations, aiming to establish the extent to which there is a prima facie case that some policies may not be in compliance with human rights norms and standards.

Fiscal and monetary policy in Mexico is considered in Chapter 1 and in the USA in Chapter 2, from the early 1980s up to and including the financial crisis and economic recession of 2008/09. In both cases the conduct of policy is cross-checked with respect to the right to work and the right to just and favourable conditions of work. More detailed examination of public expenditure is provided for Mexico in Chapter 3 and the USA in Chapter 4, with a focus on the composition of expenditure. The conduct of policy is cross-checked with respect to the right to health and the right to food. Taxation is the subject of Chapters 5 and 6, in Mexico and the USA respectively. The conduct of policy is not cross-checked with any particular rights, as most taxes are not specifically linked to any particular right, but are relevant to the realization of all economic and social rights. International trade policy is considered in Chapters 7 (for Mexico) and 8 (for the USA), with a particular focus on the North American Free Trade Agreement. This policy is cross-checked against the right to work and the right to just and favourable conditions of work in both countries, and the implications for migration from Mexico to the USA are discussed. The implications of NAFTA for the right to food in Mexico are examined, providing an opportunity to discuss the extraterritorial obligations of the government of the USA towards people living in Mexico, as well as the obligations of the Mexican government. Chapters 9 and 10 consider the issue of regulation of the private sector, using the case of pension reform in Mexico and the USA respectively. The conduct of policy is cross-checked against the right to social security.

Key findings

The overall orientation of fiscal and monetary policy is particularly important for the realization of the right to work and the right to just and favourable remuneration, but the conduct of fiscal and monetary policy in both Mexico and the USA has fallen short of what is required for the progressive realization of these rights. In both countries policy has prioritized keeping inflation very low over creating more jobs. Though both governments made some attempts to counteract the impact of the 2008 financial crisis and the global slowdown in growth that followed, neither did enough to prevent job prospects from worsening even further.

In Mexico, conduct of fiscal and monetary policy over the last thirty years has been constrained by decisions to open the economy to foreign competition. Fiscal policy has focused on maintaining a balanced federal budget and generating a primary budget surplus to cover interest payments on public debt, in a context where fiscal reform initiatives have largely failed to expand and deepen the tax base and improve tax collection. Adhering to these principles has reduced the margin of action for the state to stimulate aggregate demand in conditions of global economic downturn; and to undertake planning and policy to develop productive activities that create decent jobs in formal employment. Monetary policy has been reduced to meeting a target for low inflation, and as a result, wage increments are seen as threats. The Bank of Mexico failed to act to counteract the contraction of credit after the financial crisis. Thirty years of restrictive fiscal and monetary policy in Mexico have demonstrated their inability to promote the kind of economic growth that generates employment with decent wages. Though open unemployment has been relatively low, there has been an increase in the proportion of jobs that are precarious; and large numbers of Mexicans have had to migrate to the USA to try to find employment. This failure to meet the obligation regarding progressive realization of the right to work and to just and favourable conditions of work cannot be excused in terms of the absence of alternatives. Unfortunately, decision-making on the objectives and strategies of fiscal and monetary policy is concentrated in the hands of the president, the Ministry of Finance and the Bank of Mexico, without sufficient opportunity for the legislature to participate and for citizens to be consulted and to put forward alternative strategies.

The government in the USA has more room for manoeuvre in fiscal and monetary policy: at the federal level, there is no requirement for a balanced budget (though there is in all but one of the states); and in theory, the Federal Reserve Bank has a dual mandate to have regard for employment as well as inflation, though in practice it has prioritized low inflation. In response to the recession that followed the financial crisis, the federal government did increase spending to stimulate the economy, but most of the stimulus spending ended after 2010; and in 2011 there was a renewed focus on decreasing the deficit through spending cuts, rather than through taxing rich people, which will increase the economic insecurity of those in need and undermine efforts to generate employment. The Federal Reserve Bank did act to provide more liquidity to both financial and non-financial institutions, but not to homeowners facing foreclosure. Neither the fiscal nor the monetary policy response was sufficient to stop a large rise in unemployment. Over the last thirty years, US fiscal and monetary policy has benefited corporations and rich people much more than low- and middle-income people. It has not prevented a widening gap between productivity and wages; and a fall in the share of decent work (i.e. jobs that are compliant with human rights obligations). The emphasis on low inflation in the conduct of monetary policy has hit African-Americans particularly hard, so that conduct has not been in compliance with the obligation regarding non-discrimination and equality. While there is a high level of formal provision for transparency and accountability in the US federal budget process and the operations of the Federal Reserve Bank, in practice powerful financial interests play an important behind-the-scenes role, especially in monetary policy. Successive US governments have fallen short of conducting fiscal and monetary policy so as to realize economic and social rights, despite the availability of alternative strategies.

Turning to trends in public expenditure, the analysis particularly focused on health expenditure and the right to health, and poverty-related expenditure and the right to an adequate standard of living, including the right to food. As a share of GDP, health expenditure was lower in Mexico in 2006 than in 1980. Per capita health expenditure in Mexico is below that of several comparable Latin American countries. In addition, the distribution of public expenditure on health does not comply with the obligations regarding non-discrimination and equality. Health spending per capita on the better-off Mexicans who are covered by contributory social insurance schemes is much higher than on the poorer Mexicans (many of whom are indigenous people), who can access only the much more limited health services supplied by the Ministry of Health. Moreover, there is evidence of failure to spend all the resources allocated to improving health infrastructure in deprived, largely indigenous, regions.

The health outcomes are disappointing. The child mortality rate has fallen, indicating progressive realization, but remains higher than in many comparable Latin American countries. Brazil has done much better than Mexico in reducing the mortality rates for children under the age of five during the last two decades. The national maternal mortality rate appears to have fallen but remains higher than that of many comparable Latin American countries, and falls far short of government targets for reduction. Moreover, data on maternal mortality by state show falls not rises in most cases, calling into question whether there has been any progressive realization with respect to this aspect of the right to health. Indigenous women are at much greater risk of dying in pregnancy than non-indigenous women, an indicator that health outcomes are not fully compliant with non-discrimination and equality in the enjoyment of the right to health.

An attempt was made to address the acute inequalities in the funding, quality and accessibility of health services through the introduction of the Popular Insurance scheme in 2004. Despite increases in the allocation of public expenditure to this new scheme, it continues to exclude much of the rural population and has been quite ineffective in prioritizing indigenous communities. The allocation and spending of public resources on health do not satisfy human rights obligations.

Public expenditure in Mexico has addressed the issue of minimum core obligations regarding ensuring enjoyment of minimum essential levels of social and economic rights, through increased allocations to anti-poverty programmes, but the allocations have not grown as fast as those to other forms of social expenditure. The main programme, *Oportunidades*, provides targeted, means-tested, conditional cash transfer. Many millions of poor people are still excluded from the programme; and many thousands have had the cash transfers withdrawn on grounds of non-compliance with the conditions. Programmes of this kind are more effective in ensuring that benefits do not go to families above the poverty line, than ensuring that the benefits do reach all families below the poverty line. The anti-poverty programmes have not yet been effective in ensuring that no child in Mexico suffers from chronic undernourishment. Although there have been declines in the rate of chronic undernourishment among children, it remains high for poor and indigenous Mexican children.

There have been improvements in the transparency of public expenditure, but Mexico still lags behind many other large middle-income countries. Accountability for public expenditure has also improved, but much of the real budget negotiation take place behind closed doors. Citizen participation in planning and implementing public programmes is very limited. Other comparable Latin American countries do better.

Per capita public expenditure on healthcare in the USA has been rising in real terms: there has been no retrogression in terms of the allocation of public expenditure to healthcare. However, there is no national health insurance programme providing universal coverage in the USA. Around 15 per cent of the population was not covered at all in the period from 1987 to 2009, calling into question the fulfilment of the obligation to ensure that everyone has access to healthcare.

Among high-income countries, the United States has by far the highest share of GDP devoted to health expenditure, when both public and private sources are taken into account. But this expenditure is not used very effectively: administration constitutes 20–30 per cent of total US healthcare expenditure. The health outcomes are disappointing: the USA had the fourth-highest infant mortality rate in the OECD after Turkey, Mexico and Chile in 2006. In terms of maternal mortality, the USA has the sixth-highest rate in the OECD. Moreover, the rate has risen since 2000, clearly indicating a lack of progressive realization with respect to maternal health.

There is evidence of a lack of compliance with obligations of non-discrimination and equality with respect to the conduct of public spending on health, with racial/ethnic minorities, women, poor people and migrants being less likely to have access to health insurance. This is matched by evidence of lack of compliance with the obligations of non-discrimination and equality in health outcomes. The healthcare reforms introduced in the USA in 2010 did not introduce a comprehensive social insurance system comparable to that of other well-off countries, and there is reason to believe that they will not succeed in ensuring that the right to health is realized in compliance with the obligation regarding non-discrimination and equality.

Though the USA is a rich country, there is evidence that the state is not complying with obligations to provide a minimum core level of enjoyment of the right to food. Despite the food stamps programme, a substantial proportion of households lack food security, and this has risen as a result of the economic crisis that began in 2008. Despite increasing needs, access to food stamps is being cut in some places. Single-mother households and those in racial/ethnic minority groups experience higher levels of food insecurity. The USA has a right-to-information law, and a lot of information is provided about expenditure once budgets have been set, especially at the federal level; but the rich and powerful have much more access to the process of setting budget priorities. There are many ways in which the government of the USA is not in compliance with its obligations with respect to the right to health.

Taxation policies have been examined here using the principles of maximum available resources, non-discrimination and equality, and transparency, accountability and participation. Neither the government of Mexico nor the government of the USA is conducting tax policy in ways that fully comply with human rights obligations. Tax revenue in Mexico is low compared to other Latin American countries; and tax administration is marred by inadequate surveillance and enforcement, poor tax management and collection, loopholes and preferential tax treatments. There is significant tax evasion and avoidance. It is true that in Mexico, a high proportion of government revenue comes from revenues and royalties from PEMEX, the state-owned oil company. However, since oil is a depleting natural resource, PEMEX will eventually no longer be able to sustain these revenues. In the absence of a comprehensive tax reform, the exhaustion of this oil revenue will significantly deplete the resources available to realize economic and social rights.

In terms of non-discrimination and equality, while income tax (which is not paid by low-income Mexicans) is progressive, value added tax, levied on most goods and services, and therefore paid by all Mexicans, is regressive. Income tax is levied on individuals, even if they are married, and this tends to put men and women income tax payers on an even footing, but there is cause for concern in the relative inability of women earners to take advantage of tax allowances (because the allowances are available only for employees and not for the self-employed).

The Federal Law of Transparency and Access to Public Information in Mexico has led to some improvements. However, the tax information that is available is still not sufficient, nor is it transparent, even though taxation and tax policy generate the most freedom-of-information requests. There have been improvements in mechanisms to hold those who break the tax law to account, but tax evasion and avoidance remain high. In order to meet the obligations to use maximum available resources to realize economic and social rights, further reform of the design and administration of the tax system is required.

In the USA, tax revenue as a share of GDP is lower than in comparable rich countries, calling into question whether the government has been mobilizing maximum available resources. Over time, the share of revenue coming from corporations has fallen, and that coming from individuals has risen. However, tax on the incomes of the very wealthy has fallen, reducing the resources available to realizing economic and social rights, and compromising the principles of equality and non-discrimination. This principle is also called into question by the way in which income tax is levied on married people, through a joint filing system, on their joint income. Insofar as married women tend to be the secondary earners in the household, this means that they face a higher effective tax rate on the first dollar they earn than they would face as an individual, because their earnings are added to those of their husband. This tends to create a disincentive for married women to participate in the labour market. Sales and local taxes are levied by state and local governments and are regressive, with low-income people paying a higher share of their income in these taxes than high-income people. African-Americans and Latinos are more likely to have lower incomes than white Americans, and are thus more likely to be harder hit by these taxes. Although the tax authorities are charged with providing information about the tax code to the public, the code is complex and opaque, so that those who cannot afford the advice of specialist tax accountants find it hard to understand; and those who can afford this advice, especially corporations, find many loopholes for tax avoidance. The tax system is tilted in favour of corporations and the very wealthy, and the principle of non-discrimination and equality is breached in several ways in the tax system. To rectify this, and to allow the state to use maximum available resources, the tax system needs to be reformed.

In examining trade policy, this book focuses on the North American Free Trade Agreement, which links Mexico, the USA and Canada, and is an investment agreement as well as a trade agreement. It also has a side agreement that is supposed to protect labour rights, but it affords labour rights far less protection than is afforded to the rights of corporations. In both Mexico and the USA, NAFTA failed to support the progressive realization of the right to work, and progressive realization of the right to just and favourable conditions of work. The rights of low-income small-scale farmers in Mexico and unskilled poorly educated workers in manufacturing and services in the USA were undermined, and there was retrogression in both countries in the enjoyment of the right to work and to just and remunerative conditions of work.

In Mexico, the conduct of trade policy could have been more compliant with human rights obligations even within the NAFTA framework. For instance, free trade in maize could have been phased in more slowly; more extensive support could have been offered to small farmers to develop exports of fruits and vegetables; a well-resourced and well-functioning development bank could have been set up to support innovation in production. These measures would have helped to support progressive realization of the right to work and to just and favourable conditions of work.

On the face of it, NAFTA might have supported securing a minimum level of enjoyment of the right to food for low-income Mexicans, as it facilitated imports of maize and other key staples from lower-cost US farmers. But this did not result in lower prices of tortillas, bread and cereals for Mexican consumers. Moreover, the relative prices of less nutritious food, likely to be injurious to health, fell, and the diet of low-income Mexicans worsened.

Although the US government introduced compensation measures for low-income workers who lost their jobs as a result of NAFTA (among whom racial/ ethnic minorities and women are over-represented), these have been grossly inadequate. Men disproportionately lost jobs, as compared to women; but women who had lost their jobs found it harder to get new comparable jobs than men who had lost their jobs. Workers of Hispanic origin were harder hit in terms of job loss than other racial/ethnic groups. All workers of colour who lost their jobs found it harder to secure new comparable jobs than did white workers. Neither conduct nor result appears to be consistent with the principle of non-discrimination and equality.

No thought appears to have been given by the US state to its extraterritorial obligations to Mexican people in relation to NAFTA. For instance, there appears to have been no study of the potential impact of NAFTA provisions on the right to food in Mexico before the agreement was signed. The gainers were large US corporations, while Mexican small-scale farmers lost their livelihoods and Mexican consumers paid higher food prices and ate more junk food. The right to a minimum level of nutritious food has been undermined in Mexico. The government of the USA is complicit in this deterioration, in the subsidies it provides to US agribusiness (especially for corn syrup) and its failure to adequately regulate corporations involved in the supply of food in Mexico.

NAFTA is unique among trade agreements in granting foreign investors the right to sue governments for introducing measures that are found to impede the investor's freedom to make profits through the NAFTA dispute settlement mechanism. There is a lack of adequate provision for accountability, transparency and participation in the operation of this mechanism. Overall, the evidence suggests that the US state has negotiated and operated a trade agreement that does not comply fully with its human rights obligations.

The lack of adequate regulation of corporations is at the heart of the problems with NAFTA, and also at the heart of problems with pension reform. In both Mexico and the USA, the government has reformed the pension system to give a greater role to the private sector. In both countries, this has gone hand in hand with the decline of defined benefit pensions, in which employees are guaranteed a particular level of pension, and the rise of defined contribution systems, in which the contributions that people must pay are specified but their eventual pension is not guaranteed but depends on financial markets. These reforms have impeded rather than promoted the progressive realization of the right to social security.

In Mexico reforms were introduced in 1997 and 2007, but neither aimed to provide a universal pension for everyone, despite the fact that the majority of the population had no access to social security. Among other things, the reforms abolished the collective funds into which employees (in formal employment, with a regular contract), employers and government had contributed, and which had been managed by public institutions. These were replaced with individual funds held by individual employees, who had to choose a private sector fund administrator (mainly provided by banks) and pay them fees to manage the funds so as to earn a return to provide a pension. While employers and the state continued to make some contribution to these funds, their contributions decreased and that of the employees had to increase. The risks are now borne by the individual employees, whose savings are at the mercy of the financial markets and who do not know what their pension will be. While the private sector pension fund managers are subject to government regulation, the regulations are inadequate. For instance, there are no clear provisions for what would happen if a pension fund manager goes bankrupt; and the regulations permit managers to charge fees even for accounts that are inactive, because the holders have lost their formal sector jobs and are no longer contributing. Pensions are now less secure. The reforms have not contributed to the progressive realization of the right to social security, though they have enriched the banks and other financial institutions.

In the USA, the state continues to provide a defined benefit pension through the social security system, funded by payroll taxes on paid employees and employers. However, for an adequate income in retirement, people also need a second private pension, based on occupational or individual pension schemes. Legislation, including tax breaks, has promoted the move in private pension provision from defined benefit plans (part funded by employers, and paying an insurance premium to the state, which in turn guarantees the benefits) to defined contribution plans, in which the individual bears the risk (and there are no state-provided guarantees). The financial crisis of 2008 dramatically reduced the pensions of holders of defined contribution plans. Although private pension providers are regulated by the state, the regulations are inadequate. Defined contribution plans have been promoted as providing higher returns, but defined benefit plans in fact provide higher returns, because of the high fees private providers charge for managing the individual accounts in defined contribution plans. The US state is failing to protect the right to social security of the millions who now have defined contribution pension plans.

Holding governments to account

The kind of analysis presented in this book can be used to hold governments to account in international, regional and national processes. At the international level, the UN Human Rights Universal Periodic Review (UPR) is an opportunity for civil society organizations to hold their governments to account. The UPR is a human rights mechanism of the Human Rights Council (HRC), created on 15 March 2006 by the UN General Assembly Resolution 60/251.1 The UPR reviews the fulfilment by all 192 UN member states (or countries) of their human rights obligations and commitments, as well as their progress, challenges and needs for improvement. Countries are reviewed every four years.

It was created in response to criticism that previous UN mechanisms focused too much on certain regions, thus the UPR was designed using a peer review formula to be applied more universally and uniformly. This process offers civil society organizations a unique opportunity to measure a country's human rights obligations and pressure governments to live up to those commitments. The UPR assesses each country's adherence to its human rights obligations under the United Nations (UN) Charter, the Universal Declaration of Human Rights (UDHR), human rights treaties ratified by the country, its voluntary commitments, and applicable international law. During the review, in addition to the 'national report' provided by the country under review and the reports of UN bodies, the Working Group considers reports from other 'stakeholders' such as civil society and national human rights institutions. The United States Human Rights Network, a network of hundreds of organizations, highlights significant and specific shortcomings in domestic compliance with international human rights standards; and makes recommendations on how the USA can better meet those standards and live up to its treaty obligations.[10]

Another opportunity is the process through which the Committee on Economic, Social and Cultural Rights monitors compliance with the ICESCR. This committee is made up of independent experts and monitors implementation of the ICESCR by its states parties. All states parties that have ratified the covenant are obliged to submit regular reports to the Committee on how the rights are being implemented. The Committee examines each report and addresses its concerns and recommendations to the state party in the form of 'concluding observations'.[11]

Regional human rights mechanisms may also be useful. For example, the Inter-American Commission on Human Rights, headquartered in Washington, DC, is one of two bodies in the inter-American system for the promotion and protection of human rights. The other human rights body is the Inter-American Court of Human Rights (IACHR), which is located in San José, Costa Rica. The IACHR is an autonomous organ of the Organization of American States (OAS). The IACHR is a permanent body which meets in ordinary and special sessions several times a year.

At the national level, research like that presented in this book can be used to educate human rights activists, so that they can hold their governments to account through publicity, campaigns and lobbying. For example, the Center for Women's Global Leadership used the methodology in this book as part of its participation in the UPR process for the United States. It took the lead in developing a cluster report on macroeconomic policy and human rights.[12] In Mexico the methodology has been used at the Mexico City level, where activists have been urging the human rights commission to examine its obligation in terms of the obligation of conduct and result.[13]

Changing the way that economists evaluate policies

In the long run, it is important to change the ways in which economists evaluate policies, so that human rights take priority and economic growth, and economic efficiency, is pursued only in ways that are consistent with human rights. This is an area where more work needs to be done, through extending the dialogue between economists and human rights advocates. One way of approaching this is by using this study as a pilot for comparable investigations in other countries, tailored, of course, to the specific conditions of each country; and taking up new challenges such as the increasing role of financial markets in mediating access to goods that are key for realizing human rights, such as food and water.

Notes

1 For accounts of this dialogue, see Balakrishnan (2004) and Balakrishnan et al. (2009).

2 For more information on these non-conformist economists, see www.open.ac.uk/socialsciences/hetecon and www.heterodoxeconomics.net and www.iaffe.org.

3 Treaties are signed by the executive part of the state, but need to be ratified by the legislature.

4 There are other important treaties that are relevant for economic and social rights, such as the Convention on the Rights of the Child, but this book will not explicitly refer to them.

5 www.state.gov/documents/organization/146379.pdf.

6 www.state.gov/s/l/releases/remarks/150677.htm.

7 The full text of all the treaties is available on the website of the UN High Commission for Human Rights, www.ohchr.org.

8 The text of the Limburg Principles and the Maastricht Guidelines can be found as Appendices to Office of UN High Commissioner for Human Rights (2005).

9 This section draws upon Balakrishnan and Elson (2008).

10 www.ushrnetwork.org/UPRbook.

11 www2.ohchr.org/english/bodies/cescr/workingmethods.htm.

12 www.cwgl.rutgers.edu/globalcenter/policy/unadvocacy/May%202010%20Macro%20Econ%20Report%20US%20UPR.pdf.

13 This was told to Radhika Balakrishnan by Alberto Serdan during a recent visit to Mexico.

References

Alston, P. (2007) Special Rapporteur on 'Extra-judicial, Summary or Arbitrary Executions', UN General Assembly, Human Rights Council, Sixth Session (A/HRC/6/7).

Balakrishnan, R. (2004) *Why MES with Human Rights? Integrating Macro Economic Strategies with Human Rights*, New York: Marymount Manhattan College.

Balakrishnan, R. and D. Elson (2008) 'Auditing economic policy in the light of obligations on economic and social rights', *Essex Human Rights Review*, 5(1): 1–19.

Balakrishnan, R., D. Elson and R. Patel (2009) *Rethinking Macro Economic Strategies from a Human Rights Perspective* (Why MES with Human Rights II), New York: Marymount Manhattan College.

CEDAW (Committee on the Elimination of All Forms of Discrimination Against Women) (2004) General Recommendation 25, Temporary Special Measures (Art. 4, para. 1 of the Covenant).

Center for Economic and Social Rights (2000) *Economic, Social and Cultural Rights: A Guide to the Legal Framework*, New York: Center for Economic and Social Rights.

CESCR (Committee on Economic, Social and Cultural Rights) General Comments:

— General Comment 3, 'The Nature of States Parties' Obligations' (Article 2, para. 1) (1990).

— General Comment 11, 'Plans of Action for Primary Education' (Article 14) (1999).

— General Comment 12, 'The Right to Adequate Food' (Article 11) (1999).

— General Comment 13, 'The Right to Education' (Article 13) (1999).

— General Comment 14, 'The Right to the Highest Attainable Standard of Health' (Article 12) (2000).

— General Comment 15, 'The Right to Water' (Articles 11 and 12) (2002).

— General Comment 16, 'The Equal Right of Men and Women to the Enjoyment of All Economic, Social and Cultural Rights' (Article 3) (2005).

— General Comment 20, 'Non-Discrimination in Economic, Social and Cultural Rights' (Article 2, para. 2) (2009).

CESCR (2001) 'Poverty and the International Covenant on Economic, Social and Cultural Rights' (E/C. 12/2001/10).

— (2007) 'An Evaluation of the Obligation to Take Steps to the "Maximum of Available Resources" Under an Optional Protocol to the Covenant' (E/C.12/2007/1).

Elson, D. (2006) *Budgeting for Women's Rights: Monitoring Government Budgets for Compliance with CEDAW*, New York: UNIFEM.

Gauri, V. (2004) 'Social rights and economics: claims to health care and education in developing countries', *World Development*, 32(3): 465–77.

Hunt, P. (2006) 'Using all the tools at our disposal: poverty reduction and the right to the highest attainable standard of health', *Development Outreach*, October.

IACHR (Inter-American Commission on Human Rights) (2007) 'Guidelines for Preparation of Progress Indicators in the Area of Economic, Social and Cultural Rights' (OEA/SER/L/V/II.129).

MacNaughton, G. (2009) 'Untangling equality and non-discrimination to promote the right to health care for all', *Health and Human Rights*, 11(2): 47–63.

Mkandawire, T. (2007) 'Targeting and universalism in poverty reduction', in J. A. Ocampo, K. S. Jomo and S. Khan (eds), *Policy Matters: Economic and Social Policies to Sustain Equitable Development*, London: Zed Books.

Morsink, J. (1999) *The Universal Declaration of Human Rights: Origins, Drafting and Intent*, Philadelphia, PA: University of Philadelphia.

Office of UN High Commissioner for Human Rights (2002) 'Globalization and Its Impact on the Full Enjoyment of Human Rights', Economic and Social Council, Commission on Human Rights, 58th Session (E/CN.4/2002/54).

— (2003) 'Human Rights, Trade and Investment', Economic and Social Council, Commission on Human Rights, Sub-Commission on the Promotion and Protection of Human Rights, 55th Session (E/CN.4/Sub.2/2003/9).

— (2005) *Economic, Social and Cultural Rights, Handbook for National Human Rights Institutions*, Geneva: United Nations.

Rowarth, K. (2001) 'Measuring human rights', *Ethics and International Affairs*, 15(1): 111–32.

Tomasevski, K. (1998) Background paper submitted by Special Rapporteur on the right to education, Committee on Economic,

Social and Cultural Rights, 19th Session (E/C.12/1998/18).

— (2005) 'Not education for all, only for those who can pay: the World Bank's model for financing primary education', www2.warwick.ac.uk/fac/soc/law/elj/lgd/2005_1/tomasevski/.

UN Secretary-General (2000) 'Globalization and Its Impact on the Full Enjoyment of Human Rights,' series of reports of the Secretary-General, UN General Assembly, 55th Session (A/55/342; A/56/254; A/57/205; A/58/257; A/59/320; A/60/301; A/61/281; A/62/222).

Valticos, N. (1998) 'International labour standards and human rights', *International Labour Review*, 137(2): 135–47.

Vienna Declaration and Programme of Action (1993) UN General Assembly, World Conference on Human Rights (A/CONF. 157/23).

1 | FISCAL AND MONETARY POLICY AND THE RIGHT TO WORK: MEXICO[1]

Kristina Pirker and Sarah Gammage

Introduction

Fiscal and monetary policy have implications for the realization of many human rights, and are particularly important for those that are related to paid employment. Here we examine fiscal and monetary policy with respect to the obligations to fulfil the right to work and to just and favourable conditions of work. The Universal Declaration of Human Rights (Article 23) and the International Covenant on Economic, Social and Cultural Rights (ICESCR) (Articles 6 and 7) oblige governments to create the conditions required to generate full and productive employment with fair wages that secure decent living conditions. The Mexican government ratified the ICESCR in 1981. Social rights have a long-standing legal basis in Mexico, having been included in the 1917 Constitution, which included the Right to Work as well as the Right to Earn a Minimally Remunerative Salary (Article 123). Mexican fiscal and monetary policy in the last thirty years or so is discussed in light of the human rights principles of progressive realization and non-retrogression; and transparency, accountability and participation.

Conduct of fiscal policy

Progressive realization and non-retrogression The ICESCR requires government to take steps 'with a view to achieving progressively' the full realization of the rights it specifies. The Committee on Economic, Social and Cultural Rights has clarified that, in general, states should not introduce 'retrogressive' measures that set back the realization of rights. If such retrogressive measures are deliberate, then the state has to show that they have been 'introduced after consideration of all alternatives and are fully justifiable by reference to totality of rights provided for in the Covenant and in context of the full use of the maximum of available resources'. How far has the conduct of fiscal policy complied with these principles?

During the 'stabilizing development' period (1958–70) and the 'debt expansion and crisis' period (1971–82), fiscal policy played an active role in promoting growth and employment creation. This focus changed, however, after the debt crisis in 1982. Under the administration of Miguel de la Madrid (1982–88), stabilization and structural adjustment programmes were introduced, and the reduction of the federal government budget deficit became a paramount objective, taking precedence over promotion of growth and employment creation. Under the administrations of Carlos Salinas (1988–94) and Ernesto Zedillo (1994–2000), these policies have continued. Macroeconomic policy has prioritized the reduction of the role of the state in the economy, trade and financial liberalization, and labour market flexibility. The administrations of Vicente Fox (2000–06) and now Felipe Calderón (2006–12) have largely followed the course laid out by their predecessors; and the commitment to a balanced budget has been enacted in law.

> The Federal Budget Law (2006) established a balanced budget as the guiding principle for fiscal policy: only under extraordinary economic and social conditions can the government incur a budget deficit, and the Federal Government must justify this before the Congress, explaining how it plans to return to a balanced budget (LFPRH, Article 17). Moreover, the Ruling of the Federal Law of Budget and Treasury Responsibility is even more specific by establishing in Article 11, 'The budget deficit should be equal to zero. Under exceptional circumstances a budget deficit different from zero can be anticipated; up to 0.5 percentage points of the estimated GDP ...'[2]

Mainstream economists argue that maintaining a balanced budget will secure lower inflation, and stable access to international capital markets; as Ocampo notes, they believe this will promote dynamic and sustainable economic growth; and consequently ensure the generation of employment (Ocampo 2005: 13). However, the requirement for a balanced budget reduces the ability of a government to take counter-cyclical action in times of economic downturn. Despite their commitment to fiscal discipline, many OECD countries continue to maintain a budget deficit: for example, in 2005, prior to the financial crisis, the USA had a budget deficit of 4.7 per cent of GDP, Germany one of 3.3 per cent, Italy 4.2 per cent and Hungary 6.1 per cent (OECD 2006: 58). Ha-Joon Chang and Ilene Grabel, after an extensive evaluation of international experiences, recommend that well-designed and strategic public expenditure programmes in developing countries should not be cut as a result of an 'obsession' with not incurring a fiscal deficit (Chang and Grabel 2004).

Chile provides an interesting example of a fiscal balance commitment that focuses on the medium term instead of the short term and that therefore can be used to implement counter-cyclical fiscal policy. Since 2001, Chile's fiscal policy has embraced a commitment to a central government 'structural balance'. Unlike the 'effective balance', which reports the current fiscal position, this balance reflects the medium-term fiscal outlook. Maintaining a structural balance involves estimating the fiscal revenue that would be obtained net of the impact of the economic cycle, and spending only the amount that would be compatible with this level of income. In practice, this means saving revenue

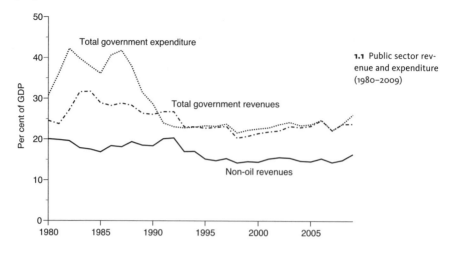

1.1 Public sector revenue and expenditure (1980–2009)

Source: Own calculations using data from the Centre for the Study of Public Finance from the Chamber of Deputies (CEFP) with data from the Federal Treasury Accounts, 1980–2006, www.cefp.gob.mx/intr/bancos deinformacion/historicas/gasto_publico/A13.xls (accessed March 2008); data 2007–09: SHCP, *Estadísticas oportunas de las finanzas públicas*, 2010, www.apartados.hacienda.gob.mx/estadisticas_oportunas/esp/index. html (accessed July 2010).

during economic upturns and spending the revenues during downturns. Mexico could draw on such an example to pursue counter-cyclical fiscal policy.

As illustrated in Figure 1.1, since the late 1980s the budget deficit has been eliminated by reducing public expenditure rather than by raising tax revenue.[3] Two considerable declines in the level of public revenue are worth mentioning, the first between 1992 and 1993 when total public revenue declined 3.1 percentage points from 26.7 per cent of GDP to 23.1 per cent. The second important fall can be seen from 1997 to 1998 – in response to the falling oil prices – with a decline of 2.8 percentage points from 21.2 to 20.4 per cent of GDP. The recovery in public sector revenue that can be seen over the last ten years is owing primarily to the strong price of oil and not to any improvement in tax revenue generation.

The current budget balance and the primary budget balance are shown in Figure 1.2.

The difference between the primary balance[4] and the current budget balance is largely accounted for by interest payments and amortization of government debt. Figure 1.2 illustrates two important points. First, the budget deficit in the period under study was primarily the result of the debt service obligations of the various governments. As can be seen, the financial crisis of 1982 prompted an immediate and sudden increase in the public deficit[5] – which demonstrated the impossible task that the administration of Miguel de la Madrid faced servicing the public debt in response to the increase in international interest rates. In order to meet these commitments in a timely manner, the resources dedicated to public investment and social development were drastically re-

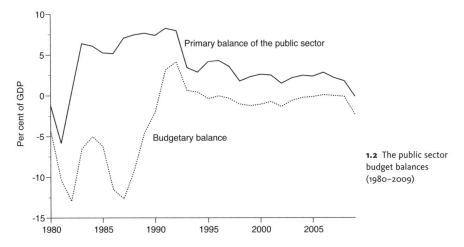

1.2 The public sector budget balances (1980–2009)

Source: Own calculations using data from the Centre for the Study of Public Finance from the Chamber of Deputies (CEFP) with data from the Federal Treasury Accounts, 1980–2006, www.cefp.gob.mx/intr/bancos deinformacion/historicas/gasto_publico/A13.xls (accessed March 2008); data 2007–09: SHCP, *Estadísticas oportunas de las finanzas públicas*, 2010, www.apartados.hacienda.gob.mx/estadisticas_oportunas/esp/index. html (accessed July 2010).

duced, even though in this period total public expenditure reached historic levels, rising to 42 per cent of GDP in 1982. Thanks to the international debt renegotiation in 1988 and 1989, these payments were reduced, which permitted the recovery of social expenditure. A balanced budget was achieved in 2006 and 2007, with a surplus in the primary balance (approximately 2 per cent of GDP) dedicated to meet the financial obligations, which means that this amount of government revenues was being transferred to holders of government debt – both within Mexico and abroad. The impact of the 2008 global financial crisis resulted in a decline in economic growth from 3.2 per cent in 2007 to 1.3 per cent in 2008 and –6.7 per cent in 2009. Not surprisingly, revenue also fell, by 6.5 per cent in 2009 (CEPAL 2010). There was an increase in the deficit associated with the primary balance (–0.1 per cent of GDP) and in the overall budgetary balance (–2.3 per cent of GDP) in 2009. Congress authorized a temporary departure from a balanced budget because the circumstances were considered exceptional.

One critical problem with Mexican public finances is the weight of financial sector liabilities in the Financing Requirements of the Public Sector (FRSP). In Figure 1.3, we can see the evolution of the FRSP and public sector expenditures from 1990 to March 2008. While public sector expenditure demonstrates few sudden increases or decreases, the historic balance declined in the early 1990s and then grew considerably from 1993 to 1995. This increase can be attributed to the fiscal cost of the 1994 banking bailout, as a result of which the Mexican government absorbed the obligations of bankrupt banks, which have cost around 6 per cent of GDP since 2006, calculated as part of the liabilities

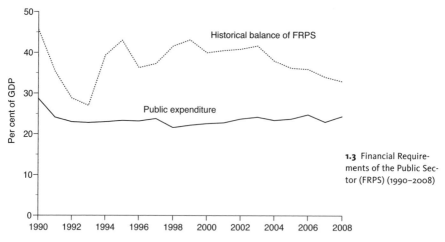

1.3 Financial Requirements of the Public Sector (FRPS) (1990–2008)

Note: Public expenditure for 2007 and 2008 refers to the approved budget

Source: Own estimates based on SHCP, *Report on the Economic Situation, Public Finances and Public Debt*, First Trimester, 2008, www.shcp.gob.mx (accessed June 2008); from the database of the Centre for the Study of Public Finance from the Chamber of Deputies (CEFP), www.cefp.gob.mx/intr/bancosdeinformacion/historicas/gasto_publico/A53.xls (accessed March 2008).

of the Institute for the Protection of Bank Savings (IPAB).[6] Marcos Chávez concludes that with respect to the FRSP:

> These [obligations] are of such a magnitude that they would fiscally destabilize any state leaving it in bankruptcy. The amortization of annual debt including the principal and interest payments would oblige the government to qualitatively sacrifice development for decades. That is to say, [to sacrifice] the quality and efficiency of the public sector, public works and social wellbeing. Under whatever circumstances, in order to finance such development, one would have to combine an increase income – taxes of whatever nature – and the prices charged for state goods and services with restraints on expenditure. (Chávez 2005: 260–1)

In Mexico, the achievement of a primary surplus has relied on cutting capital expenditure on public infrastructure, which fell in 1981, from 11.5 per cent of GDP to 5.5 per cent of GDP in 2009. This means that capital expenditures made by the federal government are significantly lower than the so called 'non-programmable expenditures' which consist primarily of financial obligations, plus some mandatory transfers to the state governments.[7] The fall in public investment is both dramatic and worrisome, and undermines the objective of expanding employment opportunities.

The contractual obligations of the state to its debtors (who directly or indirectly are mainly higher-income individuals and many of whom are foreigners) have taken precedence over its obligations with respect to the right to work and to just and favourable conditions of work.

Expenditure on programmes that directly support economic growth and the creation of employment (including agriculture and forestry and communications and transport) fell from just over 15 per cent of GDP in 1980 to only 5.5 per cent of GDP in 2005 (Cabrera Adame 2008). The most marked decline was in agriculture and forestry, which fell from 3.2 per cent to 0.6 per cent, indicating a retreat from policies that foster agricultural development, just at a time when Mexico needed policies to deal with the opening up of the agricultural sector in the context of trade liberalization. In particular, economic measures were needed to assist small farmers and producers of staples and basic grains on small plots of land with little access to technology who were unable to compete with more mechanized and efficient overseas producers (Nadal 2000). But instead of expanding support for agriculture and forestry, relative to GDP, the opposite happened.

The current administration of Felipe Calderón does includes among its objectives fostering 'a competitive economy that generates employment'. In order to achieve this, the government says it will pursue three priority actions: investment in physical capital, investment in human capital by improving investment in education, health and fighting poverty, and the promotion of economic growth through a more competitive economy that fosters those conditions favourable to the development and take-up of new technologies. But the requirement to balance the budget, while continuing to meet the ongoing costs of the 1994 banking bailout, puts stringent limits on the contribution that fiscal policy can make to this.

The Calderón government did attempt to increase public investment somewhat to counteract the impact of the 2008 global economic crisis, via the Programme to Stimulate Growth and Employment. The first two components, announced in March and October 2008, provided support to firms and households, via reduced social security contributions, as well as reductions in income taxes and other tax payments made by enterprises and an electricity subsidy for poor households. The programme also contained a commitment to increase investment in infrastructure and provide support for small and medium-sized enterprises. However, data from the Ministry of Finance show that the National Fund for Infrastructure had spent, until August 2009, less than 1 per cent of its funds. At the same time the government announced cuts in other areas of public expenditure, including for the Ministry of Health, the Ministry of Social Development and the Ministry of Agriculture (FUNDAR 2009).

These measures were insufficient to compensate for the impact of global stagnation, the sharply falling demand for Mexican exports, and the contraction of credit, savings and investment worldwide. Non-programmable expenditure remained above capital expenditure as a share of GDP in 2008 and 2009, as shown in Figure 1.4, indicating that guaranteeing the payment of debt service is a fundamental policy of the state and, to the extent possible, it

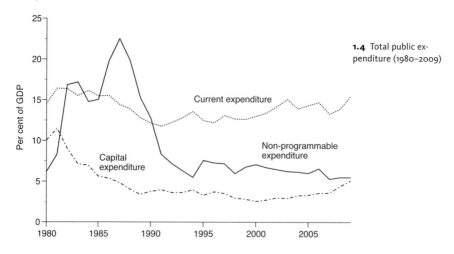

1.4 Total public expenditure (1980–2009)

Source: Centre for the Study of Public Finance from the Chamber of Deputies (CEFP), www.cefp.gob.mx/intr/bancosdeinformacion/historicas/gasto_publico/A53.xls (accessed March 2008); data 2007–09: SHCP, *Estadísticas oportunas de las finanzas públicas*, 2010, www.apartados.hacienda.gob.mx/estadisticas_oportunas/esp/index.html (accessed July 2010).

operates independently of political and electoral cycles. GDP growth declined throughout 2009 and only became positive in the first quarter of 2010. Tax rates were increased in January 2010; income tax rates rose temporarily from 28 per cent to 30 per cent; VAT rose from 15 to 16 per cent; and other indirect taxes also rose. The government forecast an increase in revenues of up to 1 per cent of GDP in 2010. The plan was to return to a balanced budget as soon as possible.

Transparency, accountability and participation From a human rights perspective, fiscal policy should be transparent; the government should be accountable to the people of Mexico for its operation; and the people should have opportunities to participate in the design and operation of policy. In Mexico, as in many countries, the design of fiscal policy is concentrated in the hands of the executive branch of government. It is the president of the republic who has the constitutional mandate to draw up the National Development Plan, where the general objectives of social and economic development are fixed and which provides guidance for fiscal policy; and to establish the mechanisms and procedures for participation and consultation.[8] Traditionally consultation with the general public is undertaken in each state in open-access public meetings.[9] It is difficult to know the level of influence that these consultative mechanisms have on the final version of the plan. The legislature does not participate in the elaboration of the plan, but it has the power to approve or to reject a budget.

The Secretary of the Treasury and Public Credit (SHCP) is in charge of drawing up the budget and presenting it to the Chamber of Deputies. The SHCP has some discretion in the use of any unanticipated extra income that results from higher than expected oil revenues; and to authorize additional payments in the Federal Budget for Expenditures (PEF), particularly for the unprogrammed expenditures (debt service and amortization). The SHCP is only obliged to *inform* the Chamber of Deputies about authorizing these expenditures.[10] The role of the legislature is weak, consisting primarily of oversight of the budgetary process, through the approval of the public accounts, one year after the budgetary process (Pérez and Romero 2006: 26).

There have been important advances in access to budgetary information in Mexico. Since 2001, the federal administration, in addition to producing the traditional budget document, also provides information about public debt, including those that result from the banking bailout. In the *Historic Accounts of Financial Requirements of the Public Sector* and the *Quarterly Reports on the Economic Situation, Public Finance and Public Debt* the full extent of the financial commitments of the public sector are made visible.[11] However, provision of this information has not led to improvements in accountability. While the Fox administration (2000–06) published data on the Financial Requirements of the Public Sector, it did not take the opportunity

> to investigate the murky and fraudulent privatization of the banking sector that was undertaken by Carlos Salinas, the bankruptcy of the [financial] intermediaries, and the bailout undertaken by Ernesto Zedillo and the subsequent re-privatization; to return the liabilities that were illegally transferred to the State and to impose legal sanctions on those involved in the violation of the laws. (Chávez 2005: 262)

The Treasury Budget and Transparency Law clearly lays out the rules and dates for the submission of budgetary information to the Chamber of Deputies, which gives more time to the commissions of the Chamber of Deputies to review the proposals of the Executive, and prepare proposals for modifications, as well as for civil society organizations to try to influence specific budget allotments.

Documents that provide some information about the loans to the Mexican federal government from the World Bank, the Inter-American Development Bank and the IMF are available on the websites of these organizations.[12] The processes through which projects and policies financed by these loans are designed are rarely participatory. At most they include a consultation with a limited selection of experts, academics and (occasionally) representatives of civil society.[13]

There are some important limits in the access to information relevant to fiscal policy. For example, even though the Federal Law for Access to Public and Governmental Information (LFTAIPG) requires the publication of information about the economic situation, public finances and debt, at the same time it includes restrictions regarding 'all information that can damage the economic, financial and monetary stability of the country'.[14] This clause is written so generally and permits such a wide definition of 'economic stability' that this can potentially place significant restrictions on access to information (Sandoval 2008). The laws governing access to information in other countries do not seem to have such a general definition of exemptions.

Another obstacle to an informed public debate is the poor quality of some of the economic and social data that the government agencies produce. While data on most key macroeconomic variables are generally very good, some of the data for employment are less reliable and consistent and much less easy to interpret. For example, according to newspaper articles, in April 2008 the Mexican Social Security Institute (IMSS) admitted to an 'error' in their methodology for measuring employment, which over a number of years contributed to an overestimation of the number of formal jobs (with formal contracts and social security benefits) created: between 2005 and 2007, the Mexican economy did not create 2.2 million formal jobs but instead only 1.6 million (Rivera and Carrillo 2008).

The limitations to transparency and participation in fiscal policy are reflected in the ratings obtained by Mexico in the Latin American Index of Budgetary Transparency, an index produced since 2003 by FUNDAR, a Mexican NGO specializing in fiscal policy. This index is based on evaluations by budget experts in academia, civil society and the legislature. Since this index was first published, Mexico has never obtained an overall rating of much above 50 per cent (see Figure 1.5).

The rating was initially higher than 60 per cent for the component of the index that relates to publication of information on macroeconomic variables, but this was because of the introduction of the transparency law: in

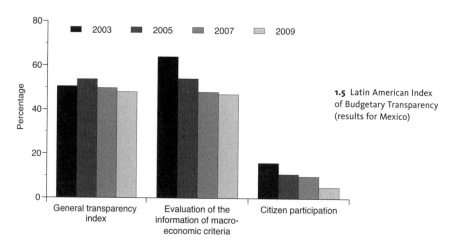

1.5 Latin American Index of Budgetary Transparency (results for Mexico)

Source: José Maria Marín (2009), *Indíce latinoamericano de transparencia presupuestaria,* 5th edn, FUNDAR, www.iltpweb.org/ (accessed July 2010)

subsequent years the rating declined because of the poor quality of much of the information.[15] The rating for citizen participation in the budget process continues to be very low because there are no formal mechanisms for citizen consultation in the development of the federal budget.

Conduct of monetary policy

Progressive realization and non-retrogression The mandate of the Bank of Mexico from 1999 onwards has been the control of inflation and the stability of prices. In this shift towards a monetary regime oriented towards controlling inflation, the financial crises of 1982 and 1994 played an important role because they gave impetus to a series of reforms in the management of external debt, and to liberalization of the exchange rate and the financial sector.

It was the administrations of Miguel de la Madrid (1982–88), Carlos Salinas de Gortari (1988–94) and Ernesto Zedillo (1994–2000) which gave rise to those policies that profoundly changed the financial structure of the country. Among these changes, the following should be highlighted: the development of the CETES[16] as new instruments of government borrowing, during the administration of de la Madrid (Suárez Dávila 2008); the reprivatization of the banking sector and the elimination of restrictions on foreign ownership in financial entities under the administration of Salinas (Gíl-Díaz and Carstens 1997); the banking bailout and the granting of autonomy to the Bank of Mexico during the administration of Zedillo; and finally, the transition towards a monetary regime based on fixing inflation targets, when the Bank of Mexico announced as a medium-term objective the control of inflation within a range of 3 (+/–1) per cent.

The monetary policy currently pursued by the Bank of Mexico, 'inflation targeting', has been introduced in many countries throughout the world at the urging of mainstream economists (Epstein 2003). The principal instrument of inflation targeting is the control of interest rates. A central bank cannot control inflation directly nor the variables that determine inflation – for example, the costs of raw materials, the costs of labour, or aggregate demand in the economy. However, central banks do have the instruments to affect a group of monetary variables that in turn affect inflation, such as interest rates. The control of interest rates can be undertaken with the intention of stimulating savings or investment. If interest rates are high, this typically stimulates savings and raises the cost of taking out loans and undertaking investment. If interest rates are low this is likely to stimulate consumption and borrowing and as a result can also increase investment. Who benefits from an increase in investment depends on how much employment is generated, the quality of this employment, the sustainability of any multiplier effects that create further jobs in other sectors, and the distribution of benefits between lenders and borrowers.

As Figure 1.6 illustrates, the Bank of Mexico's policies regarding its

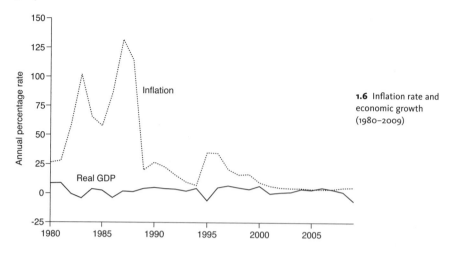

1.6 Inflation rate and economic growth (1980–2009)

Source: Annual inflation: data from the Centre for the Study of Public Finance, Chamber of Deputies, with data from the Bank of Mexico; GDP growth: CEPALSTAT

objectives of securing purchasing power and controlling inflation have been successful. It can be seen that after the financial disequilibria of the 1980s and 1990s, inflation was low after 2000. However, contrary to the expectations of mainstream economists, GDP growth continued to be erratic, and after the onset of the financial crisis in 2008, became sharply negative.

The restriction of monetary policy to inflation targeting has sidelined other objectives such as the generation of employment, and the selective stimulation of strategic economic sectors. Epstein (2003) and Pollin (1998, 1993) argue that there is no evidence that inflation rates lower than 20 per cent have significantly large negative effects on the real economy, nor on low-income people. However, low and controlled inflation benefits investors and the rentier classes.

Inflation targeting is based on the Taylor rule (after the economist John B. Taylor), which states that the central bank should alter interest rates to respond to deviations between actual and potential GDP and between actual and desired inflation rates (Taylor 1993). Potential GDP is defined as the level of national output that could be obtained if all markets in the economy were in equilibrium and all inputs were fully employed and used in the most efficient way. Mainstream economic theory suggests that markets do tend to equilibrium with full employment of all resources. Heterodox economists dispute this, and argue that disequilibrium and underemployment are more likely to characterize market economies, unless public policy is used to counteract these tendencies.

Currently, the Bank of Mexico adjusts the short-term interest rate in response to changes in the inflation rate. When the inflation rate rises, the Bank of Mexico increases the short-term rate of interest and vice versa. Similarly, when real GDP rises and it is thought to be converging towards potential GDP, the Bank of Mexico raises the rate of interest, dampening down expansion.

The Bank of Mexico is concerned about rises in prices of imports (which are mainly priced in US dollars) because these can feed through into rises in the peso prices of domestic goods that are produced using imported inputs. Rises in the dollar price of imports can be offset by allowing the exchange rate to appreciate, since that means that a peso is worth more in terms of US dollar (and a US dollar is worth fewer pesos). When interest rates are kept high to choke off inflation, this can attract short-term capital flows which will contribute to an appreciation of the exchange rate. Frequently, the Central Bank of Mexico allows appreciation to happen: from 1987 onwards the real exchange rate with the USA has tended to appreciate.

Galindo and Ros (2008) find that this has constrained economic growth in Mexico, because it makes Mexican exports more expensive in dollar terms and thus less able to compete in the USA and other international markets. They observe that the downward effect of the real exchange rate on output significantly increased after the signing of the North American Free Trade Agreement (NAFTA) in 1994, leaving the Mexican economy more sensitive to exchange rate changes today than in the past. The conclusion reached by Galindo and Ros (ibid.) is that inflation has indeed declined, in part owing to the implementation of an inflation targeting regime, and that there has been a slight reduction in pass-through from the raises in the price of imports to inflation. But this has come at a cost with the almost continuous appreciation of the real exchange rate, which has had contractionary effects on output in the long run. This is likely to weaken the creation of jobs that have just and favourable conditions.

At the beginning of June 2008, President Calderón urged the Bank of Mexico to lower interest rates as a strategy to stimulate economic growth. The Secretary of the Treasury, Agustin Carstens, reinforced this presidential request, highlighting that the difference between the rates of interest in Mexico and the United States had widened significantly, and as a result the Bank of Mexico should 'consider' this possibility. However, the Bank of Mexico was more concerned about inflation than stagnation. Following the onset of the global financial crisis of September 2008, the value of the peso fell by 17 per cent in real terms in October 2008, despite attempts by the central bank to prevent this. The real value of the peso declined by over a third during 2008. Thus, notwithstanding the requests from the government, the Bank of Mexico announced an increase in the one-day interbank lending rate from 7.5 to 7.75 per cent in an attempt to control inflation brought about by rises in the dollar price of imports (Meré 2008; González Amador and Rodríguez 2008).[17] In 2009, in response to the worldwide decline in growth rates, the Bank did lower the interest rate to 4.5 per cent, but maintained its focus on inflation as the primary objective of monetary policy.

Transparency, accountability and participation The Transparency Law also applies to the Bank of Mexico, and this creates improved opportunities for public scrutiny of monetary policy information by academics, civil society organizations, social movements and interested citizens.[18] However, the autonomy of the Bank means that it is not fully subject to the Federal Institute for Access to Public Information (IFAI).[19] The Information Committee of the Bank of Mexico, the body that decides about appeals in cases where information has been denied by the administrative divisions of the Bank, is made up of three functionaries who report directly to the governor of the Bank (Sandoval 2008).

Furthermore, as Sandoval (ibid.) shows, the mechanisms meant to secure the accountability of the Bank to the legislature are weak, starting with the nomination of the Board of Governors: Article 28 of the constitution stipulates that the five members of the Board of Governors are appointed by the president of the republic and approved by the Senate. Neither the constitution nor the law governing the Bank of Mexico clearly sets the procedures for the selection of the members of the board, which permits a wide margin of discretion on the part of the president.[20] The accountability mechanisms are limited to the submission of three reports to the president and the Congress: two general reports (one in September and the other in April) and an annual forecast of prices, economic activity and other macroeconomic data in January of each year. However, the Senate and the Chamber of Deputies can call the governor of the Bank before them to testify on specific matters.

Results of fiscal and monetary policy with respect to the right to work and to just and favourable conditions of work

The fiscal and monetary policies adopted since the early 1980s were supposed to support employment through fostering macroeconomic stability. This, it was argued, would promote economic growth, and this in turn would generate more employment. Here we assess whether this happened, and whether the rights to work and to just and favourable conditions of work were progressively realized, without policy causing any retrogression.

A summary of key macroeconomic indicators from 1993 to 2009 is provided in Table 1.1. Economic growth has been disappointing. There was a slight recovery after the 1994/95 crises, but in 2001 there was another significant downturn, and since then the average rate of growth has been low. The impact of the global economic crisis that began in 2008 can be seen in the dramatic fall in GDP in 2009. Private consumption also fell dramatically in 2009, and although public consumption increased, it was not sufficient to offset the fall in private consumption. The weak growth of public consumption as a component of aggregate demand highlights that the state plays a contingent or secondary role in promoting economic growth. That is, public consumption has not played a strong counter-cyclical role oriented towards stimulating

TABLE 1.1 Macroeconomic indicators (1993–2009)

	1994	1995	1996	1997	1998	1999	2000	2001	2002	2003	2004	2005	2006	2007	2008	2009
Annual rate of change																
Total GDP	4.8	-6.2	5.5	7.3	5	3.6	6	-1	0.1	1.3	4	3.2	4.9	3.3	1.5	-6.5
GDP per capita	3	-7.7	3.9	5.7	3.5	2.2	4.5	-2.2	-1.1	0.3	3	2.3	4	2.4	0.6	-7.3
Consumption	4.4	-8.4	1.8	6	5	4.4	7.4	1.9	1.4	2.1	4.4	4.5	5.1	3.9	1.7	-5
Public consumption	2.9	-1.3	-0.7	2.9	2.3	4.7	2.4	-2	-0.3	0.8	-2.8	2.5	1.9	3.1	0.9	2.3
Private consumption	4.6	-9.5	2.2	6.5	5.4	4.3	8.2	2.5	1.6	2.2	5.6	4.8	5.6	4	1.9	-6.1
Other components of aggregate demand																
Gross national investment, public and private	8.4	-29	16.4	21	10.3	7.7	11.4	-5.6	-0.6	0.4	8	7.5	9.9	6.9	4.4	-10.1
Exports of goods and services	17.8	30.2	18.2	10.7	12.2	12.3	16.3	-3.6	1.4	2.7	11.5	6.8	10.9	5.7	0.5	-14.8
Imports of goods and services	21.3	-15	22.9	22.7	16.6	14.1	21.5	-1.6	1.5	0.7	10.7	8.5	12.6	7.1	2.8	-18.2
Employment																
Activity rates (%)[1]	54.7	55	55.4	56.2	56.6	55.8	56.3	57.3	56.9	57.1	57.7	57.9	58.8	58.8	58.7	58.6
Open unemployment rates (%)[2]	3.6	6.3	5.5	3.7	3.2	2.5	2.2	2.8	3	3.4	3.9	3.6	3.6	3.7	4	5.5

Notes: 1. Ratio of the economically active to the working-age population, urban areas   2. As a percentage of the economically active population, urban areas. From 2003 onwards thirty-two areas were considered urban instead of the forty-eight that were defined as urban previously. From 2005 onwards the unemployment rate was unified, ENOE.

Source: Centre for the Study of Public Finance from the Chamber of Deputies (CEFP) database, www3.diputados.gob.mx/camara/001_diputados/006_centros_de_estudio/02_centro_de_estudios_de_finanzas_publicas/03_bancos_de_informacion/01_estadisticas_historicas/01_indicadores_macroeconomicos_1980_2010/01_principales_indicadores_economicos (accessed July 2010)

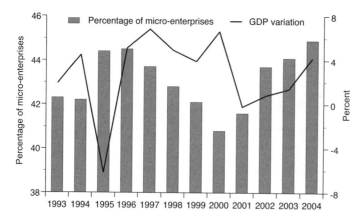

1.7 Economic growth and employment in micro-enterprises as a share of total urban employment (1993–2004)

Source: Percentage of employment in micro-enterprise: Salas and Zepeda (2006: 136); GDP growth rate: Centre for the Study of Public Finance from the Chamber of Deputies (CEFP) database, www3.diputados.gob. mx/camara/001_diputados/006_centros_de_estudio/02_centro_de_estudios_de_finanzas_publicas/03_bancos_ de_informacion/01_estadisticas_historicas/01_indicadores_macroeconomicos_1980_2010/01_principales_ indicadores_economicos, accessed July 2010

aggregate demand. The peso value of exports did increase in 2009, but the value of imports increased even more.

The rate of open unemployment reported in Table 1.1 is low, but this is attributable to the tiny proportion of workers who are covered by unemployment insurance. Only these workers are counted in the official unemployment rate. A large number of job seekers end up in the informal micro-enterprise sector characterized by precarious and low earnings (Salas 2008). Moreover, migration acts as an absorber of unemployment. More than three-quarters of Mexican migrants to the USA in 2008 were adults of working age (Terrazas 2010).

The relationship between GDP and the growth in the number of workers employed in the micro-enterprise sector in urban areas is shown in Figure 1.7: with the 1995 crisis, the proportion of urban workers occupied in this sector rose to 44 per cent. The economic recovery in the second half of the 1990s was accompanied by a reduction in this share, but from 2000 to 2004 the recovery of GDP was not accompanied by a reduction in the proportion of urban workers employed in the micro-enterprise sector. This highlights the failure of this type of economic growth to create sufficient jobs in the formal sector for those people seeking employment.

Employment growth by type of contract is shown in Table 1.2. Between 1995 and 2000, total employment grew 27.8 per cent; between 2000 and 2007 the increase was only 14.8 per cent. Moreover, the increase in permanent employment was much less in the later period than in the earlier period, whereas the increase in temporary employment was much greater in the later period than in the earlier period. By 2007, permanent employment was less than half of total employment.

TABLE 1.2 Structure of employment by type of contract, 1995, 2000, 2007

	Permanent contract	% change	Temporary contract	% change	Verbal contract	% change	Total	% change
1995	6,805,400		1,527,695		10,665,996		18,999,091	
2000	10,366,229	52.3	1,818,223	19	12,094,887	13.4	24,279,339	27.8
2007	12,058,356	16.3	2,557,576	40.7	13,259,870	9.6	27,875,802	14.8

Source: Taken from Salas (2008)

The global economic crisis of 2008 put further pressure on the creation of jobs with just and remunerative conditions. There was a fall in the rate of growth in the number of workers covered by the Mexican Social Security Institute (IMSS) in 2008. Comparing the first quarters of 2007 and 2008, there was an increase of 2.9 per cent in the numbers of workers covered by the IMSS. Comparing the second quarters over the same period, this had declined to 2.7 per cent, and by the third quarter the rate of growth had declined to 1.6 percent (BANXICO 2008). The ability to find a job in the USA fell, as unemployment rose in the USA. The number of Mexicans leaving in search of employment abroad (primarily to the USA) fell; it was 8 per cent lower in the third quarter of 2009 than it had been in the third quarter of 2008, and 39 per cent lower than it had been in the third quarter of 2007 (Terrazas 2010).

Not only has neoliberal fiscal and monetary policy constrained the creation of secure employment, it has also depressed wages. The minimum wage in Mexico was originally set in the 1917 Constitution. The current definition is specified in Article 123, Clause 6 of the Mexican Constitution: 'The generally applicable minimum wages should be sufficient to meet the normal needs of a head of household, in terms of their material, social and cultural needs, as well as to provide for the obligatory education of their children.'

In December 1986, the National Commission for Minimum Wages (CONASAMI) was set up, and it was established that 'minimum wages will be fixed by a national commission made up of representatives of workers, employers and the government ...'[21] The minimum wage is intended to fix a floor for wages and is a point of reference for collective bargaining.

The institutions charged with managing fiscal and monetary policy (the Treasury and the Bank of Mexico) influence the setting of the minimum wage. In the Consultative Commission for the modernization of the system for setting minimum wages, brought into being in 2001 by the federal government to evaluate the possibilities of raising minimum wages, the representative of the Bank of Mexico maintained that raising the minimum wage above the expected inflation rate and productivity growth rate would have a negative effect on employment, firm competitiveness and the overall macroeconomic environment. The strategy outlined by the Bank of Mexico was to raise the well-being of the population through measures to stimulate productivity of and demand for workers: 'such as training and skills building, achieving flexible labour markets, and promoting a stable macroeconomic environment' (Baqueiro Cárdenas 2002).

The imposition of wage ceilings, which began under the government of López Portillo (1976–82; Guillén 2000: 44–5) in order to keep wage rises below the inflation rate, contributed in the 1980s to the accelerated deterioration in real wages, shown in Figure 1.8. In 2007, approximately 12.6 per cent of the economically active population earned a salary of up to the value one minimum

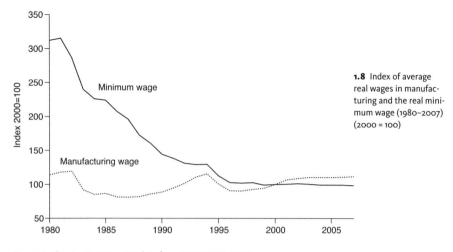

1.8 Index of average real wages in manufacturing and the real minimum wage (1980–2007) (2000 = 100)

Source: Authors' estimates using data from CEPALSTAT, CEPAL

wage and a further 20.6 per cent earned between one and two minimum wages.[22] The average real wage in manufacturing is also shown in Figure 1.8; it fell during the 1982 crisis, and recovered somewhat thereafter. However, in 1994 this recovery was undermined; and from 2000 onwards, the average real wage in manufacturing stabilized at a level no higher than in 1980.

The relationship between the minimum wage and national poverty lines is expressed in Table 1.3.[23]

TABLE 1.3 National poverty lines as a percentage of the minimum wage (1992–2008)

	1992	2000	2006	2008
Food poverty	44	61.8	59.1	66.6
Capacity poverty	53.5	75.1	72	81.1
Asset poverty	86.2	1.21	1.17	1.31

Note: Consolidated poverty lines using population weighted averages for rural and urban populations.
Source: National Commission on Minimum Wages and CONEVAL

While in 1992 an individual needed to earn only a little less than half of the minimum wage (44.0 per cent) to command an income that exceeded the food poverty line (extreme poverty), in 2008 the same individual needed to earn 66.6 per cent of the minimum wage to avoid food poverty. In 2000, one needed to earn 1.2 times the minimum wage and in 2008 1.3 times the minimum wage to be above the asset poverty line. These data indicate, despite a slight recovery in 2006, that the requirement established in the Constitution, that minimum wages should be sufficient to meet the normal needs of a family,[24] is far from being met. The strategy of most working families to cope with the decline in real wages has been the diversification of sources of income by increasing the number of family members in the labour market, especially women and youth (Salas 2008; Cortés 2006: 102–6).

The strategy of restrictive fiscal and monetary policy coupled with that of keeping rises in the minimum wage below the rate of inflation is clearly not fulfilling the right to just and favourable conditions of work, which includes 'a decent living for themselves and their families' (ICESCR, Article 7). Moreover, as Ibarra observes, these policies have contributed to the concentration of income:

> The population with incomes of up to two times the minimum wage has grown to almost 10 million and those who do not receive any income to 3.6 million (data from 2004). As a result, the distribution of income, taking into account minor fluctuations, has moved to the detriment of workers and in favour of income generated by enterprises and through property ownership. Placing aside the question of direct and indirect taxes and subsidies, the national income available to workers was 41 percent in 1980 and by 2003 this had shrunk to 30 percent. The opposite occurs with profits from enterprises and property ownership which rose from 54 percent to 61 percent. (Ibarra 2008: 546)

The Committee for Economic, Social and Cultural Rights expressed its concern about the value of the minimum wage in their Concluding Observations in the fourth report submitted to the Committee by Mexico in 2006:

> [Mexico should] ensure that wages fixed by the National Wages Commission or negotiated between workers and employers secure for all workers and employees, in particular women and indigenous workers, a decent living for themselves and their families, in accordance with Article 7(a)(ii) of the Covenant.[25]

However, it seems that the strategy of wage repression has not changed: in 2009 the official minimum wage was only 71.87 per cent of the minimum wage of 1994, and 2.65 per cent below its 2007 level (CONASAMI 2011).

It is likely that any recovery from the impact of the US financial crisis will begin to be seen only towards the end of 2010. If the crisis of 1995 provides any indication of how conditions are likely to worsen, unemployment and underemployment will continue to rise, and informality of employment will increase dramatically. Poverty rates increased between 2006 and 2009 and began to diminish only in 2010 (CONEVAL 2009, 2010).

Conclusion

Fiscal policy in Mexico over the last three decades has focused on maintaining a balanced budget and generating a primary budget surplus to cover interest payments on public debt. This occurs in a context where fiscal reform initiatives have largely failed to expand and deepen the tax base and improve collection (see Chapter 5). Adhering to these principles has reduced the margin of action for the state to stimulate aggregate demand in conditions of global economic downturn; and to undertake planning and policy to develop productive activities that create decent jobs in formal employment. This places at risk the principle of no retrogression and the progressive realization of social and economic rights.

Since 1999, monetary policy in Mexico has been reduced to meeting a target for low inflation, and as a result wage increments are seen as threats. In a recession, this approach limits the ability of the government to undertake counter-cyclical policy to stimulate aggregate demand. In this context the autonomy of the Bank of Mexico becomes problematic because it impedes adequate coordination between the Ministry of Finance and the central bank to enable them to confront an economic downturn.

In times of recession, it would be best for the Bank of Mexico to abandon its focus on inflation targets and concentrate on providing liquidity, and trying to counteract the contraction of credit and lending to productive sectors of the economy.

Macroeconomic strategies are not neutral with respect to the fulfilment of economic and social rights. Thirty years of a restrictive fiscal and monetary policy have demonstrated their inability to promote the kind of economic growth that generates employment with decent wages. The evidence presented in this chapter shows that fiscal and monetary policy has not been conducted in ways that contribute to the fulfilment of the right to work and to just and favourable conditions of work. This failure deserves to be discussed in a broad social dialogue to consider alternatives. Unfortunately, the decision-making on the objectives and strategies of fiscal and monetary policy is concentrated in the hands of the president, the Ministry of Finance and the Bank of Mexico, without sufficient opportunity for the legislature to participate and for citizens to be consulted.

Notes

1 The authors would like to thank Radhika Balakrishnan, Diane Elson, James Heintz, Juan Carlos Moreno-Brid, Ignacio Perrotini and Carlos Salas for their support and comments on previous versions of this document.

2 Ruling of the Federal Law of Budget and Treasury Responsibility, Article 11, *Diario Oficial de la Federación*, 28 June 2006, www. insp.mx/Portal/Centros/daf/normateca/regla_3. pdf. The specific ruling for exceptional reasons under which the Executive can incur a deficit include: rising financial costs to the public sector because of increases in interest rates; the costs of reconstruction after a natural disaster, where these costs exceed the resources available to the Natural Disaster Fund; the foreseen increment in costs in excess of 2 per cent of those programmable expenditures approved in the Expenditures Budget, including those expenditures destined for the payment of liabilities incurred because of similar events or to implement fiscal policy that contributes to reducing the budget deficit; and a foreseen fall in incomes from non-oil tax revenues that

exceeds 2.5 per cent of the amount approved in the Incomes Law as a result of the weak performance of the economy.

3 In 1980 the proportion of public sector income from oil revenues and royalties was 18 per cent of total revenue. This proportion increased to 34 per cent in 2008. The considerable importance of oil revenues in public sector income is partly attributed to the fiscal regime governing Petróleos Mexicanos (PEMEX) through which the federal government recovers 86 per cent of oil revenues through the Rights to Hydrocarbons. E. Caballero Urdiales (2007), 'El aporte de PEMEX a los ingresos del sector público de México', www.economia.unam.mx/cempe/EL%20APORTE%20DE%20PEMEX%2014%2003%2008%20final.pdf (accessed May 2008). It is important to note that resistance to tax reform in Mexico has persisted for some time. Antonio Ortiz Mena, Secretary of Treasury and Public Credit from 1958 to 1970, reports in his memoirs that the tax reform of 1961, overseen by the international expert Nicholas Kaldor, could not be achieved because of the resistance from the business sector, which considered these reforms as part of a strategy to implement 'socialist'-style reforms in Mexico (Mena Ortiz 1998: 156).

4 The primary balance is the fiscal balance excluding the cost of financing the public debt and loans guaranteed by the federal government.

5 This deficit was exacerbated by decisions taken in 1981 to increase both expenditures and revenues based on forecast changes in oil prices.

6 Journalists, opinion leaders and the opposition parties have criticized the state intervention in the 1994 banking crisis, focusing primarily on the disproportionate response and the magnitude of the rescue effort and the size of the losses that the public sector had to take on (Nava-Campos 2004: 475).

7 Non-programmable expenditures include that part of the federal government passed over to the states and municipalities, debt financing and other debts from fiscal corrections taken on previously.

8 See Article 26 of the Political Constitution of the United States of Mexico.

9 Under the administration of Vicente Fox an Internet consultation was implemented as an additional method of citizen participation, so that the citizenry could make their opinions known on approximately 110 national topics.

10 See LFPRH, Article 19(1).

11 See SHCP, *Report on the Economic Situation, Public Finance and Public Debt, First Quarter of 2008*, www.shcp.gob.mx (accessed June 2008).

12 These documents include, for example, the last 'Letter of Intent' signed by the Mexican government and sent to the IMF and signed in June 1999 (www.imf.org/external/np/loi/1999/061799.htm), as well as the *Country Partnership Strategy for the United Mexican States, 2008–2013*, 4 March 2008, which constitutes the guidelines for cooperation between the World Bank and the current administration (www-wds.worldbank.org).

13 For example, in the process of introducing results-based budgeting, which was overseen by the Inter-American Development Bank, the IDB invited representatives of civil society organizations, among these FUNDAR, to participate in seminars on the topic. But it is not clear to what extent the participation of civil society organizations has had any impact on the design of the results-based budgeting framework and reporting.

14 See the Federal Law for Transparency and Access to Public Governmental Information, Article 7(9) and Article 13(3), in the *Official Journal of the Federation*, 11 June 2002.

15 For example, during the last years of high oil revenues the Executive continually underestimated the price of oil, which allowed for excess earnings during the budget cycle, which the Secretary of the Treasury could distribute without consulting the legislature.

16 CETES are treasury certificates issued by the Mexican government.

17 Food, fertilizer and oil prices have been rising significantly in Latin America since 2007, placing pressure on inflation rates throughout the region.

18 For example, in 2007 the Bank of Mexico received 615 requests, and information was provided in 480 cases. Almost 18 per cent of the questions were about inflation estimates and requests for information about the National Consumer Price Index (INPC) and the National Producer Price Index (INPP), and just over 18 per cent about various interest rates (BANXICO 2008).

19 However, the Bank of Mexico does

provide accounts to the IFAI about meeting its obligations established in the LFTAIPG with respect to transparency and the right to information. See the Bank of Mexico's website on transparency: www.banxico.gob.mx/footer/leyTransparencia/LeyTransparencia.htm.

20 The mechanism for ensuring the autonomy of the Board of Governors of the Bank of Mexico is the appointment of members in stepped periods. For example, the period of the governor is six years, starting on 1 January of the fourth year of every presidential term.

21 See www.conasami.gob.mx/.

22 Data from Info-Laboral at the National Institute for Statistics and Geography (INEGI).

23 Following the definition applied by the Technical Committee for the Measurement of Poverty, food poverty includes those households that do not have sufficient income to acquire the basic basket of food items; capability poverty includes those families that are unable to meet other basic needs beyond nutrition, such as education and health; asset poverty includes those families that cannot meet other needs such as clothing, footwear, housing, energy and public transport. In 2006, the poverty lines established by the Technical Committee in rural areas were 18.27 pesos per person per day for food poverty, 21.70 for capability poverty, and 33.30 pesos for asset poverty. In urban areas these three lines were 24.70, 30.30 and 49.60 pesos per person per day respectively.

24 Average family size in 2006 was 4.5 members with an average of less than two income earners per family. Data from INEGI.

25 See United Nations, E/C.12/CO/MEX/4, Committee on Economic, Social and Cultural Rights, Concluding Observations, Mexico, 17 May 2006, www.ohchr.org/english/bodies/cescr/docs/E.C.12.co.mex.4.pdf.

References

BANXICO (2008) *Informe sobre la Inflación Julio–Septiembre 2008*, 29 October, www.banxico.org.mx/documents/{FB0916B3-BB2E-9883-BA6D-466667371809}.pdf (accessed January 2009).

Baqueiro Cárdenas, A. (2002) 'Consideraciones sobre el salario mínimo, el empleo y la estabilidad macroeconómica en México', Comisión Consultiva para la Modernización del Sistema de los Salarios Mínimos, *Estudios y ponencias*, STPS/CNSM, www.conasami.gob.mx (accessed June 2008).

Cabrera Adame, C. (2008) 'Gasto público (1982–2006)', in R. Cordera and C. J. Cabrera Adame (eds), *El papel de las ideas y las políticas en el cambio estructural en México*, El Trimestre Económico no. 99, Mexico: UNAM/FCE, pp. 138–72.

CEPAL (2008) 'Balance preliminar de las economías de América Latina y el Caribe – 2008', CEPAL Santiago, December.

— (2009a) *Preliminary Overview of the Economics of Latin America and the Caribbean 2009*, CEPAL, Santiago, December.

— (2009b) *México, Estudio Económico de América Latina y el Caribe 2008–2009*, CEPAL, Santiago, July.

— (2009c) *Panorama Social de América Latina 2009*, CEPAL, Santiago, November.

— (2010) 'Estudio económico de América Latina y el Caribe 2009–2010', CEPAL, Santiago, July.

Chang, H. and I. Grabel (2004) *Reclaiming Development. An Alternative Economic Policy Manual*, London: Zed Books.

Chávez, M. (2005) 'Las finanzas públicas en México, 1970–2000. Crónica del Fracaso de la política fiscal', in L. A. Aguilar and L. Jáuregui (eds), *Penurias sin fin. Historia de los impuestos en México. Siglos XVIII–XX*, Instituto Mora, pp. 211–302.

CONASAMI (2011) Índice del Salario Mínimo Real (1994=100), México/STPS, www.conasami.gob.mx/pdf/salario_minimo/sal_min_real.pdf.

CONEVAL (2009) Press release 006/09, July.

— (2010) 'Tendencias económicas y sociales de Corto Plazo, Agosto 2010', CONEVAL, August.

Cortés, F. (2006) 'La incidencia de la pobreza y la concentración del ingreso en México', in E. de la Garza and C. Salas (eds), *La situación del trabajo en México, 2006*, Mexico: Plaza y Valdés, pp. 91–123.

Epstein, G. (2003) 'Alternatives to inflation targeting monetary policy for stable and egalitarian growth: a brief research summary', Working Paper Series no. 62, Political Economy Research Institute, University of Massachusetts, Amherst.

FUNDAR Centro de Análisis e Investigación (2009) 'Incongruencia y contradicciones en la política económica del gobierno',

Working paper, 19 August, www.fundar.org. mx/pdf/IncongruenciaPoliticaEconomica. pdf (accessed October 2009).

Galindo, L. M. and J. Ros (2008) 'Alternatives to inflation targeting in Mexico', *International Review of Applied Economics*, March.

Gíl-Díaz, F. and A. Carstens (1997) 'Pride and prejudice: the economics profession and Mexico's financial crisis', in S. Edwards and M. Naím (eds), *Anatomy of an Emerging Market Crash*, Washington, DC: Carnegie Endowment for International Peace, pp. 165–200.

González Amador, R. and I. Rodríguez (2008) 'Eleva BdeM en 0.25% la tasa de interés; ignora pedido de Calderón', *La Jornada*, 21 June, p. 22.

Guillén, A. (2000) *México hacia el siglo XXI. Crisis y modelo económico alternativo*, Mexico: Plaza y Valdés.

Ibarra, D. (2008) 'Derechos humanos y realidades sociales', in R. Cordera and C. J. Cabrera Adame (eds), *El papel de las ideas y las políticas en el cambio estructural en México*, El Trimestre Económico no. 99, Mexico: UNAM/FCE, pp. 519–57.

IMF (2006) *Mexico: Selected Issues*, IMF Country Report no. 06/351, Washington, DC.

López González, T. (2005) 'Efectos de la desregulación financiera en la política fiscal. Implicaciones de política económica en México', in I. Manrique and T. López (eds), *Política fiscal y financiera en el contexto de la reforma del Estado y de la desregulación económica en América Latina*, Mexico: UNAM/Ed. Porrúa, pp. 19–102.

Marín, J. M. (2009) *Indíce latinoamericano de transparencia presupuestaria*, 5th edn, FUNDAR, www.iltpweb.org/ (accessed July 2010).

Mena Ortiz, A. (1998) *El desarrollo estabilizador: reflexiones sobre una época*, Mexico: FCE.

Meré, D. (2008) 'Piden a Banxico meditar', *Reforma. Sección Negocios*, 10 June.

Nadal, A. (2000) 'The environmental and social impacts of economic liberalization on corn production in Mexico', Study commissioned by Oxfam GB and WWF International.

Nava-Campos, G. (2004), 'Implicaciones fiscales del rescate bancario en México, 1994–1998', in J. P. Guerrero (ed.), *Impuestos y gasto público en México desde una perspectiva multidisciplinaria*, Mexico: CIDE.

Notimex/La Jornada online (2008) 'Disminuyó 31.2% crédito bancario al consumo en noviembre. BdeM', *La Jornada Online*, 31 December, www.jornada.unam.mx/ ultimas/2008/12/31/cae-en-noviembre-31-2-credito-bancario-al-consumo (accessed January 2009).

Ocampo, J. A. (2005) *Más allá del Consenso de Washington: una agenda de desarrollo para América Latina*, Estudios y Perspectivas series no. 26, CEPAL.

OECD (2006) *OECD in Figures 2006–2007*, Paris: OECD Publications, www.oecd.org/ infigures (accessed March 2008).

Pérez, M. and J. Romero (2006) 'Transparencia en el presupuesto público. Los desafíos de la rendición de cuenta', in H. Hofbauer and V. Zebadua (eds), *Avances y retrocesos, una evaluación ciudadana del sexenio 2000–2006*, 1, Mexico: FUNDAR.

Perrotini Hernández, I. (2008) 'El nuevo paradigma monetario', *Economía*, 4(11): 64–82.

Pollin, R. (1993) 'Public credit allocation through the Federal Reserve: why is it needed; how should it be done', in G. Dymski, G. Epsetin and R. Pollin (eds), *Transforming the U.S. Financial System: Equity and Efficiency for the 21st Century*, Armonk, NY: M. E. Sharpe.

— (1998) 'Can domestic expansionary policy succeed in a globally integrated environment? An examination of alternatives', in D. Baker, G. Epstein and R. Pollin (eds), *Globalization and Progressive Economic Policy*, Cambridge: Cambridge University Press.

Presidencia de la República (2007) *Plan Nacional de Desarrollo 2007–2012*, Mexico, www. pnd.presidencia.gob.mx (accessed April 2008).

Rivera, A. and L. Carrillo (2008) 'Inflan cifra de empleo', *Reforma*, 14 May.

Salas, C. (2008) *Tendencias salariales en México*, Mimeo, February.

Salas, C. and E. Zepeda (2006) 'Ocupación e ingresos en México, 2000–2004', in E. de la Garza and C. Salas (eds), *La situación del trabajo en México, 2006*, Mexico: Instituto de Estudios del Trabajo, pp. 125–50.

Sandoval, I. E. (2008) 'Autonomía, transparencia y rendición de cuentas en organismos financieros: el caso del Banco de México', in J. Ackerman (ed.), *Más allá del acceso a la información: transparencia, rendición de cuentas y Estado de derecho*, Mexico: Siglo XXI, pp. 199–217.

SHCP (2008) *Informe sobre la situación económica, las finanzas públicas y la deuda pública. Primer Trimestre de 2008*, www.shcp.gob.mx (accessed June 2008).

Suárez Dávila, F. (2008) 'Retroceso estructural del sistema financiero (1940–2005). Tragicomedia nacional en tres actos', in R. Cordera and C. J. Cabrera Adame (eds), *El papel de las ideas y las políticas en el cambio estructural en México*, El Trimestre Económico no. 99, Mexico: UNAM/FCE, pp. 227–57.

Taylor, J. B. (1993) 'Discretion versus policy rules in practice', *Carnegie-Rochester Conference Series on Public Policy*, 39: 195–214.

Terrazas, A. (2010) 'Mexican immigrants in the United States', Migration Information Source, Migration Policy Institute, www.migrationinformation.org.

Legislative documents

Constitución Política de los Estados Unidos Mexicanos.

Ley del Banco de México (current text), www.banxico.org.mx/tipo/disposiciones/marconormativo/leyBM/TextoVigente.html#c4 (accessed June 2008).

Ley Federal de Presupuesto y Responsabilidad Hacendaria, *Diario Oficial de la Federación*, 30 March 2006.

Ley Federal de Transparencia y Acceso a la Información Pública Gubernamental, *Diario Oficial de la Federación*, 11 June 2002.

Ley General de Desarrollo Social, *Diario Oficial de la Federación*, 20 January 2004.

Reglamento de la Ley Federal de Presupuesto y Responsabilidad Hacendaria, *Diario Oficial de la Federación*, 28 June 2006.

United Nations, E/C.12/CO/MEX/4, Committee on Economic, Social and Cultural Rights, Concluding Observations, Mexico, 17 May 2006, www.ohchr.org/english/bodies/cescr/docs/E.C.12.co.mex.4.pdf.

2 | HUMAN RIGHTS DIMENSIONS OF FISCAL AND MONETARY POLICIES: UNITED STATES

Radhika Balakrishnan and James Heintz

Introduction

This chapter analyses the human rights dimensions of fiscal and monetary policy in the USA over the past three decades. Fiscal and monetary policies have implications for the realization of all economic and social rights, but to make the analysis manageable, we shall concentrate on the implications for the right to work and just and favourable conditions of work. We analyse the conduct of policy in terms of the principles of progressive realization and non-retrogression, transparency, accountability and participation; and the results in terms of progressive realization of the right to work and to just and favourable conditions of work, paying attention to equality and non-discrimination.

The Universal Declaration of Human Rights (1948) includes the right to work (Article 23). It is further spelled out in the International Covenant on Economic Social and Cultural Rights (1966), which defines the right to work in Article 6 (which details the actions required by governments to fulfil this right, including 'policies and techniques to achieve steady economic, social and cultural development and full and productive employment'); and the right to just and favourable conditions of work in Article 7. The elimination of discrimination in the enjoyment of these rights is covered by Article 5 of the Convention on the Elimination of All Forms of Racial Discrimination (1965) and Article 11 of the Convention on the Elimination of All Forms of Discrimination Against Women.

The UN Committee on Economic, Social and Cultural Rights has clarified that the right to work requires the implementation of policies and measures aimed at securing work for all who are available for work; and that the right to just and favourable conditions of work means that wages must be sufficient to guarantee a decent living (Committee on Economic, Social and Cultural Rights 1993). The Committee has also referred to the relevance of International Labour Organization conventions in interpreting the right to work and to just and favourable conditions of work. Particularly relevant is the International Labour Organization's concept of decent work:

> It involves opportunities for work that is productive and delivers a fair income, security in the workplace and social protection for families, better prospects

for personal development and social integration, freedom for people to express their concerns, organize and participate in the decisions that affect their lives and equality of opportunity and treatment for all women and men. (ILO 2010)

It is clear that the human rights approach to employment emphasizes the quality as well as the quantity of employment: full employment, at wages that provide a decent living.

Fiscal and monetary policy and the right to work and to just and favourable conditions of work

Fiscal and monetary policies affect the levels of overall supply and demand in an economy, and through this the levels of output, inflation and employment. Fiscal policy is the management of the government budget, including expenditure and revenue, and also public borrowing, especially via the issuing of government bonds and bills. Monetary policy allows the government to influence the supply of money, interest rates and the exchange rate between a country's currency and those of other countries. Monetary policy also includes regulation of the financial sector, including regulations on the amount of capital that commercial banks must hold in reserve; and also decisions on the size of reserves of foreign currency held by the government in order to maintain capacity to pay for essential imports in the face of fluctuations in foreign exchange earnings. Fiscal policy is the responsibility of the ministry of finance (or equivalent institution, such as the US Treasury), while monetary policy is the responsibility of the central bank (in the USA, this is the Federal Reserve System).

A central goal of fiscal and monetary policy on which all economists agree is to try to maintain overall economic stability, and smooth out the fluctuations in the overall level of output and prices, to which capitalist market economies are inherently prone. However, economists disagree about whether 'full employment' is an appropriate goal of fiscal and monetary policy. Instead of full employment, neoclassical economists often refer to an economy with no 'involuntary unemployment'. They assume that liberalized markets will eliminate involuntary unemployment: according to neoclassical theories, the excess supply of labour associated with unemployment will disappear as long as wages are allowed to adjust.

For example, Milton Friedman (1968), a neoclassical macroeconomist, argued that the economy would tend to move towards a 'natural rate of un-employment'. The natural rate of unemployment is the level of unemployment that would prevail, taking into account natural turnover from jobs, the effort it takes to find new employment, and the time it may take for workers to move from one job to another. If unemployment rose above this natural rate, wages would begin to fall. Lower wages are supposed to increase demand for labour by employers and reduce supply of labour from workers. Eventually, unemployment would return to its 'natural' rate.

Thus neoclassical economics proposes that there is a trade-off between the quantity of jobs and the level of wages – in Friedman's framework, wage increases would drive unemployment above its natural rate, but then the higher rate of unemployment would eventually put downward pressure on wages. They are also concerned that low unemployment will lead to a rise in the rate of inflation. When unemployment falls below its natural rate, wages would begin to rise. Higher wages may push up prices. However, in the long run, higher wages would also reduce labour demand and eventually unemployment would rise back to its natural rate. This approach to economics calls into question the possibility of full compliance with the provisions of the right to work and to just and favourable conditions of work, particularly when the wages and working conditions associated with the so-called natural rate of unemployment are substandard in human rights terms.

Progressive economists offer an alternative that is more congruent with those rights. They point to theories and evidence supporting the view that full employment depends not only on the cost of labour but on the overall level of demand in an economy. They argue that capitalist market economies have an inherent tendency to fail to generate enough demand to secure full employment. They show that fiscal policy can counteract this tendency through increasing public expenditure and cutting taxes when output falls and unemployment rises, putting more purchasing power into the hands of businesses and households, and making job creation at decent pay more likely. The idea that unemployment may remain at high levels owing to inadequate demand in the economy is most closely associated with the work of John Maynard Keynes (1964). If the government is to support overall demand by increasing spending during a downturn, it may have to borrow in order to do so. In other words, the government may have to run a budget deficit, with expenditure greater than revenue, until full employment is restored.

Thus, budget deficits are not necessarily bad: a budget surplus will act as an impediment to restoring full employment in times of recession. An appropriate policy is counter-cyclical, with deficits to combat unemployment in downturns and surpluses to combat inflationary over-expansion of demand in upturns.

However, progressive economists do emphasize that the way in which governments expand demand matters. Budget deficits that are caused by decreasing taxes on wealthier households will be less effective in creating jobs than those caused by increases in government spending. This is because rich people tend not to spend much of the additional after-tax income. The impact on employment will also vary depending on where the expenditure is allocated. Military spending has the effect of contributing to GDP growth, but the positive impact on job creation may not be as large as spending on health, education and infrastructure.

Fiscal policy also has an impact on the aggregate supply in an economy. Here again there are disagreements between economists. Neoclassical economists argue that government spending tends to displace private sector spending, and that the latter would be more productive. For example, Milton Friedman (2002) argues that if government spends money on something which private individuals would have purchased themselves, then increases in public expenditure reduce private expenditures, and there will be no impact on the economy.

Progressive economists argue that much government spending serves to increase the productive capacity of an economy, through investment in physical and human resources, such as transportation infrastructure and a trained and healthy labour force, which private sector businesses would be reluctant to undertake. Similarly, private individuals may not be able to invest in their own education, if they do not have the resources to do so and lack access to long-term credit from the private sector in the absence of government policies. The revenue side of the budget may also have an impact on aggregate supply through the impact of taxation on incentives to produce. Neoclassical economists argue that high levels of income tax and profits tax discourage people from producing, thus reducing aggregate supply. However, this effect should be evaluated relative to the positive effect that taxation-financed public investment has on aggregate supply. Progressive economists argue that the bigger problem is a focus on achieving a balanced budget or a budget surplus without regard to employment levels.

> There is a clear need for fiscal discipline, defined as responsible fiscal policy that levies taxes fairly and efficiently and spends wisely. However, that is a very different proposition from making balancing the budget the primary focus of fiscal policy. Moreover, deficits should be recognized as a rational and reasonable tool of fiscal policy. (Palley 2002: 17)

Monetary policy also has an impact on the level of aggregate demand and supply. Central banks influence aggregate demand by adjusting the interest rate that they charge to commercial banks when the latter borrow on overnight markets in order to meet the requirements for holding a minimum quantity of financial resources that are stipulated by the central bank. In the USA, this interest rate is called the Federal Funds Rate. The Federal Funds Rate influences, to some extent, the interest rates commercial banks charge on loans: if the Federal Funds Rate rises, the rates of interest charged by commercial banks also tend to rise. Higher interest rates decrease the demand for loans by borrowers; and as the amount of credit made available by the banks contracts, so does the money supply.

The money supply is determined by the financial resources that can quickly be converted into cash to finance purchases and sales. Therefore, it includes all the savings and checking deposits in the banking system. When credit expands (or falls), it increases (or decreases) the total financial resources available – i.e. the money supply changes with the amount of credit available.

The money supply, in turn, determines the financial purchasing power available in the economy. Just as with fiscal policy, monetary policy can be expansionary or contractionary; increasing or decreasing aggregate demand. Neoclassical economists argue that the impact of monetary policy is only on the level of prices; and that monetary policy is ineffective in increasing (or decreasing) employment. Again, we can use the theories of Milton Friedman (1968) as an example. He argues that increases in the money supply may, in the very short run, raise the demand for labour (ibid.). However, as discussed earlier, this leads to pressures on wages and inflation. Higher wages and inflationary pressures counteract the effect of an expansion in the money supply. Neoclassical economists therefore argue that what money supply primarily affects is the rate of inflation, not the level of employment. Many central banks now focus exclusively on managing the rate of inflation, and often have explicit inflation targets.

Monetary policy can also have an impact on the supply side of the economy. Lower interest rates may encourage private sector investment and expand the economy's capacity to produce goods and services and create jobs. However, progressive economists caution that private sector investment also depends on the expected level of demand for what is produced. If there is a downturn in the economy, businesses may not invest, even if interest rates are very low. Moreover, during a downturn, banks may not lend when they are worried that borrowers will default on their loans (Stiglitz 1999). The result is a situation in which banks do not lend and investors are wary of an uncertain economy. Monetary policy, by itself, may be unable to fix this situation. Unless there is an expansionary fiscal policy, monetary policy may be ineffective.

The approach of progressive economists is thus more congruent with the human rights approach, emphasizing the risk that capitalist market economies will fail to create decent jobs for all who want them; and the ability of governments to offset this with appropriate fiscal and monetary policies.

In a globalized economy, in which international financial markets have been liberalized, many governments do face constraints in using fiscal and monetary policy to fulfil the right to work and to just and favourable conditions of work. To use these policies in a proactive way, governments need to be able to borrow to finance deficits in downturns, by selling government bonds. Particularly in conditions of economic crisis, private sector financial institutions operating in international financial markets may be unwilling to buy these bonds in large enough quantities. They may instead speculate against the bonds, driving up the cost of borrowing to unsustainable levels. Of course, government policy has reinforced the power of bond holders by liberalizing financial markets. But we must recognize that many governments in developing countries have done this reluctantly, as a condition for receiving loans from the International

Monetary Fund. If international bond dealers are preventing governments from fulfilling their human rights obligations, then governments have a responsibility to help one another create an international system which is more supportive of full employment and decent wages.

Fiscal and monetary policy in the United States

The obligation of conduct requires the US government to use fiscal and monetary policy so as to fulfil human rights. It must conduct these policies in ways that are reasonably calculated to realize human rights (General Comment 3, 'The Nature of States Parties' Obligations', 1990). Here we will examine conduct bearing in mind the obligation to progressively realize the right to work, and the right to just and favourable conditions of work, without retrogression. We will also examine the extent to which the conduct of policy has satisfied the principles of transparency, accountability and participation.

Progressive realization and non-retrogression
OBLIGATION OF CONDUCT These principles suggest that fiscal and monetary policy should be conducted so as to offset the ups and downs of the market economy, so as to maintain and expand the enjoyment of the right to work. In other words, policy should be counter-cyclical rather than pro-cyclical, expanding aggregate demand in a downturn and contracting it in an upturn; and should have a concern with the impact of policy on employment.

First we examine whether budget legislation permits this. At the federal level, there is currently no specific legislation requiring the US Treasury (i.e. the US equivalent of a ministry of finance) to balance the federal budget. However, legislation to limit spending by the federal government has been introduced in the past, and political discourse in late 2010 indicates that the drive to cut spending in order to eliminate budget deficits has surfaced again with renewed fervour, similar to the 2011 debates on the budget. The debates of 2010 regarding the need to cut spending in order to reduce the deficit and balance the budget were very much a part of the mid-term election debate and had a great deal to do with the results of the elections. The Gramm-Rudman-Hollings Emergency Deficit Control Act of 1985 attempted to contain budget deficits by limiting spending and established a maximum deficit beyond which the president had to limit certain spending. In the Balanced Budget and Emergency Deficit Control Reaffirmation Act (1987) the maximum deficit amounts were extended to 1992.

These laws have been introduced as temporary measures with finite expiration dates and as such have had little binding power. In spite of this legislation, deficits continued to grow. In 1990 the Budget Enforcement Act replaced the system of deficit limits with two independent enforcement regimens: caps on discretionary spending[1] and a pay-as-you-go requirement for direct spending[2] and revenue legislation (Committee on the Budget, US Senate, 1998).

Both have remained throughout subsequent budget acts. In 2005, the Deficit Reduction Act instituted cuts in mandatory programmes to take place over the subsequent five years. The 2005 Act adjusted the growth rate of the public health insurance programmes, Medicare and Medicaid, and modified the way in which government-guaranteed student loans were administered. The bulk of these cuts affect social spending to marginalized and vulnerable social groups.

All states, with the exception of Vermont, have balanced budget requirements. The source of these requirements varies from state to state: some are enshrined in the state Constitution, others were the result of laws being passed, and still others were the outcome of a judiciary ruling. A balanced budget requirement means the expenditures cannot exceed revenues, except for very specific categories of spending (e.g. certain categories of public investment in infrastructure). As a result, state budgets are often pro-cyclical rather than counter-cyclical. During an economic downturn, tax revenues fall, which means that, to keep the budget balanced, government spending must decline. During good times, high tax revenues encourage governments to lower average tax rates. Therefore, state spending is often cut during a downturn and taxes are reduced during economic upturns.

Now we turn from examining legislation to examining whether government policy has operated so as to offset economic downturns (counter-cyclical) or reinforce them (pro-cyclical).

In practice, the United States stands apart from nearly every other nation in terms of the fiscal policies it is able to pursue. The budget deficit rose to well over $1 trillion beginning in 2009, owing largely to falling tax revenues and increased spending associated with the economic crisis. This is the highest peacetime deficit, both in absolute value and relative to the size of the economy, in US history. The USA is able to finance this level of borrowing because of the role of the dollar as an international reserve currency. Other countries need dollars to buy imports, make debt payments, and participate in global markets. Countries often guard against global economic risks by accumulating reserves of dollars through the buying of US government-issued bonds. This effectively means that the central banks in other countries as well as private sector actors have been willing to finance US deficits as a type of insurance policy.

Figure 2.1 shows information on the US deficit in three categories: (1) the federal deficit, (2) state and local government deficits, and (3) deficits from all levels of government combined. Negative numbers in the figure indicate budget deficits. Positive numbers show surpluses. Figure 2.1 indicates that fiscal policy at the federal level has responded counter-cyclically. That is, the deficit has increased during economic downturns and fallen during boom years. For example, the economic downturns in the early 1980s and the early 1990s were associated with notable increases in the deficit (i.e. the budget balance became more negative). During the second half of the 1990s, the US economy

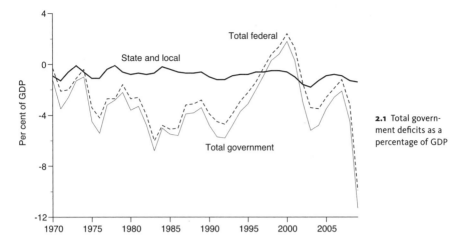

2.1 Total government deficits as a percentage of GDP

Source: Office of Management and Budget, Historical Tables, Table 15.6: 'Total government surpluses or deficits in absolute amounts and percentages of GDP: 1948–2009', www.whitehouse.gov/omb/budget/Historicals/

performed well and the federal budget went into surplus for the first time since the end of the Second World War. Notice that the budget balance for state and local governments does not show the same counter-cyclical behaviour.

Although fiscal and monetary policies have responded counter-cyclically, deficit spending has been increasingly concerned with financing non-social expenditures, such as the military. Figure 2.1 shows that throughout the 1980s the deficit remained sizeable, even when the economy was not in recession. This was due to high levels of defence spending. Sustained areas of expenditure, such as military spending, can create deficits across the booms and busts of the economy. Such deficits are often called 'structural deficits'.

For example, the US government allocated an estimated \$624 billion to the military in 2008 (Pollin and Garrett-Peltier 2009), accounting for 4.3 per cent of GDP. Such spending often has a relatively small impact on the realization of social and economic rights, such as the right to work.

A recent study of the relative employment impact of military spending relative to social spending and public investment found that 'Spending \$1 billion on personal consumption, clean energy, health care, and education will all create significantly more jobs within the US economy than would the same \$1 billion spent on the military' (ibid.: 3).

The study estimated that \$1 billion in defence spending would generate 11,600 jobs, compared to 19,600 jobs from \$1 billion in healthcare spending and 29,100 jobs from the same of amount of spending on educational services. Moreover, borrowing to finance ongoing military spending is not sensitive to the state of the economy, but rather contributes to structural deficits – long-run deficits which are the outcome of structural features of taxation and spending.

Concerns over securing a balanced budget were pushed temporarily to the sidelines by the severity of the 2008 financial crisis and its aftermath. The enactment of the American Recovery and Reinvestment Act (ARRA) in February 2009 demonstrated that the federal government was willing to introduce a substantial fiscal stimulus in response to the crisis. The ARRA authorized nearly $790 billion in combined government spending and tax cuts to counteract the recession. From a human rights perspective, it is important to stress that there were good parts and 'less good' parts of the ARRA. A significant portion of the stimulus package went towards aid to states (supporting Medicaid and education). This was good – a partial response to the pro-cyclical nature of state-level spending. There was also a sizeable amount of direct spending aimed at job creation. This was important – since it helped prevent retrogression in terms of the right to work.

However, tax cuts comprised a sizeable share of the stimulus package. In December 2010, in order to maintain unemployment benefits, the Obama administration agreed to maintain tax cuts on the very rich for two more years. This will certainly reduce the amount of money available to increase government spending, and the amount of money that the top 1 per cent will spend owing to the tax cuts will not be sufficient to help increase aggregate demand. This raises questions about whether the right to work could have been better protected by further increases in spending.

So far, the federal government is not constrained by rigid balanced budget laws that would prevent a pro-employment response to downturns and recessions. However, in 2010 pressures to reduce the deficit by cutting government spending have grown, even when unemployment remains at 9 to 10 per cent. In 2011, the Republican Party will control the House of Representatives, the lower chamber of the federal legislature, making it almost impossible for President Obama to introduce a further fiscal stimulus, even if there is high unemployment.

One of the major objectives of the ARRA was employment creation. Again, this is positive from a human rights perspective. However, the type of employment generated needs to be closely examined to ensure that there are no discriminatory impacts where a certain group, men as opposed to women, is privileged in the type of spending.

Monetary policy in the USA is conducted by the Federal Reserve System, the key management of which is appointed by the president. It consists of a seven-member Board of Governors, a Federal Open Market Committee and twelve Federal Reserve Banks located in major cities. In formal terms, the Federal Reserve operates under a dual mandate: it is responsible for maintaining the maximum level of employment possible and managing inflation to ensure price stability. Full employment was codified as a responsibility of the Federal Reserve with the 1978 Full Employment and Balanced Growth Act. The law mandates that the Federal Reserve 'promote full employment … and reasonable price stability' (Thorbecke 2000: 6).

However, there have been some attempts by lawmakers to overturn the legal mandate of the Federal Reserve in order to institute price stability as the chief objective of monetary policy. In 1999, House of Representatives member Jim Saxton introduced the Price Stability Act to mandate price stability as the 'primary and overriding goal' of monetary policy. As Thorbecke (ibid.: 10) argues, 'It would require the Federal Reserve to establish an explicit numerical goal for inflation and specify the time frame for achieving this goal.' The Price Stability Act was reintroduced in 2008, but the proposed legislation never became law.

In practice, the Federal Reserve has for some time put more emphasis on combating inflation, beginning with Paul Volker's term as the chair of the Federal Reserve Board of Governors (1979–87). The two subsequent chairs, Alan Greenspan (1987–2006) and Ben Bernanke (2006 to the present), continued this tradition. In 2007, Bernanke was described by the business journal *The Economist* as pursuing a policy of 'low cal inflation targeting' or 'inflation targeting lite'; i.e. putting the emphasis on low inflation, without having an explicit inflation target.[3]

Proponents of inflation targeting argue that monetary policy cannot influence employment or standards of living in the long run. They also advocate for central bank action to control inflationary threats of rising wages. Critics of the Federal Reserve such as progressive economists claim that 'rising wages are actually viewed as cause for concern on the grounds that they may be inflationary, but the same standard is never applied to rising profit rates' (Palley 2007: 5). They report that 'When wages lag, the Fed expresses sympathy for the failure of wages to rise. But once they start rising, then the Fed says there's an inflation danger and we have to step on the brake. So it really actually has sort of a trap for wages built into it.'[4] It seems that the Federal Reserve interprets tightening of the labour market as cause for alarm.

Figure 2.2 shows how the Federal Funds Rate, the policy interest rate described above, has changed from 1960 to 2009. The figure shows both the nominal Federal Funds Rate (the actual interest rate) and the real Federal Funds Rate (the interest rate minus the inflation rate). Many economists argue that the real Federal Funds Rate is more important in influencing investment and employment outcomes. The most significant shift in monetary policy over this period began in the late 1970s. The 1970s were a period of relatively high rates of both inflation and unemployment. The Federal Reserve chose to focus on battling inflation. Figure 2.2 shows the dramatic rise in interest rates that resulted from the Federal Reserve's policies. These policy choices caused the most severe recession since the end of the Second World War, until the recent crisis that unfolded in 2008 came along.

While no one would argue that inflation, in itself, is a good thing, it is important to consider the trade-offs involved. If maintaining inflation in the very low single digits requires high interest rates, slower growth and more

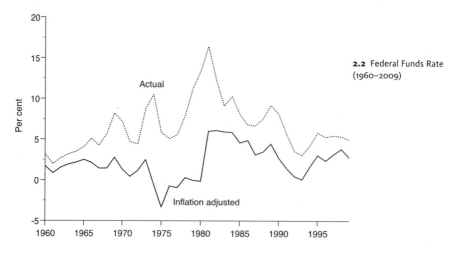

2.2 Federal Funds Rate (1960–2009)

Source: Table H, '15 selected interest rates', Federal Reserve Statistical Release, Board of Governors of the Federal Reserve System, www.federalreserve.gov/releases/h15/data.htm

unemployment, the costs of the policy will exceed any possible benefits. Moderate rates of inflation up to 20 per cent have not been proved to do any harm (Bruno and Easterly 1996 and Epstein 2000, 2002, cited in Epstein 2003: 4).

Since the 1980s, Federal Reserve policy has emphasized inflation control over unemployment. This does not mean that the Federal Reserve has been completely unresponsive to recessions. For example, the Federal Funds Rate dropped in the early 1990s in response to an economic downturn. Worries about inflation and what the Federal Reserve considered to be overly low rates of unemployment led to a rise in interest rates beginning in 2005. This increase in interest rates helped trigger the crisis in sub-prime mortgages which eventually caused the current financial crisis.

Federal Reserve policy changed significantly in response to the financial crisis, the true extent of which became evident in the second half of 2008. Bernanke introduced trillions of dollars into the US economy in an effort to prevent a systemic financial collapse. The direct injection of financial resources into the economy – in contrast to conducting monetary policy by adjusting the Federal Funds Rate – is called 'quantitative easing'. Both financial institutions and non-financial institutions borrowed money from the Federal Reserve – including corporations like Goldman Sachs, Citigroup, General Electric and Harley Davidson (Chane and McGinty 2010). However, quantitative easing did not provide direct credit to ordinary homeowners facing foreclosure.

OBLIGATION OF RESULT First we examine trends in unemployment, as this is an important indicator of whether the right to work is being realized.

Figure 2.3 shows the rate of unemployment since 1979 – rising in recession and falling as the level of output in the economy has recovered. It also shows

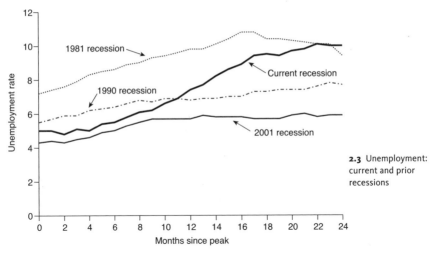

2.3 Unemployment: current and prior recessions

Source: Data from Economic Policy Institute, *Resources: Economy Track Data*, www.epi.org/resources/ economy_track_data

the long-term unemployment (those who are unemployed for twenty-seven weeks or over) as a share of total unemployment. Since 1979 the share of long-term unemployment in total unemployment has risen from below 4 per cent to about 18 per cent in 2006. The rate at which long-term unemployment rose during the 2001 recession was also greater than during the two previous recessions.

Job growth in the 2001 business cycle lagged behind that of all the previous business cycles for the past forty years (see Figure 2.3).

It is clear from Figure 2.3 that the impact of the current recession in terms of unemployment rate is going towards the levels of the 1981 recession. Other than the official unemployment rate there is also a problem of underemployment and those who have left the labour force. The underemployment rate as of 2008 was already at 11 per cent: this includes the unemployed as well as those who are looking for full-time work but can only find part-time work, as well as those marginally connected to the labour market (Mahalia 2008).

The rate of unemployment is clearly an important indicator as to whether the right to work is being realized, but it does not tell us whether the right to just and favourable conditions of work is being realized. The rate of unemployment may be low but available jobs may not provide just and favourable conditions of work. In countries that do not have unemployment benefits or other forms of social security, usually only wealthier people can afford to be unemployed for any length of time (Balakrishnan et al. 2009: 38). Poor and middle-income people have to find some way to survive through informal employment, even though this type of employment may be poorly paid and insecure (ibid.: 38). Unemployment, underemployment and inadequate

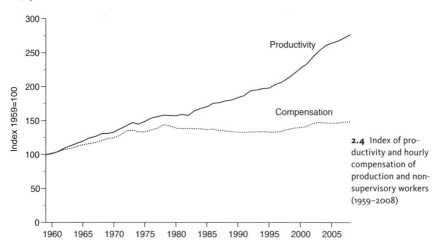

2.4 Index of productivity and hourly compensation of production and non-supervisory workers (1959–2008)

Source: Figure 3B from Mishel et al. (2009)

employment depress wages by negatively impacting on the bargaining power of labour associations (Palley 2007: 2).

As the risk of joblessness increases, employers are better able to moderate or reduce wages, since workers will be less likely to credibly threaten to leave and find a better job. Over the past thirty years productivity (non-farm business sector) continued to grow at a steady rate, but worker compensation did not. Figure 2.4 demonstrates that prior to 1979 worker compensation for production and non-supervisory workers, a group of workers with lower levels of pay, grew in close relation to productivity. From 1979 a gap emerged and continuously widened. This means that more and more of the fruits of productivity increases are going to other, more advantaged, social groups, such as managers and stockholders (who benefit from increased profits). This does not seem consistent with the right to just and favourable conditions of work, which calls for fair wages which must be just and equitable.

There has been a change in the share of good jobs over time. A good job is defined as one that pays at least $17 per hour (the inflation-adjusted median male earnings in 1979) and offers employer-provided health insurance and a pension. In Figure 2.5 there has been a decline in the share of good jobs in the cycle from 2000 to 2006 (2.3 percentage points), following much smaller drops over the same period in the 1980s (down 0.5 percentage points) and 1990s (down 0.1 percentage points) business cycles. The most current data do not include the current recession but the trend in terms of decent work has shown that there has been a decrease in work that is paid a decent wage and has benefits. The deterioration in good jobs in the 2000s business cycle has been particularly sharp for men, down 4.4 percentage points, compared to a 3.4 percentage point decline in the 1980s and a 1.9 percentage point drop in the 1990s. Over the 2000s business cycle to date,

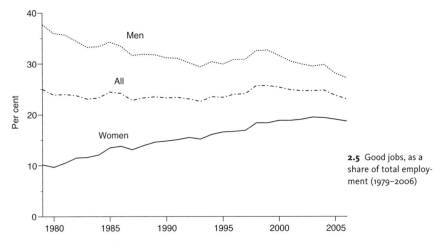

2.5 Good jobs, as a share of total employment (1979–2006)

Source: Figure 6 in Schmitt (2007)

the share of women in good jobs fell (0.2 percentage points), reversing the solid positive trends over comparable periods in the preceding two business cycles (up 3.3 percentage points in the 1980s cycle and 2.0 percentage points in the 1990s cycle).

The biggest impact of the decline in the share of good jobs has been the decrease in the number of jobs that offer health insurance and pension benefits. In the 2000s there was a sharp deterioration in employer-provided health insurance (3.1 percentage points) and employer-sponsored pension and retirement savings plans (4.9 percentage points). The fall-off in health and pension benefits has been sharper in the 2000s than it was over comparable periods in the earlier two decades. Though the new healthcare bill might reverse some of these trends in the coming years, the decline in pensions will continue. Health insurance coverage declined 3.1 percentage points in the 2000s, compared to a 0.7 percentage point drop over a comparable period in the 1980s and a 1.5 percentage point fall in the 1990s. Pension coverage trends have also been worse in the current decade (down 4.9 percentage points) than they were over corresponding periods in earlier cycles (down 3.1 percentage points in the 1980s and up 1.6 percentage points in the 1990s) (Schmitt 2007: 11).

Non-discrimination and equality

Obligation of conduct There has been little work done on the obligation of conduct with regard to macroeconomic policies and specifically the principle of non-discrimination. There is some evidence that the Federal Reserve responds to higher rates of unemployment by lowering the Federal Funds Rate in an effort to stimulate the economy. However, the response of the Federal Reserve to higher unemployment appears to be smaller if the unemployment rate of

African-American population rises relative to the unemployment rate of the white population (Heintz and Seguino 2011). In other words, the response of the Federal Reserve to rising unemployment depends on who is unemployed.

Fiscal policy in terms of conduct in some instances is structured in a way to be discriminatory. For example, the bulk of educational spending in the USA is financed through local property taxes. This financial arrangement exists along with national (federal) mandates with regard to primary and secondary education. The dependence on local property taxes results in poor neighbourhoods having inadequately financed schools and wealthier districts having much better schools. Communities of colour are disproportionately concentrated in low-income school districts. Given these structural realities, the failure of the government to put in place policies that would equalize revenues across school districts may be considered a violation of the obligation of conduct.

Obligation of result Fiscal and monetary policies that operate with disinflationary bias have negative consequences for employment and adequate standards of living. It would also be a mistake to believe that these unfavourable consequences are neutral to race, ethnicity or sex. Studies conducted in developing and industrial economies demonstrate that women and communities of colour pay disproportionately for disinflationary monetary policy.

Although an adjustment in the Federal Funds Rate may not outwardly seem biased towards any particular group, it has real effects that place an undue burden on minorities. Studies have shown that African-Americans and women are more vulnerable to job loss than white men when the Federal Reserve tightens monetary policy. A host of factors may contribute to the unevenness of job security with respect to race and gender, including discrimination, differences in educational attainment, and unequal access to information.

For the USA, the real Federal Funds Rate has a significant effect on the overall unemployment rate, the female-to-white male unemployment ratio and the black-to-white male unemployment ratio. An increase in the Federal Funds Rate slows aggregate activity and increases the unemployment rate. Although this is not overtly discriminatory, social structures prevail in the United States that tend to make women and minorities the last to be hired and the first to be fired. On average, African-American workers have lower job tenure than white workers. Because the policy is uniform and there are no targeted measures to compensate for societal and cultural factors, a slowdown in aggregate activity working through either the money or the credit channel would burden low-income workers more than high-income workers. Since minorities tend to have lower wages than whites, disinflationary policy should disproportionately affect them. Human rights principles of non-discrimination necessitate the absence of a discriminatory legal framework, while mandating that policies cannot be discriminatory in effect.

Transparency, accountability, participation: fiscal policy

Each year the US government publishes the President's Budget Proposal, in-year reports, a mid-year review, a year-end report and an auditor's report. Though it does not provide a non-technical budget report that is more accessible to ordinary citizens, in 2010 the Open Budget Survey ranked the United States very high, along with South Africa, New Zealand, the United Kingdom, France, Norway and Sweden (Open Budget Survey 2010).

The budget process in the USA involves both the executive and legislative branches of the government. The executive branch submits a budget to Congress, which then passes legislation that will authorize the spending of the approved budget. The Congressional Budget Office (CBO), which was established in 1974, provides each house with projections on the impact of taxation and spending on the economy. The particular committees in both houses use the information provided by the CBO to decide on the budget resolution. This process takes a great deal of negotiation, and both the Senate and the House have to agree on a final budget resolution which sets limits on spending. During the process of negotiating the budget resolution people can contact Congress and give opinions on what the budget priorities should be. This of course requires a detailed knowledge of the budget. Several non-governmental organizations monitor the process and provide information on the budget.[5] Though there is some information that is made available, and access to legislatures, the budgeting process is weighted in the interests of those who have better access to those in government. The final budget will then have to be signed by the president.

The response to the financial crisis that unfolded in 2008 has raised serious questions of transparency and accountability. The bailout of the financial sector, the Troubled Assets Relief Program (TARP), authorized hundreds of billions of dollars to prop up the financial sector. Only a fraction of the authorized amount was spent, and the net cost to taxpayers is likely to be small relative to the approved size of the programme. This is because corporations that received government loans are paying them back. However, there was almost no transparency, accountability or participation in the processes that led to the mobilization of these funds, the selection of institutions to save, the use of the funds once they had been allocated, or the internal management of these resources by the financial institutions themselves. In a well-publicized controversy, the giant insurer, AIG, planned to grant large bonuses to its executives shortly after receiving the bailout money. Although the US Treasury has reported on the allocation of funds after the fact, there was very limited transparency with regard to the decision-making process for the initial allocation of funds to financial institutions and the terms under which the resources were advanced.[6]

Similarly, there are formal provisions for transparency, accountability and participation with regard to monetary policy, but in practice there are significant limitations. The Board of Governors of the Federal Reserve is a central governmental agency comprised of seven members, appointed by the president for a term of fourteen years. In appointing members to the board, 'the President shall have due regard to a fair representation of the financial, agricultural, industrial, and commercial interests, and geographical divisions of the country'.[7] Only one member from any one region may be appointed to the board at any given time.[8] After the president appoints a chair and vice-chair, the Senate confirms these two appointments. The individuals chosen to occupy these positions are typically economists with long-standing connections to the banking sector and financial institutions.

The overwhelming majority of the decision-makers in the Federal Reserve system come either from the financial sector or have long-standing ties to the sector. Each of the twelve Reserve Banks has a board of directors with nine members. The board of directors is divided into three classes with three directors in each class. The letters A, B and C designate different categories. The first class of directors represents the interests of commercial banks, while B and C represent the interests of business in other sectors, labour and consumers. However, the banking sector has disproportionate influence over the choice of directors. For example, classes A and B are elected by member banks from the district. Directors are responsible for supervising the Reserve Bank and making monetary policy recommendations.

The Federal Open Market Committee (FOMC) is the body that makes the most important decisions regarding monetary policy. 'By statute the FOMC determines its own organization, and by tradition it elects the Chair of the Board of Governors as its Chair and the President of the New York Bank as its Vice Chairman.'[9] There are twelve voting members on the committee. The seven members of the board constitute the majority of the FOMC. The other five representatives are presidents of regional Reserve Banks who serve on a one-year rotating basis. The exception is the president of the Federal Reserve Bank of New York, who has a permanent seat on the FOMC. The other four positions are filled on the basis of one representative from each of four other major regions of the country.[10] The FOMC is required by law to meet at least four times each year. However, attendance at FOMC meetings is restricted.

Under the Federal Reserve Act of 1913, the Federal Reserve must report annually to Congress on its activities and twice annually to congressional banking committees on its plans for monetary policy. Twice annually the board must submit a written report to Congress on the state of the economy and the course of monetary policy, and the chair must testify on the report.[11] In addition, Congress may request the testimony of Federal Reserve officials at any time. In accordance with Section 10 para. 10 of the Federal Reserve Act, all action taken in relation to open market operations must be recorded. The record must include the votes of the board and the Committee and provide the underlying reasons for actions taken. The Board of Governors must keep a similar record pertaining to the policy that it determines, and a full account of actions must be included in the Board's annual report to Congress (12 USC § 247a).[12]

The Federal Reserve is subject to the Government in the Sunshine Act of 1976, designed to promote openness in governmental affairs. The law codified a policy of conducting open meetings of the board but also provided for exceptions. The board may conduct 'closed-door' meetings when they consider matters related to information that would 'lead to significant financial speculation in currencies, securities, or commodities, or significantly endanger the stability of any financial institution' (5 USC § 552b). Under the same exceptions, the FOMC is allowed to conduct its meetings behind closed doors. Since 1994, the transcripts of closed-door meetings are released with a lag of five years.

Members of the Board of Governors are in contact with other policy-makers in government. They frequently testify before congressional committees on the economy, monetary policy, banking supervision and regulation, consumer credit protection, financial markets and other matters.[13] For instance, as required by the Federal Reserve Act, the chair of the Board of Governors testifies before the Senate Committee on Banking, Housing, and Urban Affairs and the House Committee on Financial Services twice a year. The chair's testimony addresses the efforts, activities, objectives and plans of the Board of Governors and the Federal Open Market Committee with respect to the conduct of monetary policy, as well as economic developments in the United States and the prospects for the future. Concurrently, the Board of Governors must submit a report on these same issues to the House and Senate committees before which the chair testifies.

The board has regular contact with members of the President's Council of Economic Advisers, which is an agency within the Executive Office of the president, and is responsible for providing the president with objective economic advice on the formulation of both domestic and international economic policy. The board also meets with other key economic officials. The chairman also meets from time to time with the president and has regular meetings with the Secretary of the Treasury. The Fed is also audited annually by a major public accounting firm. In addition, the Government Accountability Office (GAO) generally exercises its authority to conduct a number of reviews each year to look at specific aspects of the Federal Reserve's activities. The audit report of the public accounting firm and a complete list of GAO reviews are available in the board's *Annual Report*, which is sent to Congress during the second quarter of each calendar year. Importantly, monetary policy is exempt from audit by the GAO on the grounds that it is monitored directly by Congress through written reports, including the semi-annual *Monetary Policy Report to the Congress*, prepared by the Board of Governors (FASAB 2008: 6). The Fed enjoys exemptions from the Freedom of Information Act; Exemption 8 of the FOIA protects matters that are 'contained in or related to examination, operating, or condition reports prepared by, on behalf of, or for the use of an agency responsible for the regulation or supervision of financial institutions'.[14] The banking industry advisers (the Federal Advisory Council) are also allowed to meet behind closed doors.

The economic crisis that unfolded in 2008 has raised a number of concerns about transparency and accountability of the Federal Reserve. For example, in response to the crisis, the Federal Reserve extended its emergency powers to inject a historic amount of financial resources into the banking industry, but initially refused to disclose the details of its operations to save the financial sector. Only towards the end of 2010 did the Federal Reserve begin to release information to the public on the scope of these activities and who the beneficiaries were (Chane and McGinty 2010).

Conclusion

Macroeconomic policy discourse has tended to show a deflationary bias in the case of both fiscal and monetary policies. The current economic crisis has brought increased attention to the need for reducing the budget deficit and a constant fear of increased inflation. Although the policies that have been carried out in terms of the American Reinvestment and Recovery Act increased spending to stimulate the economy, most of the stimulus spending ends after 2010. At the time of writing this chapter, the debate in the government is about keeping a tax cut that was introduced during the Bush administration, which would decrease taxes to the richest 1 per cent of the US population. At the same time, there is a renewed focus on decreasing the deficit through spending cuts that would increase the economic insecurity of those in need and undermine efforts to generate employment.

The recent financial and economic crises powerfully demonstrate the reasons why using human rights as an ethical lens to evaluate macroeconomic policy is necessary. The biggest economic meltdown in the USA since the Great Depression has eroded fundamental economic and social rights in terms of housing, employment, poverty, health and education. The crisis destroyed jobs, reduced standards of living, heightened economic risks for ordinary people, and has driven more people into poverty, especially women and people of colour. While the crisis makes these issues obvious, macroeconomic policy affects the realization of rights in the long run, not just during the bad times. Fiscal and monetary policies influence levels of employment, living standards and social spending. They can directly impact the distribution of income. Increasingly divergent income disparities exacerbate ethnic and regional differences – raising important questions about the obligation of non-discrimination with respect to the conduct of monetary policy. For too long, macroeconomic policy has been conducted with a bias towards the narrow interests of corporations, the financial sector and wealth-holders, bypassing consideration of basic human rights obligations. What is needed is to have macroeconomic policy respond to the human rights obligations regarding the right to work and just and favourable remuneration. If monetary and fiscal policy prioritized the right to work as a primary objective, the kind of policies that have been carried out over the last thirty years would have been considerably different. We need a paradigm shift that holds macroeconomic policy accountable for basic human rights.

Notes

1 Discretionary spending includes defence, education, environment and natural resources, health research and services, housing, WIC (Women, Infants, Children – Special Supplemental Nutrition Program), other income support and veterans' medical benefits.

2 This requires budget neutrality in increases in spending.

3 In 'Letting light in', *The Economist*, 15 November 2007.

4 From the edited transcript of the 'Agenda for Shared Prosperity: More Jobs, Good Jobs' forum, Washington, DC, 22 June 2007.

5 See National Priorities Project for an example of work on the budget by non-governmental organizations; nationalpriorities. org/resources/federal-budget-101/budget-briefs/federal-budget-timeline/.

6 A report from the US General Accountability Office in early 2009 found that 'Treasury has made limited progress in formatting, articulating and communicating an overall strategy for TARP, continuing to respond to institution- and industry-specific needs by, for example, making further capital purchases and offering loans to the automobile industry. In addition, it has not yet developed a strategic approach to explain how its various programs work together to fulfill TARP's purposes or how it will use the remaining TARP funds ... the lack of a clearly articulated vision has complicated Treasury's ability to effectively communicate to Congress, the financial markets, and the public on the benefits of TARP' (GAO 2009).

7 As amended by Acts of 3 June 1922 (42 Stat. 620); 23 August 1935 (49 Stat. 704); www. federalreserve.gov/aboutthefed/section%20 10.htm.

8 See the online resource about the structure of the Federal Reserve system: www. federalreserve.gov/pubs/frseries/frseri.htm.

9 Ibid.

10 The four groupings are as follows: Boston, Philadelphia and Richmond; Cleveland and Chicago; Atlanta, St Louis and Dallas; and Minneapolis, Kansas City and San Francisco.

11 www.federalreserve.gov/Pubs/frseries/ frseri2.htm.

12 Ibid.

13 Ibid.

14 See USC § 552(b)(8) (2000).

References

Balakrishnan, R., D. Elson and R. Patel (2009) *Rethinking Macroeconomic Policies from a Human Rights Perspective (Why MES with Human Rights II)*, New York: Marymount Manhattan College.

Chane, S. and J. McGinty (2010) 'Fed documents breadth of emergency measures', *New York Times*, 1 December.

Economic Policy Institute (EPI) (n.d.) *Resources: Economy Track Data*, www.epi. org/resources/economy_track_data.

Economist (2007) 'Letting light in', *The Economist*, 15 November.

Elson, D. (2006) *Budgeting for Women's Rights: Monitoring Government Budgets for Compliance with CEDAW*, New York: UNIFEM.

Epstein, G. (2003) 'Alternatives to inflation targeting monetary policy for stable growth: a brief research summary', Working Paper Series, Political Economy Research Institute (PERI).

FASAB (Federal Accounting Standards Advisory Board) (2008) Memorandum, 3 December, www.fasab.gov/pdffiles/tabe_federalentity. pdf.

Federal Reserve Act, USC 12, Chapter 3, Subchapter II, § 241, www.law.cornell.edu/ uscode/12/usc_sec_12_00000241----000-. html.

Friedman, M. (1968) 'The role of monetary policy', *American Economic Review*, 58(1): 1–17.

— (2002) *Capitalism and Freedom*, Chicago, IL: University of Chicago Press.

GAO (2009) 'Troubled Asset Relief Program: status of efforts to address transparency and accountability issues', GAO-09-296, Washington, DC: General Accountability Office, January.

Heintz, J. and S. Seguino (2011) 'Federal Reserve policy and inflation dynamics in the US: racial inequalities in unemployment', Working Paper Series, Political Economy Research Institute (PERI), January.

ILO (International Labour Organization) (2010) Online resource, www.ilo.org/global/ Themes/Decentwork/lang-en/index.htm (accessed 5 November 2010).

Keynes, J. M. (1964) *The General Theory of Employment, Interest, and Money*, New York: Harcourt, Brace, & World.

Mahalia, M. (2008) 'Stimulus now! Underemployment at 14-year high', Snapshot for 15 October, Economic Policy Institute (EPI).

Mishel, L., J. Bernstein and H. Shierholz (2009) *The State of Working America 2008/2009*, Economic Policy Institute Book, Ithaca, NY: Cornell University Press.

Office of Management and Budget (n.d.) *The Budget/Historical Tables*, www.whitehouse. gov/omb/budget/Historicals/.

Open Budget Survey (2010) *International Budget Partnership, Open Budget Survey: Country Info: United States*, www. internationalbudget.org/what-we-do/open-budget-survey/?fa=countryDetails&id=2319 &countryID=US.

Palley, T. (2002) 'Economic contradictions coming home to roost? Does the U.S. economy face a long-term aggregate demand generation problem?', *Journal of Post Keynesian Economics*, 25(1): 9–32. http://www.thomas palley.com/docs/articles/macro_policy/ economic_contradictions.pdf.

— (2007) 'Reviving full employment policy: challenging the Wall Street paradigm', Briefing Paper, Economic Policy Institute (EPI).

Pollin, R. and H. Garrett-Peltier (2009) *The US Employment Effects of Military and Domestic Spending Priorities: An Updated Analysis*, Political Economy Research Institute Publications, October.

Price, L. (2005) 'The boom that wasn't: the economy has little to show for $860 billion in tax cuts', Briefing Paper no. 168, Economic Policy Institute (EPI).

Schmitt, J. (2007) *The Good, the Bad, and the Ugly: Job Quality in the United States over the Three Most Recent Business Cycles*, Center for Economic and Policy Research (CEPR) Report, November.

Stiglitz, J. (1999) 'Interest rates, risk, and imperfect markets: puzzles and policies', *Oxford Review of Economic Policy*, 15(2): 59–76.

Thorbecke, W. (2000) 'A dual mandate for the Federal Reserve: the pursuit of price stability and full employment', Public Policy Brief no. 60, Jerome Levy Economics Institute of Bard College.

3 | HUMAN RIGHTS AND PUBLIC EXPENDITURE IN MEXICO

Daniela Ramírez Camacho

Introduction

International and national laws bind the Mexican government to respect, protect and fulfil economic and social rights. Mexico has signed and ratified three key international treaties that cover economic and social rights.[1] Moreover, during the twentieth century, economic and social rights have been gradually included in Mexico's constitution.[2] This chapter examines the conduct of public expenditure in Mexico since the early 1980s in light of the human rights principles of progressive realization and non-discrimination. It also examines compliance with minimum core obligations, as well as transparency, accountability and participation in the budget process. Obligations of result are examined with respect to the right to health (ICESCR, Article 12) and the right to food (ICESCR, Article 11). The two rights are linked: the right to health does not imply solely the right to have access to healthcare. General Comment 14 of the Committee on Economic, Social and Cultural Rights refers to the multiple factors that contribute to the creation of conditions that allow for a person to be healthy. States have the obligation 'to ensure equal access for all to the underlying determinants of health, such as nutritiously safe food and potable drinking water, basic sanitation and adequate housing and living conditions' (General Comment 14, para. 36).

Progressive realization and non-retrogression

Obligation of conduct The Mexican federal budget is organized into three major functional groups: government, economic development and social development. Expenditure on economic development comprises expenditure on programmes related to job creation and support of economic livelihoods. Expenditure on social expenditure comprises expenditure on education, health, social security, housing, urban planning, regional development, potable water and sewerage services and other social services.

After the 1980s debt crisis, the federal government substantially reduced total public expenditure. While in 1980 total public expenditure represented 30.8 per cent of GDP, by 2008 it had dropped to 23.9 per cent of GDP (Cabrera 2008). The composition of public expenditure changed: social development spending was prioritized over economic development spending, as Figure 3.1

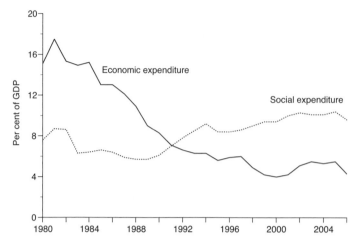

3.1 Public expenditure on social development and economic development

Source: Author, based on data from *Cuenta de la Hacienda Pública Federal, Centro de Estudios de las Finanzas Públicas, Cámara de Diputados. VI Informe de Gobierno del Ejecutivo Federal, México, 2006*, in Cabrera (2008: Appendix A6)

shows. In the 1980s, economic development expenditure was much higher than social development expenditure, averaging 13.6 per cent of GDP; in the 1990s this was reduced by half to 6.1 per cent of GDP; and from 2000 to 2006 the average share fell to 4.8 per cent. The share of social expenditure in GDP fell after 1982 but had recovered to its 1981 level by 1994. From 2000 to 2006 the share averaged 10 per cent of GDP, a couple of percentage points higher than in the early 1980s.

Per capita social expenditure more than doubled between 1990 and 2005, as illustrated in Figure 3.2. While in 1990 government spent $298 per person (2000

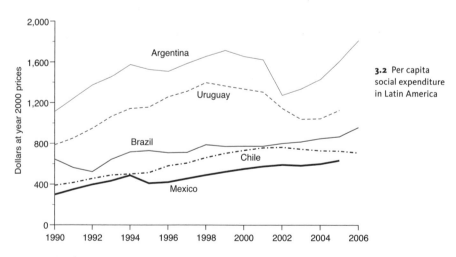

3.2 Per capita social expenditure in Latin America

Source: Author, based on data from the Economic Commission for Latin American and the Caribbean, Social Statistics Database, www.eclac.org/estadisticas/bases/ (accessed 23 October 2009)

real terms), by 2005 per capita social expenditure had risen to $634 (2000 real terms). In 2004, Congress approved the General Law on Social Development (Ley General de Desarrollo Social) so as to guarantee the social rights in the Constitution (education, health, food, housing, clean environment, work, social security and non-discrimination). This General Law mandates that allocations to social development programmes will not be reduced unless Congress instructs it. This has established some protection for social expenditure, but it is conditional upon the 'availability of budgetary resources', which opens a legal door for possible retrogression if a government prioritizes a balanced budget rather than the maintenance of social expenditure after a substantial fall in revenue. Moreover, when there is surplus revenue from oil, social expenditure does not necessarily benefit from it, as explained by Rocío Moreno (2006).

Despite the fact that Mexico's per capita social expenditure has steadily increased, it is still low compared to other large Latin American countries, as is shown in Figure 3.2. Mexico's per capita social expenditure averaged $488 (2000 real terms) in the period 1990–2005; a figure well below per capita expenditure in Argentina ($1,481), Uruguay ($1,143), Brazil ($731) and Chile ($611).

Public expenditure on health has not followed the same upward trajectory as social expenditure as a whole, though expenditure on education has. In the mid-1980s the shares of health and education spending in GDP both fell, though the share of health was a little higher. In the early 1990s the shares of both rose, but the share of education rose more. The mid-1990s economic crisis led to falls in the share of both, but hit health particularly hard, as shown in Figure 3.3. Public health expenditure as a share of GDP fell from 3.5 per cent to 2.4 per cent, recovering somewhat to 2.7 per cent in 2005, considerably

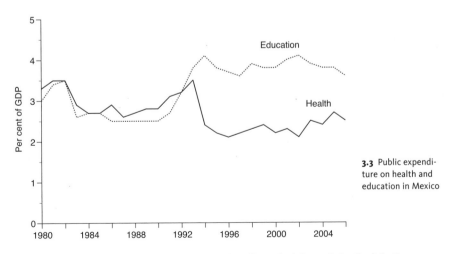

3.3 Public expenditure on health and education in Mexico

Source: Author, based on data from *Cuenta de la Hacienda Pública Federal, Centro de Estudios de las Finanzas Públicas, Cámara de Diputados. VI Informe de Gobierno del Ejecutivo Federal, México, septiembre 2006,* Cabrera (2008: Appendix A8)

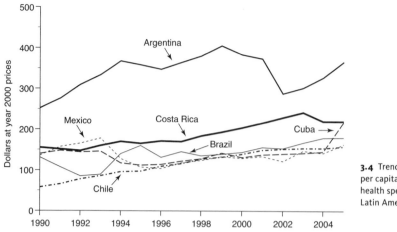

3.4 Trends in real per capita public health spending in Latin America

Source: Author, based on data from the Economic Commission for Latin American and the Caribbean, Social Statistics Database, www.eclac.org/estadisticas/bases/ (accessed 23 October 2009)

below the share of health in 1980. The trajectory of education expenditure was different. After falling in the early 1980s, the share of education expenditure rose to 4.1 per cent of GDP in 1994, and on average has maintained a share of between 4 and 3.5 per cent, a higher share than in 1980.

Mexico does not have a unified public health system. Urban formal workers achieved social security rights and access to a full range of healthcare services offered by social security institutions as early as 1943.[3] However, people working in the urban informal sector and most of those working in agriculture were not covered by this system. For this uninsured[4] population, the state provided basic healthcare free of charge through public facilities funded by the Ministry of Health. The right to health became a constitutional right in 1983. In 1984 the Mexican government approved the General Health Bill detailing the different dimensions of the right to health and the various responsibilities of the government. Article 25 establishes as a national priority of the public health system 'the quantitative and qualitative extension of health services, preferably to vulnerable groups'. By services it refers to all actions directed to protect, promote and restore the health of individuals and the collectivity (Article 23). Services will be granted by public institutions based on universality and cost-free principles (Article 35). User fees will be collected considering 'the cost of the services provided and the user's socioeconomic condition [...] exempting those who cannot afford to pay them, or [those living] in areas of less economic and social development, according to the dispositions of the Ministry of Health' (Article 36).[5]

Compared to many other Latin American countries, Mexico lags behind in public health expenditure per capita, as shown in Figure 3.4. Argentina, Costa Rica, Cuba and Brazil all have consistently higher per capita health spending in real terms. In Mexico, per capita spending fell substantially between 1993 and 1995, and since then has recovered slowly to its previous level.

The government did not take steps to safeguard allocations to health in adjusting to the 2008 economic crisis. In August 2009 the Executive informed Congress of new reductions in the original budgets of several ministries, including Social Development, Agriculture and Health. The health budget was cut by 3 per cent; and 69 per cent of the cutbacks were concentrated on federal health subsidies to the states, which are a major source of funding health programmes directed at vulnerable groups (women and the uninsured) (FUNDAR 2009: 7). The budget proposal for 2010 follows the same trend, reducing federal health subsidies to states by 84 per cent and cutting capital investment under the Ministry of Health in half.[6]

Obligation of result The mortality rate of under-five children (deaths per 1,000 births) has decreased substantially from 78 in 1980 to 35 in 2007. However, this rate is still relatively high for a middle-income country such as Mexico. In 2005 gastrointestinal and respiratory infections were still prime causes of death for children under five and undernourishment remained listed as the sixth main cause.[7] As shown in Figure 3.5, other Latin American countries have considerably lower under-five child mortality rates and achieved faster progress between 1990 and 2007. This evidence shows that the government of Mexico has not taken measures sufficient to guarantee the healthy development of children, as required by ICESCR, Article 12.

The maternal mortality rate serves as an indicator of the effectiveness of actions taken by governments to guarantee women's health during pregnancy, birth and the period after birth as required by Article 12 of CEDAW. There are various factors that contribute to the tragic phenomenon of maternal mortality, and not all of them are related to public expenditure on health.

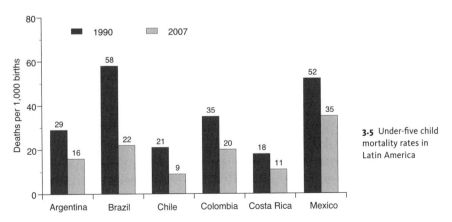

3.5 Under-five child mortality rates in Latin America

Source: Author, based on data from the Economic Commission for Latin American and the Caribbean, Social Statistics Database, www.eclac.org/estadisticas/bases/ (accessed 24 October 2009)

However, several studies show that well-planned health policies, services and programmes do make a difference in diminishing maternal mortality rates (Melendez Navarro 2006). In 2005, a study committee on maternal mortality in Mexico reported the following:

> 75 per cent of maternal deaths were due to complications in the last period of pregnancy and these lives were not saved because among other things there exist deficiencies in medical and technological equipment, shortage of safe blood, obstetric care that does not follow technical protocols and guidelines, inexistence of basic supplies to control haemorrhage, mistaken diagnosis and lack of transport for women who are giving birth. (Castañeda 2007: 208)

The Mexican government has committed itself to reducing the maternal mortality rate by three-quarters of that of 1990 by 2015. However, by 2005 the national maternal mortality rate was reported to have decreased by only 28.8 per cent from the 89 deaths per 100,000 births registered in 1990. From 2002 to 2005 the rate apparently remained stagnant at 63 deaths per 100,000 births (Meneses Navarro 2007). The latest figure available is a rate of 57.2 maternal deaths in 2008, a fall of only 35.7 per cent from 1990.[8]

Moreover, there are discrepancies between data for the Mexican average rate, which show a slow progressive trend, and sub-national-level data, which show alarming retrogressions. As Table 3.1 shows, in 2008 the fourteen states

TABLE 3.1 Registered maternal deaths at the sub-national level (maternal deaths per 100,000 births)

Subnational	2002	2008	Increase in reported deaths (%)
Aguascalientes	24.8	39.7	60.5
Baja California	30	43.4	44.6
Chiapas	89.5	96.8	8.1
Colima	17.9	39.3	119.7
Distrito Federal	52.5	52.9	0.8
Durango	40.9	78.3	91.7
Hidalgo	61.4	62.2	1.3
Jalisco	35.1	40.4	15.2
Michoacán	43.1	59.1	36.9
Nuevo León	27.4	30.1	10.1
Quintana Roo	51.8	67.2	29.6
Sinaloa	34.7	39.4	13.5
Tabasco	34.1	72.6	112.9
Tamaulipas	37.5	58.7	56.5

Source: Author, based on data from Sistema Nacional de Información en Salud, *Maternal Deaths 2002–2008*, sinais.salud.gob.mx/mortalidad/index.html (accessed 24 October 2009)

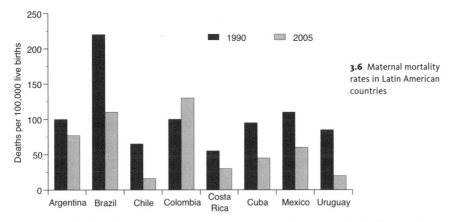

3.6 Maternal mortality rates in Latin American countries

Source: Author, based on data from the Economic Commission for Latin American and the Caribbean, Social Statistics Database, www.eclac.org/estadisticas/bases/ (accessed 24 October 2009)

registered an increase in maternal mortality rates compared to six years earlier, ranging from 0.8 per cent to 112 per cent.

In comparison with other Latin American countries, Mexico does better than Brazil, Argentina and Colombia; but worse than Chile, Cuba, Costa Rica and Uruguay, as shown in Figure 3.6. In 2005 Chile had only about one fourth of the maternal deaths (per 100,000 live births) that took place in Mexico.

Thus, while the evidence on child mortality does indicate some progress in relation to the right to health, it is slow, and Mexico lags behind comparable Latin American countries. In the case of maternal mortality, there is some uncertainty about whether there has been progress, given the discrepancy between national and sub-national-level data.

Non-discrimination and equality

Obligation of conduct The distribution of social development expenditure in Mexico is very unequal, as shown in Table 3.2. In 2000 households in the three lowest deciles received 25.8 per cent of total social expenditure while the three top deciles (middle and upper middle classes) received 34.8 per cent. The same unequal distribution characterizes education, health and social security.

As noted earlier, the public health system is not unified: different public health providers administer different amounts of public resources and assist different groups. The social security institutions, ISSSTE (for the public sector employees) and IMSS (for private sector employees with formal contracts), meet the health needs of the formally employed through better-funded and relatively good-quality health services. In 2000, the three top deciles that have a high concentration of government employees got most of the ISSSTE health budget (66.1 per cent), while the three bottom deciles received only 4.9 per cent. The same happens with the IMSS health budget, of which 40.6 per cent goes to the three top deciles, while the poorest share only 14.3 per cent. It is

TABLE 3.2 Shares of public expenditure by deciles (2000), ordered according to income per capita (%)

	I	II	III	IV	V	VI	VII	VIII	IX	X
Total social expenditure	7.8	8.5	9.5	9.4	9.5	9.7	10.8	11.8	11.2	11.8
Education	8.6	8.4	8.7	9.6	9.6	10.6	11.6	12.6	9.6	10.8
Health	7	7.6	8.4	8.6	9.1	10	12.8	12.1	13.4	11
Social security	0.4	2	4.3	6.1	8.6	10.3	13	16	19.2	19.9
Targeted social expenditure	21	21.1	24.8	16.8	12.3	4.1	0	0	0	0

Source: Adapted from John Scot Andretta, 'La otra cara de la reforma fiscal', Programa de Presupuesto y Gasto Público, Centro de Investigación y Docencia Económicas, Mexico, 2001

only through the Ministry of Health services for the uninsured that the three lowest deciles benefit much from public health resources, consuming half of the ministry's budget (50.8 per cent). It is important to note that deciles do not necessarily mean social classes. Income information organized in deciles omits the real better-off sector in Mexican society, as demonstrated by the percentage of public health resources allocated to the three top deciles of the Mexican population.

Considered as a group, the insured population receives a disproportionate share of public health spending, as is shown in Table 3.3. By 2002, the insured received almost twice as much in terms of public resources as the uninsured in per capita terms.

In the richest states, such as Colima, Aguascalientes and Nuevo León, the uninsured are a minority (26, 27 and 28 per cent of total population respectively in 2005). In contrast, the uninsured population represents a vast majority in the poorest states. In both Oaxaca and Chiapas the uninsured represented 76 per cent of total population.

In 2003 Mexico's Federal Congress reformed the General Health Bill and introduced a new programme, the Popular Insurance (Seguro Popular or

TABLE 3.3 Health spending by group, 2002 (%)

	Population	Total health spending
Insured population	50.81	65.08
Uninsured population	49.19	34.92

Source: Hofbauer and Lara (2002)

Sistema de Protección Social en Salud), which consists of a limited health protection plan directed at the uninsured population. The government claimed that the purpose of the Popular Insurance was to help make effective the right to health.[9] Through this Popular Insurance people receive primary-care medical services offered by the Ministry of Health, and medical coverage for 95 per cent of hospitalization cases and the serious illnesses included in the Catastrophic Spending Protection Fund.[10] The federal government claimed that the Popular Insurance contributed to equity since people can obtain health insurance without being formally employed. They claimed that the Popular Insurance allowed access to a wide series of health services with only a modest monetary contribution, from which households in the two lowest deciles were exempted.

However, the Popular Insurance has been criticized because it does not cover all illnesses. 'It creates a separate form of entitlement in an already segmented rights-based health system while creating a group of relatively less excluded people among the excluded' (Lavielle et al. 2004: 50).

Since 2004 the Ministry of Health has been allocated increasing resources with which to run the Popular Insurance programme, but it has failed to spend all of this money. For instance, the Popular Insurance has an investment fund reserved for the construction of health facilities where they are lacking; but from 2004 to 2009 only 25 per cent of the fund was spent.[11] Underspending has also been identified in the administration of the federal funds that are channelled to the states. As shown in Figure 3.7, from 2001 to 2004 the underspending of the Ministry of Health represented less than 5 per cent of the approved budget; but from 2004 to 2009, the ministry, together with the Contribution Fund for Health Services, which channels federal resources to the states, registered underspending that ranged from 8 to 18 per cent of the approved budget. The population that is uninsured or uses the Popular Insurance is mainly rural, as Table 3.4 shows.

In 2007, 75 per cent of total beneficiaries of the Popular Insurance lived

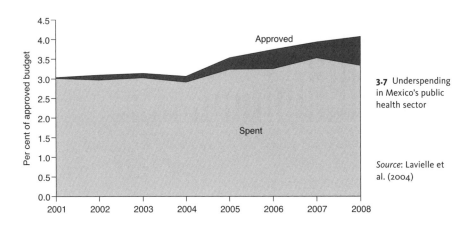

3.7 Underspending in Mexico's public health sector

Source: Lavielle et al. (2004)

TABLE 3.4 Distribution of population by insurance and locality (2005) (%)

	Uninsured	Insured	Voluntary insurance
Rural (less than 2,500 inhabitants)	84.9	12.9	1.6
Urban (2,500 to 100,000 inhabitants)	66.7	31.8	0.8
City (more than 100,000)	45.7	51.4	1.1
TOTAL	60	37.5	1.2

Source: E. Puentes et al., 'Estimación de la población con seguro de salud en México mediante una encuesta nacional', *Salud pública de México*, 47(1), 2005

in urban areas (Pérez Arguelles 2009: 23). As shown in Figure 3.8, the states with the largest uninsured rural population have done quite poorly at affiliating the target population. For example, Veracruz, with the largest uninsured population (2,816,514 inhabitants), had affiliated only 27 per cent. Mexico State was able to affiliate only 24 per cent of its 2,529,367 rural uninsured. Chiapas and Oaxaca, the ones with the lowest human development index and with a high concentration of indigenous population, had done even worse, affiliating a scant 19 and 10 per cent of total rural uninsured respectively. Popular Insurance is not reaching the most deprived people.

In Mexico, the indigenous population has historically been left at the margin of social and economic development; and this is reflected in access to healthcare, as shown in Table 3.5. In 2005, only 16 per cent of indigenous

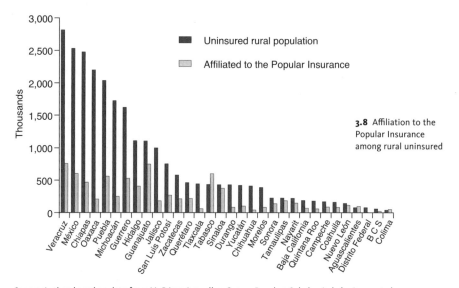

3.8 Affiliation to the Popular Insurance among rural uninsured

Source: Author, based on data from M. Pérez Arguelles, *Seguro Popular ¿Salud y ciudadanía para todos y todas?*, FUNDAR, 2009

TABLE 3.5 Social security entitlements among the indigenous and non-indigenous population, 2005 (%)

	Insured	Not insured	Popular insurance
Indigenous population	16	72	11
Non-indigenous population	44	49	7

Source: Author, based on data from Instituto Nacional de Estadística Geografía e Informática, *Conteo de Población y Vivienda*, 2005

people enjoyed healthcare through the social security system, well below the percentage of non-indigenous people who enjoy this kind of access.

In states like Guerrero, Chiapas and Oaxaca, the percentage of indigenous population that does not access healthcare via the social security system is higher than the national average, reaching 91 per cent, 86 per cent and 85 per cent respectively.[12] By law, the Popular Insurance system must prioritize the inclusion of vulnerable groups, specifically those living in rural and indigenous areas. Nevertheless, most states have failed to do this. By 2007, indigenous affiliates in Oaxaca represented only 40 per cent of the total indigenous population living in indigenous areas (defined as areas whose population is more than 40 per cent indigenous). In some other states it was even lower: Hidalgo reported that indigenous affiliates represented 38 per cent of indigenous people living in indigenous areas, Chihuahua reported 23 per cent, Tlaxcala 12 per cent and Guanajuato 4 per cent.[13]

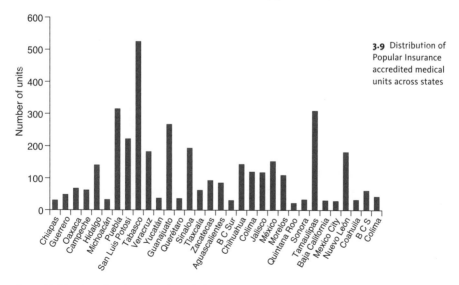

3.9 Distribution of Popular Insurance accredited medical units across states

Source: M. Pérez Arguelles, *Seguro Popular ¿Salud y ciudadanía para todos y todas?*, FUNDAR, 2009

One of the reasons for this continued exclusion of the most deprived groups is because of lack of health infrastructure. The Popular Insurance has established mechanisms to evaluate existing health units' capacities, and accredit them to become part of the Popular Insurance provider network. In 2007 Chiapas had only 31 accredited health units while Nuevo León had 181 accredited units. The number of Popular Insurance medical units per state is shown in Figure 3.9, in which states are ordered left to right from the highest level of deprivation to the lowest. Notice that Chiapas, Guerrero and Oaxaca, states with the highest levels of deprivation, have very few accredited health units.

Expenditure has been allocated to improve infrastructure deficits but much of it has not been spent, as noted above. The problem of unequal distribution of health infrastructure remains unresolved.

Obligation of result Mexico has few health indicators disaggregated by sex, race, ethnicity, or income quintile. Here we examine maternal mortality with a focus on indigenous women. The number of maternal deaths per 100,000 live births in Oaxaca, Guerrero and Chiapas, three states with high levels of deprivation and large indigenous populations, is shown in Table 3.6, together with the national average mortality rate and that of Nuevo León, one of the states with the lowest maternal mortality rate.

TABLE 3.6 Distribution of maternal deaths in the country (maternal mortality rate per 100,000 live births)

	2002	2003	2004	2005	2006	2007	2008
Chiapas	90	105	98	84	85	82	97
Guerrero	97	114	97	124	126	98	97
Oaxaca	99	65	88	99	78	102	99
National	60	63	61	62	59	56	57
Nuevo León	27	13	15	26	31	22	30

Source: Author, based on data from Instituto Nacional de Estadística Geografía e Informática and Dirección General de Información en Salud, Secretaría de Salud, *Estimated births by Consejo Nacional de Población*

Indigenous women face the greatest risk of dying before, during or after pregnancy. According to official figures, indigenous women have triple the risk of dying from maternity-related causes compared to non-indigenous women (Meneses Navarro 2007: 19). Research has shown that, in Oaxaca, 'From 2000 to 2005, 50.5 per cent of the women who died due to maternity causes lived in predominantly indigenous municipalities (70 per cent or more indigenous inhabitants). Furthermore, 75 per cent of those women lived in municipalities with 90 per cent indigenous population' (Castañeda 2007: 112). This is related to lack of health insurance and poor health facilities. In a previous study of Oaxaca, Castañeda had reported that 90 per cent of the women who died owing to maternal causes from 1999 to 2001 did not have health insurance; and that 44 per cent of the maternal deaths occurred inside the hospitals, 47 per cent in homes and the rest on the road to the health centre or hospital (Castañeda et al. 2004: 130).

According to the international human rights framework, discrimination is also expressed in the lack of quality and acceptability of health services. According to the Committee on Economic, Social and Cultural Rights, 'indigenous peoples have the right to specific measures to improve their access to health services and care. These health services should be culturally appropriate, taking into account traditional preventive care, healing practices and medicines. States should provide resources for indigenous peoples to design, deliver and control such services so that they may enjoy the highest attainable standard of physical and mental health' (General Comment 14, para. 27, E/C.12/2000/411, August 2000). However, Castañeda reports a lack of awareness and understanding of the local culture by medical practitioners in the public health system. Consequently, people prefer to be attended by local health healers or to pay for private treatment rather than attend the public health centres. Government efforts in tackling this problem have been scant. Health programmes do not take community participation and cultural diversity into account; there are no official indicators evaluating acceptability of health services and people's testimonies on cultural discrimination by the public health system keep piling up (Espinosa Damián 2004).

Minimum core obligations: the right to an adequate standard of living, especially the right to food

As noted in the introduction, the right to health does not imply only the right to have access to healthcare. It also implies the right to an adequate standard of living, including nutritious food, potable drinking water, basic sanitation and adequate housing conditions. This section evaluates conduct and results in relation to the minimum core obligation to ensure enjoyment of a minimum essential level of living, with a particular focus on food. The right to food goes beyond having the sufficient amounts of calories, proteins and nutrition. The state must warrant availability, accessibility and security of safe, nutritious and culturally accepted food. 'States have a core obligation to take the necessary action to mitigate and alleviate hunger as provided for in Paragraph 2 of Article 11, even in times of natural or other disasters' (General Comment 11, para. 6).

Access to food is the basis for defining poverty in Mexico. The Technical Committee of Poverty Measurement created by the Ministry of Social Development defines the most deprived as those households whose income is insufficient to buy enough food to meet their basic needs (their income is below the 'alimentary poverty line'). Two other dimensions of poverty are also captured by two other (higher) poverty lines: households below the capacities poverty line do not have enough income to meet health and education needs; and households below the assets poverty line do not have enough income to cover housing, clothing and transportation.

Obligation of conduct Targeted anti-poverty expenditure has been increasing steadily in absolute terms; in 2009 it was almost five times the level of 1990. In 2003 anti-poverty expenditure was equivalent to 15 per cent of total social expenditure; it grew to 17 per cent in 2006, but fell again to 15 per cent in 2008. In the face of the global economic recession the government has expanded it to 19 per cent of social expenditure.

Capacity-building programmes absorb on average 48 per cent of total anti-poverty expenditure, as is evident from Figure 3.10. Capacity-building is mostly focused on schooling, health and food aid programmes. The underlying premise of this expenditure is that the lack of human capital is the root cause of poverty since it prevents people from entering the market and integrating into development. The other main anti-poverty strategy since 1997 comprises means-tested conditional cash transfers to low-income families, through the *Oportunidades* programme (Programa Desarrollo Humano Oportunidades), whose official objective is to break the 'intergenerational transmission of poverty' through the formation of 'human capital'.[14] The programme offers several cash transfers, averaging 58 dollars per month per family, on the condition that family members undergo regular health check-ups in the nearest public health centre and that children attend school.[15] The programme has been widened to cover the urban population and to grant scholarships to the youth studying at

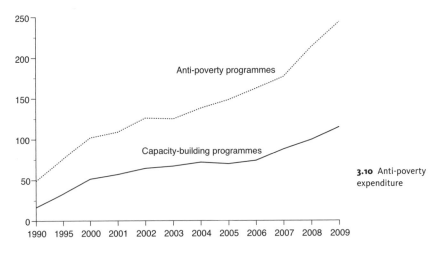

3.10 Anti-poverty expenditure

Source: Author, based on data from Tercer Informe del Gobierno Federal (2009). Figures for 2009 refer to the approved budget allocations, not to actual expenditure.

high school. It also includes nutritional supplements for under-five children, and pregnant and breastfeeding women. The payments are made to mothers in the families that qualify. The programme began with 300,000 rural families and by 2009 it covered 5,200,000 families, of which 65 per cent live in rural areas, 17 per cent in semi-urban areas and 18 per cent in urban localities. This programme alone absorbed 26 per cent of anti-poverty expenditure in 2003 and currently it receives 20 per cent. From 2003 to 2009, *Oportunidades* expenditure increased by just over a half (51.3 per cent in 2009 real terms).[16]

Although targeted, means-tested programmes are supposed to lead to more effective use of scarce resources, *Oportunidades* includes exclusionary practices that violate the principle of equal rights for all. For example, *Oportunidades* targets areas with a high degree of deprivation, and consequently it excludes households in extreme poverty who do not live in these areas. While *Oportunidades* has been quite successful in keeping inclusion of non-poor households low, 6.4 per cent in 2002 and 8.4 per cent in 2004, it has excluded many households whose incomes are below the capacities poverty line. In 2002, 64.3 per cent of such households had no access to *Oportunidades*, and in 2004 63.7 per cent did not (Espinosa Damián 2004: 332). By 2008, *Oportunidades* reached around 20,800,000 individuals. Supposing that all these people were part of the population estimated to be living under the alimentary and capacities poverty lines (26,765,222 individuals), coverage would still exclude 5,965,222 poor people.

Furthermore, conditional cash transfer programmes have potential for violating people's rights, when families are suspended from the programme for supposedly failing to comply with the conditions. From 2007 to August 2009, 217,412 families lost their cash transfers because they were deemed to have failed to meet the conditions related to participation in health check-ups. The income of these families was reduced regardless of the fact that they cannot pay for minimum essential levels of food and cover health- and education-related expenses by themselves. By 2008, *Oportunidades* transfers represented 10 per cent of total real income for each individual in the two lowest deciles.[17]

The anti-poverty strategy also excludes the people whose household income is above the alimentary and capacities poverty line but below the assets poverty line. In other words, the 23,785,607 people who can afford basic food, health and education but whose income is not enough to secure basic housing, dress and transportation are left out.

Obligation of result There has been significant progress during the last two decades in reducing undernourishment of children under the age of five. As shown in Table 3.7, in 1988 6 per cent of such children suffered from acute undernourishment, while in 2006 this rate had fallen to 1.6 per cent; while 22.8 per cent of children under five were diagnosed with chronic undernourishment in 1988 and by 2006 this rate had fallen to 12.7 per cent. In spite of these achievements, chronic undernourishment has not disappeared in Mexico. By 2006, approximately 1.2 million children under the age of five suffered from undernourishment.

TABLE 3.7 Undernourishment of children aged under five (%)

	1988	1999	2006
Acute undernourishment	6	2	1.60
Cronic undernourishment	22.80	17.80	12.70

Source: Author, based on data from Consejo Nacional de Evaluación de la Política de Desarrollo Social, *Informe de la evolución histórica de la situación nutricional de la población y los programas de nutrición y abasto en México*, p. 16, www.cedrssa.gob.mx/ (accessed 16 November 2009)

As Figure 3.11 illustrates, the southern region registered the biggest decrease in undernourishment rates from 1988 to 2006, but it still has the highest rates in the country. Four states (Oaxaca, Chiapas, Guerrero and Yucatán) continue to have child undernourishment rates above 20 per cent.[18]

Children in households in the two bottom deciles experienced the highest reduction in chronic undernourishment. Nevertheless, the rate of child undernourishment in the two bottom deciles is still 6.6 times above the undernourishment rate of the top decile. Undernourishment of children is still considerable in households from the first to the fifth deciles, with rates above 10 per cent, as shown in Figure 3.12.

Undernourishment among indigenous children decreased considerably from

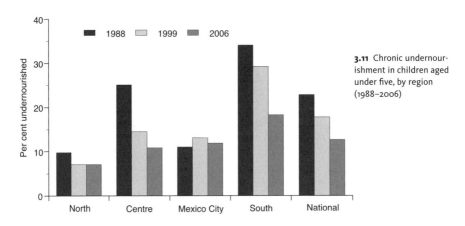

3.11 Chronic undernourishment in children aged under five, by region (1988–2006)

Source: Consejo Nacional de Evaluación de la Política de Desarrollo Social, *Informe de la evolución histórica de la situación nutricional de la población y los programas de nutrición y abasto en México*, pp. 17, 16, www.cedrssa. gob.mx/ (accessed 16 November 2009)

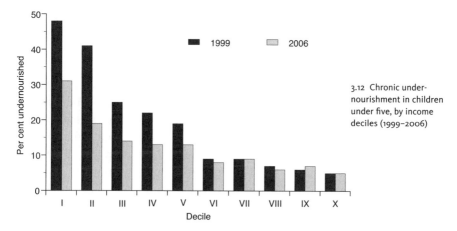

3.12 Chronic under-nourishment in children under five, by income deciles (1999–2006)

Source: Consejo Nacional de Evaluación de la Política de Desarrollo Social, *Informe de la evolución histórica de la situación nutricional de la población y los programas de nutrición y abasto en México*, pp. 18–19, www.cedrssa.gob.mx/ (accessed 16 November 2009)

1999 to 2006; however, the prevalence of undernourishment among this group continues to be higher (2.8 times) than in non-indigenous children, as shown in Figure 3.13.

'If this rate continues decreasing at the same speed we would need to wait 22 years to see undernourishment rates of the indigenous at 2.5 per cent or below'.[19] This slow rate of progress is not in compliance with the state obligation 'to move as expeditiously as possible towards' ensuring everyone 'the minimum essential food which is sufficient, nutritionally adequate and safe, to ensure their freedom from hunger' (General Comment 12, para. 14). This result also shows the failure of the targeted anti-poverty programmes

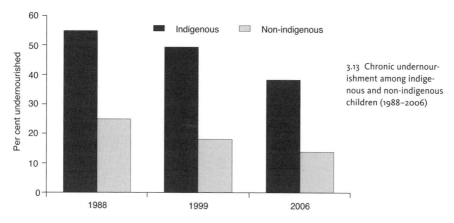

3.13 Chronic undernour-ishment among indige-nous and non-indigenous children (1988–2006)

Source: Consejo Nacional de Evaluación de la Política de Desarrollo Social, México, *Informe de la evolución histórica de la situación nutricional de la población y los programas de nutrición y abasto en México*, p. 31

since they have evidently not been able to guarantee access to sufficient food for everyone.

Transparency, accountability and participation

During the last decade, there have been significant improvements regarding transparency and the right to access public information. The right to information was introduced in the constitutional reforms of 1977. However, no mechanisms were then established to actually exercise the right. In 2002, the Federal Law for Access to Public and Governmental Information (LFTAIPG) allowed citizens' access to information from all public institutions; and provided for its enforcement through the Federal Institute for Access to Public Information (IFAI). In 2007, the right to information was incorporated in the Constitution.

The LFTAIPG establishes specific transparency obligations to be fulfilled by all agencies of the federal government. Every ministry must publish online reports on expenditure, including employees' salaries, terms of access to social benefits, and the operational rules, beneficiaries and results indicators for each social programme. However, when a ministry has presented unclear or delayed information, the IFAI has not served to sanction and correct the ministry's behaviour (Romero 2007: 167). Ministries continue publishing information that is not always complete, updated or in formats that allow for comparative analysis across time or regions.

Efforts to improve budget transparency took a step forward with the enactment of the Federal Law on Budgets and Fiscal Responsibility in 2006. This law specifies which budget documents must be made public and the information that must be included in each of them. The law also establishes specific guidelines for the expenditure of surplus income generated by unforeseen changes in oil revenue. The law also sets criteria for medium-term planning and makes it mandatory for the Executive to conduct a budgetary impact analysis whenever a reform initiative is presented (Pérez Arguelles and Romero León 2006: 23–5).

Despite the progress in the development of a transparency legal framework, there is still much to do to turn transparency into an institutional practice. The delivery of information by public institutions is not enough if it is not done in a timely fashion. There are only brief moments in the decision-making processes where information can make a difference; once these moments are passed information loses its importance. For instance, indicators showing the impact of social expenditure are key during the formulation and negotiation of the budget, since these indicators should be informing the allocations among different social programmes. However, while there have been some initial attempts to introduce a results-based budget system, the development of impact indicators is incomplete (ibid.: 26).

The Open Budget Index, elaborated by the International Budget Project,

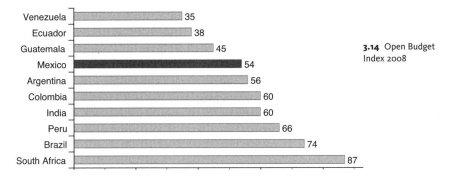

3.14 Open Budget Index 2008

Source: International Budget Partnership, Open Budget Index 2008, www.budgetindex.org (accessed 13 November 2009)

is a useful overall indicator of budget transparency. It evaluates the amount and quality of budgetary information that government makes available to its citizenry. Mexico's budget transparency is compared with other countries in Figure 3.14. In 2008, the Open Budget Index gave Mexico a score of 54 per cent, better than Guatemala, Ecuador and Venezuela; close to, but below, Argentina and Colombia; and well beneath other middle-income countries like Brazil and South Africa.

The Federal Law on Budgets and Fiscal Responsibility somewhat strengthened the capacities of legislators to decide on budget allocations (Dávila and Romero 2007: 171). Nevertheless, the Executive still has the greatest power over budget decisions. The Treasury (i.e. Ministry of Finance) has significant leeway to reallocate resources during the financial year. Although it has to inform Congress of reductions and additions made to approved budgets whenever they surpass a legal limit, usually information arrives with Congress too late for members to be able to intervene in the reallocation of resources. The 2006 Budget Law gives more certainty regarding the use of any unexpected surplus of revenue. It states that once any unexpected costs are subtracted, 25 per cent of surplus revenue must be channelled to the State Trust Fund for Infrastructure to aid infrastructure investments at the sub-national level. However, the extent of unexpected costs is still estimated and decided by the Treasury (Moreno 2007).

There is no possibility of re-election in Mexico and members of the lower house of Congress remain in their positions for only three years. This period is very short for them to become acquainted with the budget process and to develop skills that allow for informed participation and oversight. The margin for deputies to reallocate resources is also constrained by the structure of the budget: between 78 and 85 per cent represents pre-committed expenditure that cannot be modified unless legal obligations and contracts are modified as well. However, there has been some increase in their influence. In 2000, they were able to make adjustments to spending that represented only 0.63 per cent of the proposed budget; by 2006, adjustments made by Congress represented 4.9 per cent of the original budget proposal (Pérez Arguelles and Romero León 2006: 43). Strengthening deputies' capacities is more difficult since they do not participate equally in the budget negotiation. Caballero Sosa and Dávila Esterfan (2007) have documented that the real budget negotiation takes place, behind closed doors, inside the Budget Commission.

The Superior Auditor's Office has become a key factor in the control of the public finances. In 2000 the Office was established with technical, financial and management autonomy to aid Congress. The Superior Auditor is able to evaluate the efficiency, effectiveness and economy of public resources management as well as the performance and results of budgetary programmes. It is mandatory that it publicizes audit results and it has legal faculties to (administratively) sanction those who harm or misuse public funds. However, only the Executive can prosecute public servants who are found guilty of corruption, so in the end whether or not corruption cases are taken to the judiciary depends on its interest and goodwill.

Citizen participation has been incorporated into some, but not all, laws that regulate policy and budget processes. Article 20 of the Planning Law holds that 'participation and consultation of the diverse social groups will take place so that the population voices its opinion on the elaboration, update and execution of the [National Development] Plan and the programmes to which this law refers'. It also establishes that indigenous communities must be consulted and may participate in the definition of federal programmes. However, there are no formal mechanisms that monitor, evaluate and sanction whenever participation does not take place or when citizen proposals are not truly considered in policy planning.

There have been a few efforts to include the people affected by policy and expenditure in monitoring of social programmes. 'The General Laws for Social Development and for Strengthening Organizations in Civil Society have specific articles [...] that recognize, promote and protect community oversight' (Hevia de la Jara 2007: 254). In addition, there have been interesting initiatives within some social programmes to translate the operational rules into user-friendly manuals. This initiative aims at allowing beneficiaries to understand how programmes are supposed to work and to identify when officials act outside the established rules. Other efforts include 'citizen attention' mechanisms and 'good governance awards for local governments which have increasingly recognized transparency and citizen oversight' (ibid.: 254). However, these are isolated efforts that have not been formalized as legal obligations of public agencies.

The government has not yet established formal mechanisms for the participation of civil society in the budget process. Citizens face various difficulties in accessing budgetary information at the local and municipal levels, and there

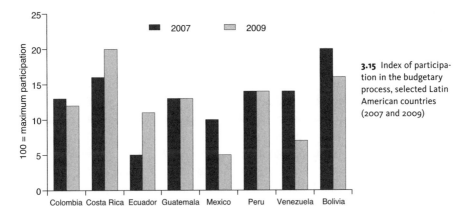

3.15 Index of participation in the budgetary process, selected Latin American countries (2007 and 2009)

Source: J. M. Marín Aguirre (ed.), Índice Latinoamericano de Transparencia Presupuestaria 2009, FUNDAR Centro de Análisis e Investigación, 2009, p. 23

are few capacities and little goodwill in local public institutions to investigate and sanction irregularities (ibid.: 256). Furthermore, the budget information published by the government appears in highly technical formats. This limits the chances of citizens to get involved, critically analyse and make proposals on public resource management and distribution. Despite these barriers, civil society groups have organized and pressured the federal government on some budgetary issues. They managed to make visible the budget lines and monitor the public resources directed to women's health, and to the control and prevention of HIV/AIDS.

According to the Latin American Budget Transparency Index 2009, Mexico does not do well in citizen participation in the budget process (see Figure 3.15). This indicator measures five dimensions: whether there exist mechanisms to incorporate public opinion in the budget formulation process; whether there are mechanisms, known by the population, to influence the approval of the budget; whether the Executive provides much information about changes it makes to the budget approved by the legislature; and whether the Executive provides information about the impact of expenditure. Compared to other countries in the region, Mexico has a low score for participation in the budget process.

The Popular Insurance programme The limitations to transparency, accountability and participation in relation to public expenditure in Mexico can be illustrated by the case of the Popular Insurance programme. It is possible to access information about the amounts allocated to each state and the amounts transferred to the states by the federal government. Nevertheless, it is not possible to get information on how resources were spent and what their impact was. The Superior Auditor had already pointed out this deficiency. Nevertheless, the authorities coordinating the programme have not resolved the problem. There are also no indicators available that link the Popular Insurance programme with the national Health Sector Programme. Thus citizens do not know how Popular Insurance will contribute to the Sector Programme's goals of reducing maternal and infant mortality rates.

One of the objectives of Popular Insurance, as stated by government, was to reduce the out-of-pocket spending of families on health services. This objective is in line with the goal of the national Health Sector Programme of reducing expenditure by 44 per cent. Nonetheless, the Popular Insurance reports do not present any information regarding progress on this; and civil social groups' efforts to obtain access to this information have been unsuccessful.

Finally, the Popular Insurance programme has no appropriate means to support the participation of the people in its design, monitoring and evaluation (Pérez Arguelles 2009: 36–8). There is a call centre and an Internet mailbox where citizens can get information on how to affiliate to the Popular Insurance programme, and register complaints. We may question whether this is an effective way to serve low-income rural people. During the first semester of 2009 the call centre received only 876 complaint calls and the Internet mailbox received 79 complaints. It is unlikely that this represents a reliable expression of people's opinion on a programme that has millions of affiliates. In addition, the Popular Insurance evaluation system reports unusual levels of satisfaction with the health services. In 2008 it recorded 96 per cent satisfaction at the national level, and the lowest score reported in the states was 91 per cent.[20] These results are inconsistent with those recorded by numerous civil society organizations and academics.

Conclusion

The Mexican state's commitment to fundamental rights risks remaining a formality. It has been almost three decades since Mexico ratified the International Covenant on Economic, Social and Cultural Rights and human rights do appear in government's discourse but do not seem to be the guidelines for policy-making and allocation and utilization of public expenditure.

Mexico's per capita social development expenditure has been rising since 1990, and this is in line with the obligations regarding progressive realization and non-retrogression, but it remains low compared to other middle-income Latin American countries. Moreover, this rise has been at the expense of a fall in expenditure on economic development, which is also relevant for the realization of economic and social rights, as discussed in Chapter 1. This can be seen as retrogression. In 1980, public expenditure amounted to around 30 per cent of GDP, but fell to about 24 per cent in 2008. If the same ratio of public expenditure to GDP had been maintained it might have been possible to avoid this retrogression.

Mexico's public expenditure on health has not risen in the same way as social expenditure. As a share of GDP it was lower in 2006 than in 1980. Per capita health expenditure is below that of several comparable Latin American countries. The obligation to conduct health expenditure in a way that is conducive to progressive realization of the right to health does not seem to have been met. In addition the distribution of public expenditure on health does not comply with the obligations regarding non-discrimination and equality. Health spending per capita on Mexicans who are covered by contributory social insurance schemes is much higher than on poorer Mexicans (the group to which most indigenous people belong), who can access only the much more limited health services supplied by the Ministry of Health. However, while increasing public expenditure on health is necessary, it is not sufficient. Resources need to be more effectively used. There is evidence of failure to spend all the resources allocated to improving health infrastructure in deprived, largely indigenous, regions.

The health outcomes are disappointing. The child mortality rate has fallen, indicating progressive realization, but remains higher than in many comparable Latin American countries. Brazil has done much better than Mexico in reducing the mortality rates for children under the age of five during the last two decades. The national maternal mortality rate appears to have fallen but remains higher than that of many comparable Latin American countries, and falls far short of government targets for reduction. Moreover, data on maternal mortality by state show rises not falls in most cases, calling into question whether there has been any progressive realization. Indigenous women are at much greater risk of dying in pregnancy than non-indigenous women, an indicator that health outcomes are not fully compliant with non-discrimination and equality in the enjoyment of the right to health.

The Popular Insurance scheme was introduced in 2004 in an attempt to address the acute inequalities in the funding, quality and accessibility of health services. It was targeted specifically at the uninsured population but failed to give them comprehensive coverage. Despite the increases in the allocations of public expenditure to this new scheme, the affiliation strategies continue to exclude much of the rural population and have been quite ineffective in prioritizing indigenous communities. Furthermore, the Popular Insurance has failed to change the health infrastructure inequalities that most affect the rural and indigenous population.

Public expenditure has addressed the issue of minimum core obligations for ensuring enjoyment of minimum essential levels of social and economic rights, through increased allocations to anti-poverty programmes, but the allocations have not grown as fast as those to other forms of social expenditure. However, the main programme, *Oportunidades*, is a targeted, means-tested, conditional cash transfer programme. Many millions of poor people are still excluded from the programme; and many thousands have had the cash transfers withdrawn on grounds of non-compliance with the conditions. Programmes of this kind are more effective in ensuring that benefits do not go to families above the poverty line than ensuring that the benefits do reach all families below the poverty line. The anti-poverty programmes have not yet been effective in ensuring that no child in Mexico suffers from chronic undernourishment. Although there have been declines in the rate of chronic undernourishment among children, it remains high for poor and indigenous Mexican children.

There have been improvements in the transparency of public expenditure, but Mexico still lags behind many other large middle-income countries. Accountability for public expenditure has also improved, but much of the real budget negotiation takes place behind closed doors. Citizen participation in planning and implementing public programmes is very limited. Other comparable Latin American countries do better. The difficulties in tracking allocations and their impact in the Popular Insurance programme illustrate many of the limits to transparency, accountability and participation.

There is much for the Mexican government still to do to ensure that Mexican public expenditure complies with human rights norms and standards.

Notes

1 The International Covenant on Economic, Social and Cultural Rights (ICESCR); the Convention on the Elimination of All Forms of Discrimination Against Women (CEDAW); and the Convention on the Elimination of all Forms of Racial Discrimination (CERD).

2 Currently, Article 1 prohibits all kinds of discrimination. Equality of rights for men and women, the right to health, adequate housing and children's right to food are recognized in Article 4. The right of all to free, secular and basic education (pre-school, primary and secondary) is established in Article 3. Equal opportunities, education and access to healthcare services for the indigenous populations are guaranteed in Article 2.

3 Instituto Mexicano del Seguro Social (IMSS) was created in 1943 to provide healthcare to the privately employed. In 1960 the Instituto de Seguridad y Servicios Sociales de los Trabajadores del Estado (ISSSTE) became the healthcare service provider for public employees. The National Oil Company (PEMEX) employees got their own healthcare services, as did those working for the Ministry of Defence and the Marine.

4 Note that in Mexico, the term 'uninsured population' has a different meaning to that in the USA. Being uninsured in Mexico means being outside the social security system; it does not mean being excluded from regular healthcare.

5 See Ley General de Salud, www.diputados.gob.mx/LeyesBiblio/pdf/142.pdf (accessed 24 October 2009).

6 Data from the approved 2009 budget and the Budget Proposal for 2010. See 'Gasto en salud' in FUNDAR Centro de Análisis e Investigación, *Observatorio de la Negociación Presupuestaria, 2009–2010*, www.fundar.org.mx/np2009/index.htm (accessed 23 October 2009).

7 Data from Sistema Nacional de Información en Salud, *Mortality Information 2000–2005*, sinais.salud.gob.mx/mortalidad/index.html (accessed 24 October 2009).

8 Data from Sistema Nacional de Información en Salud, *Maternal Deaths 2002–2008*, sinais.salud.gob.mx/mortalidad/index.html (accessed 24 October 2009).

9 Dictamen de la Comisión de Salud de la Cámara de Diputados, *Gaceta Parlamentaria*, Cámara de Diputados, no. 1240-II, 29 March–29 April 2003.

10 The Catastrophic Spending Protection Fund covers a series of high-cost illnesses such as HIV/AIDS, cataracts, congenital or acquired disorders, children or adolescents' cancer, uterine and breast cancer.

11 On this issue, see 'Tendencias del gasto en salud y en infraestructura sanitaria', in FUNDAR Centro de Análisis e Investigación, *Observatorio de la Negociación Presupuestaria, 2009–2010*, www.fundar.org.mx/np2009/index.htm (accessed 23 October 2009).

12 Figures from Instituto Nacional de Estadística Geografía e Informática, *Conteo de Población y Vivienda*, 2005.

13 'Indigenous localities' refers to those areas where 40 per cent of the population or more are speakers of an indigenous language. These are estimates calculated by the number of indigenous affiliates reported by the National Commission coordinating the Popular Insurance and the total number of indigenes living in predominantly indigenous localities (Pérez Arguelles 2009).

14 From 1997 to 2001 its name was PROGRESA. The first cash transfer programme targeting the poor was Pronasol. This programme started to be implemented in 1989, granting funds for public works in the most marginalized regions of the country, conditioned on the community's participation and grant cooperation on the part of the municipal and state governments. This programme, however, lacked the rigorous focalization mechanisms of the latter ones.

15 Data from Tercer Informe de Gobierno Federal (2009).

16 Data from Secretaría de Hacienda y Crédito Público, *Cuenta de la Hacienda Pública Federal 2004* and *Presupuesto de Egresos de la Federación 2009*.

17 Estimates based on data in 'Evolución de la pobreza en México', Consejo Nacional de Evaluación de la Política de Desarrollo Social, PowerPoint presentation, August 2009.

18 Data from Consejo Nacional de Evaluación de la Política de Desarrollo Social, *Informe de la evolución histórica de la situación nutricional de la población y los programas de nutrición y abasto en México*, pp. 17–19, www.cedrssa.gob.mx/ (accessed 16 November 2009).

19 Figures for 2006 for the indigenous population are not representative of the total indigenous population since the sample of people interviewed is not representative, but serves as a proxy for comparative purposes. Data from *Informe de la evolución histórica de la situación nutricional de la población*, Consejo Nacional de Evaluación de la Política Desarollo Social (CONEVAL) 2008, México. http://www.coneval.gob.mx/cmsconeval/rw/resource/coneval/eval_mon/ Informe%20de%2 oevolucion % 20historica%20 de%20la%20 situacion%20 nutricional%20de %20la%20poblacion.pdf?view=true (accessed 16 November 2009).

20 See Comisión Nacional de Protección Social en Salud, *Informe de resultados del primer semestre de 2009*, www.seguro-popular.salud. gob.mx/index.php?option=com_weblinks& view=category&id=35&Itemid=128 (accessed 16 November 2009).

References

BIE-INEGI, Instituto Nacional de Geografía, Estadistica e Informatica, Sistema Nacional de Información en Salud (n.d.) *Maternal Deaths 2002–2008*, sinais.salud.gob.mx/mortalidad/index.html (accessed 24 October 2009).

Caballero Sosa, L. and D. Dávila Estefan (2007) *Diagnóstico de la negociación presupuestaria 2006–2007*, FUNDAR Centro de Análisis e Investigación.

Cabrera, C. J. (2008) 'Gasto público (1982–2006)', in R. Cordera and C. J. Cabrera Adame (eds), *El papel de las ideas y las políticas en el cambio estructural en México*, Universidad Nacional Autónoma de México, Fondo de Cultura Económica, pp. 138–72.

Castañeda Pérez, M. (2007) 'El Seguro Popular en la atención materna en Oaxaca: los pendientes del sexenio', in D. Díaz (ed.), *Muerte materna y Seguro Popular*, FUNDAR, Centro de Análisis e Investigación, México, pp. 105–28.

Castañeda, M., D. Díaz, G. Espinosa, G. Freyermuth, D. Sánchez-Hidalgo and C. de la Torre (2004) *La mortalidad materna en México. Cuatro visiones críticas*, FUNDAR Centro de Análisis e Investigación, Kinal Antzetik, Foro Nacional de Mujeres y Políticas de Población, Universidad Autónoma Metropolitana, Coordinadora Nacional de Mujeres Indígenas.

Centro de Estudios de las Finanzas Públicas, Cámara de Diputados (2009) *Evolución del Gasto Público por Ramos 2003–2009*.

Centro de Estudios para el Desarrollo Rural Sustentable y la Soberanía Alimentaria (n.d.) *Informe de la evolución histórica de la situación nutricional de la población y los programas de nutrición y abasto en México*, Consejo Nacional de Evaluación de la Política de Desarrollo Social.

Dávila Estefan, D. and J. Romero León (2007) 'The policy debate over Mexico´s budget', in J. Fox, L. Hight, H. Hofbauer and T. Sánchez-Andrade (eds), *Mexico's Right-to-*

know Reforms, Civil Society Perspectives, FUNDAR Centro de Análisis e Investigación, Woodrow Wilson International Center for Scholars, Mexico, pp. 170–6.

Economic Commission for Latin American and the Caribbean (n.d.) Social Statistics Database, www.eclac.org/estadisticas/bases/ (accessed 23 October 2009).

Espinosa Damián, G. (2004) 'Doscientas trece voces contra la muerte. Mortalidad materna en zonas indígenas', in M. Castañeda, D. Díaz, G. Espinosa, G. Freyermuth, D. Sánchez-Hidalgo and C. de la Torre, *La mortalidad materna en México. Cuatro visiones críticas*, FUNDAR Centro de Análisis e Investigación, Kinal Antzetik, Foro Nacional de Mujeres y Políticas de Población, Universidad Autónoma Metropolitana, Coordinadora Nacional de Mujeres Indígenas, pp. 161–237.

FUNDAR (2009) 'Incongruencia y contradicciones en la politica economia del gobierno', FUNDAR Centro de Análisis e Investigación.

Hevia de la Jara, F. (2007) 'Social audit mechanisms in Mexico', in J. Fox, L. Haight, H. Hofbauer and T. Sánchez Andrade (eds), *Mexico's Right-to-know Reforms. Civil Society Perspectives*, Woodrow Wilson International Centre for Scholars.

Hofbauer, H. and G. Lara (2002) *Health Care: A Question of Human Rights, Not Charity*, FUNDAR Centro de Análisis e Investigación.

Instituto Nacional de Estadística Geografía e Informática (2005) *Conteo de Población y Vivienda*.

International Budget Partnership (n.d.) Open Budget Index 2008, www.budegtindex.org (accessed 13 November 2009).

Lavielle, B., R. Moreno, M. Garza and D. Díaz (2004) *Gasto en Salud: Propuesta para la Mesa de Gasto de la Convención Nacional Hacendaria*, FUNDAR Centro de Análisis e Investigación.

Marín Aguirre, J. M. (2009) (ed.) *Índice Latinoamericano de Transparencia Presupuestaria 2009*, FUNDAR Centro de Análisis e Investigación.

Melendez Navarro, D. (2006) 'La atención obstétrica de emergencia: una estrategia viable para disminuir la muerte materna ante las insuficiencias, ineficiencias e inequidades del sistema de salud en Guerrero', in D. Díaz (ed.), *Muerte Materna y Presupuesto Público*, FUNDAR Centro de Análisis e Investigación, pp. 63–80.

Meneses Navarro, S. (2007) '¿Acceso universal a la atención obstétrica? El Seguro Popular de Salud frente al reto de la muerte materna en Los Altos de Chiapas', in D. Díaz (ed.), *Muerte materna y Seguro Popular*, FUNDAR Centro de Análisis e Investigación, pp. 13–62.

Moreno, R. (2006) 'Ingresos petroleros y gasto público. La dependencia continúa', in H. Hofbauer and V. Zebadúa (eds), *Avances y retrocesos. Una evaluación ciudadana del sexenio 2000–2006*, FUNDAR Centro de Análisis e Investigación.

— (2007) 'The lack of transparency and accountability mechanisms for Mexico's oil income', in J. Fox, L. Haight, H. Hofbauer and T. Sánchez Andrade (eds), *Mexico's Right-to-know Reforms. Civil Society Perspectives*, Woodrow Wilson International Centre for Scholars, pp. 186–9.

Pérez Arguelles, M. (2009) *Seguro Popular ¿Salud y ciudadanía para todos y todas?*, FUNDAR Centro de Análisis e Investigación.

Pérez Arguelles, M. and J. Romero León (2006) 'Transparencia en el presupuesto público. Los desafíos de la rendición de cuentas', in H. Hofbauer and M. Zebadúa (eds), *Avances y retrocesos. Una evaluación ciudadana del sexenio 2000–2006*, FUNDAR Centro de Análisis e Investigación.

Puentes-Rosas, E., S. Sesma and O. Gómez Dantés (2005) 'Estimación de la población con seguro de salud en México mediante una encuesta nacional', *Salud pública de México*, 47(1): 22–6.

Scot Andretta, J. (2001) 'La otra cara de la reforma fiscal', *Programa de Presupuesto y Gasto Público*, Centro de Investigación y Docencia Económicas.

Romero León, J. (2007) 'One step forward, two steps back? budget transparency and access to information in Mexico', in J. Fox, L. Hight, H. Hofbauer and T. Sánchez-Andrade (eds), *Mexico's Right-to-know Reforms, Civil Society Perspectives*, FUNDAR Centro de Análisis e Investigación, Woodrow Wilson International Center for Scholars, Mexico, pp. 164–9.

Tercer Informe del Gobierno Federal (2009) *Anexo Estadístico, Gobierno Federal de la República Mexicana*.

4 | HUMAN RIGHTS AND PUBLIC EXPENDITURE IN THE USA

Nursel Aydiner-Avsar and Diane Elson

Introduction

Public expenditure has implications for the realization of many human rights. In this chapter, we look at public expenditure in relation to the right to health and the right to food, which is closely related to the right to health. The right to health was first articulated in the 1946 Constitution of the World Health Organization as follows (WHO Constitution Preamble): 'the enjoyment of the highest attainable standard of health is one of the fundamental rights of every human being without distinction of race, political belief, economic or social condition'. Article 25 of the Universal Declaration of Human Rights (UDHR) (1948) and Article 12 of the International Covenant on Economic, Social and Cultural Rights (ICESCR) (1966) oblige governments to protect, promote and fulfil this right. Article 12 places emphasis on equal access to healthcare and minimum guarantees of healthcare in the event of sickness.

General Comment 14 of the Committee on Economic, Social and Cultural Rights (2000) clarifies that the right to health consists of four major elements. First, health facilities, goods and services must be *available* in sufficient quantity. Secondly, these facilities must be *accessible* to everyone without discrimination and need to be affordable for all. Thirdly, they must be *appropriate* from a cultural and societal perspective. Fourthly, they must be scientifically appropriate and of good *quality*.

However, the right to the highest possible attainable standard of health refers not only to health facilities. The Committee on Economic, Social and Cultural Rights has clarified that it also refers to access to the underlying determinants of health, 'such as nutritiously safe food and potable drinking water, basic sanitation and adequate housing and living conditions' (General Comment 14, para. 36). Here we focus on food, and on income poverty as a proxy for other underlying determinants of health. The right to food is included in Article 25 of UDHR, and in Article 11 of ICESCR. The right to food refers to the right to have regular access to sufficient, nutritionally adequate and culturally acceptable food for an active, healthy life. General Comment 12 of the Committee on Economic, Social and Cultural Rights (1999) sets the framework for both national and international obligations.

Unlike the Mexican Constitution the US Federal Constitution does not have any explicit mention of economic and social rights. Constitutional scholars distinguish between negative rights (prohibiting government from interfering with individual behaviour) and positive rights (the obligation of government to provide some benefit). The satisfaction of negative rights does not require the government to take any action. On the other hand, positive rights always require some type of affirmative governmental action. While the US Federal Constitution contains only negative rights, twenty-three state constitutions implicitly or explicitly establish protections for the poor, with provisions ranging from categorical statements of an affirmative obligation on the state to care for the needy to the creation of public agencies to address this issue. However, state courts lack the institutional incentives to vigorously enforce welfare rights and instead rely on more individual rights claims (Pascal 2008).

An investigation of constitutional commitments to five social rights has been carried out for sixty-eight countries by Ben-Bassat and Dahan (2008). The rights considered were the rights to social security, education, health and housing, and workers' rights. The study defined a constitutional social right as one that grants a personal entitlement to monetary transfers or transfer in kind on a universal basis. A rank of 0 was given if a right is absent from the Constitution; a rank of 1 was given if the Constitution includes a general statement with regard to a particular social right; a rank of 2 was given if the Constitution guarantees a minimal level with respect to that right (such as the case of minimum income as part of the right to social security); and a rank of 3 was given if the Constitution has a high degree of commitment and specificity (such as a detailed description of the specifics of a minimum standard of living in terms of food, housing, etc.). The constitutional right to education occurs in fifty-one out of sixty-eight countries analysed; and the right to social security appears in the constitutions of forty-seven countries; while the right to health as well as the right to housing and workers' rights appear in fewer than half the countries. Not surprisingly, the USA gets zero for five social rights with an overall score of 0, while countries such as Portugal and Switzerland have a high constitutional commitment to social rights. On the other hand, Mexico received a score of 0.86 for social security, 3 for education, 1 for health, 3 for housing, 2 for workers' rights and a summary score of 1.97, ranking it higher than the USA.

The International Covenant on Economic, Social and Cultural Rights (ICESCR) was signed by the US president in 1977, but has not been ratified by Congress. The International Covenant on Civil and Political Rights (ICCPR) was ratified by the USA in 1992, and the International Convention on the Elimination of All Forms of Racial Discrimination (ICERD) ratified by the USA in 1994. The International Convention on the Elimination of All Forms of Discrimination Against Women has not been ratified by the USA. Nevertheless, the US government has obligations to realize economic and social rights conferred by the Universal Declaration of Human Rights (NESRI 2006).

Progressive realization and non-retrogression: public expenditure and the right to health

The realization of the right to health and the right to food is influenced by many factors, but public expenditure can play an important role in securing the progressive realization of these rights in a way that is non-discriminatory and ensures minimum core standards. Xu (2006), analysing data from 2001, finds significant variations across the states of the USA in income-related inequality in health and health achievement. He found that per capita state and local government spending, particularly the proportion spent on public health, was positively associated with better health achievement.

Obligation of conduct While increases in public expenditure are unlikely to be a sufficient condition for the progressive realization of economic and social rights, stagnation or decreases in public expenditures most strongly related to economic and social rights are unlikely to be conducive to improvements in the enjoyment of these rights. Figure 4.1 presents federal government expenditure by function as a share of GDP. National defence spending had the largest share in GDP until the early 1990s, when the end of the Cold War was followed by steep decline in the share of defence; it increased sharply in the early 2000s, and by 2009 had almost equalled social security spending.[1] However, the share of expenditure that goes to social security, income security and Medicare and other health programmes now outweighs the share for national defence.

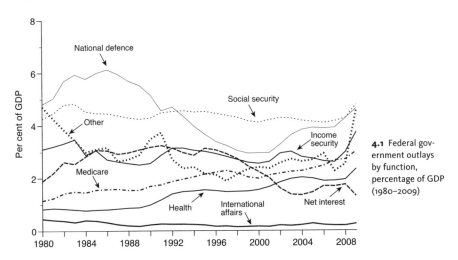

4.1 Federal government outlays by function, percentage of GDP (1980–2009)

Source: Created by the authors using data from *Economic Report of the President: 2010 Report Spreadsheet Tables*, Table B-80, www.gpoaccess.gov/eop/tables10.html (accessed 18 December 2010)

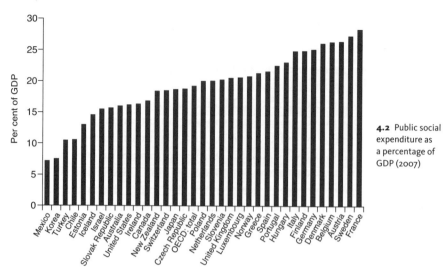

4.2 Public social expenditure as a percentage of GDP (2007)

Source: Created by the authors using data from OECD, *Social Expenditure Database (SOCX) 2010*, Aggregated Data, stats.oecd.org/Index.aspx?datasetcode=SOCX_AGG (accessed 18 December 2010)

The share of social expenditure in the USA is less than the share of the social expenditure[2] of other OECD countries, as shown in Figure 4.2. In 2007, the USA ranks tenth from the bottom with a value of 16.2 per cent, which is below the OECD average of 19.3 per cent.[3] When this figure is compared with those for other developed countries, the difference is striking, particularly compared to France, Sweden, Austria and Germany, which respectively devote 28.4, 27.3, 26.4 and 25.2 per cent of their GDP to social expenditure. The only

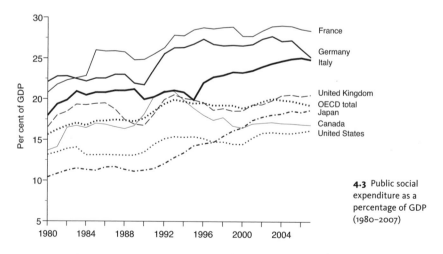

4.3 Public social expenditure as a percentage of GDP (1980–2007)

Source: Created by the authors using OECD, *Social Expenditure Database (SOCX) 2010*, Aggregated Data, stats.oecd.org/Index.aspx?datasetcode=SOCX_AGG (accessed 18 December 2010)

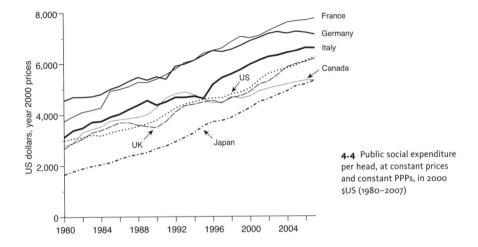

4.4 Public social expenditure per head, at constant prices and constant PPPs, in 2000 $US (1980–2007)

Source: Created by the authors using OECD, *Social Expenditure Database (SOCX) 2010*, Aggregated Data, stats.oecd.org/Index.aspx?datasetcode=SOCX_AGG (accessed 18 December 2010)

developed countries with shares close to that of the USA are New Zealand and Canada with a share of 18.4 and 15.9 per cent respectively.

The evolution of the share of social expenditure in GDP over the period 1980–2007 is shown in Figure 4.3 for G7 countries (USA, Germany, France, UK, Japan, Italy and Canada). The US share fell in the early 1980s followed by a moderate rise starting in the early 1990s. However, overall the share of social expenditure stayed below that of other G7 countries for most of the time (except for Japan).

The level of US real per capita social expenditure has been rising but it is lower than in France, Germany and Italy, while similar to that of Canada and the UK, and higher than in Japan (see Figure 4.4).[4]

We now turn to public expenditure on health services. There is no national health insurance programme providing universal coverage in the USA; however, the federal government does fund two major health insurance programmes: Medicare and Medicaid. Medicare was enacted in 1965 as the federal health insurance programme for all people at or over the age of sixty-five regardless of their income or medical history, and expanded in 1972 to include people with permanent disabilities under the age of sixty-five. Medicare is a universal entitlement for everyone over the age of sixty-five and those with permanent disabilities. Around 47 million Americans received Medicare benefits in 2009; 17 per cent of the people receiving Medicare were under the age of sixty-five and permanently disabled, and 47 per cent had incomes below 200 per cent of poverty-level income (Kaiser Family Foundation 2010a); 17 per cent were African-American or Hispanic (Kaiser Family Foundation 2007).

Medicaid was established in 1965 to provide health insurance to low-income

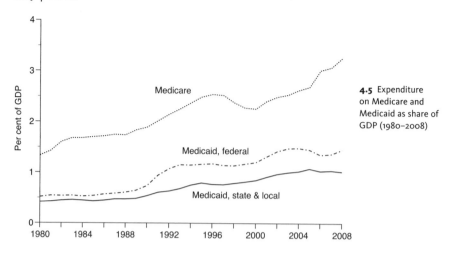

4.5 Expenditure on Medicare and Medicaid as share of GDP (1980–2008)

Source: Created by the authors using data from US Department of Health and Human Services, Centers for Medicare and Medicaid, *National Heath Expenditure Historical Data, National Health Expenditures by type of service and source of funds*, CY 1960–2008, www.cms.gov/nationalhealthexpenddata/02_nationalhealth accountshistorical.asp (accessed 19 December 2010); and Bureau of Economic Analysis, *National Income and Product Accounts*, Table 1.1.5, Gross Domestic Product, www.bea.gov/national/nipaweb/SelectTable. asp?Selected=N (accessed 19 December 2010)

Americans. It is a targeted and means-tested programme, not a universal entitlement. Medicaid is jointly financed by the federal and state governments, and states design and administer their own Medicaid programmes within broad federal rules (Kaiser Family Foundation 2010b). The federal government contributes at least 50 per cent of total costs in every state, but a higher share in poorer states, reaching 76 per cent in the poorest state; the federal share of costs is 57 per cent on average (ibid.). States are facing difficulties in providing and maintaining their current health systems because healthcare is the largest and most expensive part of their budgets. Figure 4.5 shows that expenditures that go to Medicare and Medicaid have been rising as a percentage of GDP. The expenditure on Medicare far outweighs the expenditure that goes to the poor via Medicaid.[5]

As well as Medicare and Medicaid, the federal government directly funds healthcare provided by the Department of Veterans Affairs, public hospitals and some public health activities (Kaiser Family Foundation 2009).

Per capita public expenditure on healthcare has been rising in real terms, as shown in Figure 4.6.[6] Thus there has not been retrogression in terms of allocation of public expenditure to health services – though this does not necessarily mean that there has been progressive realization of the right to health. That also depends on how effective this expenditure has been.

Publicly financed health programmes play a relatively small role in healthcare provision. As is shown in Figure 4.7, in the USA the private sector plays the dominant role in terms of providing insurance coverage; and most healthcare

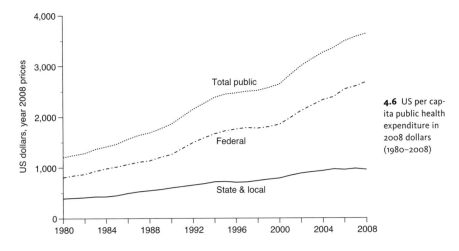

4.6 US per capita public health expenditure in 2008 dollars (1980–2008)

Source: Created by the authors using data from US Department of Health and Human Services, Centers for Medicare and Medicaid, *National Heath Expenditure Historical Data, NHE summary including share of GDP, CY 1960–2008*, www.cms.gov/nationalhealthexpenddata/02_nationalhealthaccountshistorical.asp (accessed 19 December 2010); and Bureau of Labor Statistics, Databases, Tables, and Calculators by Subject, Consumer Price Index, All Urban Consumers, data.bls.gov/PDQ/servlet/SurveyOutputServlet?data_tool=latest_numbers&series_id=CUUR0000SA0&output_view=pct_1mth (accessed 19 December 2010)

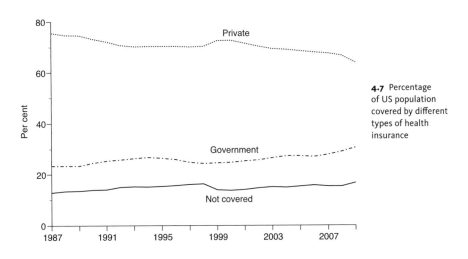

4.7 Percentage of US population covered by different types of health insurance

Note: The survey underwent some changes in 1999, therefore two series are combined to get the full series.

Source: US Census Bureau, Health Insurance Historical Tables (HIA series), HIA-1. Health Insurance Coverage Status and Type of Coverage – All Persons by Sex, Race and Hispanic Origin: 1999 to 2009, www.census.gov/hhes/www/hlthins/data/historical/index.html (accessed 19 December 2010); and Health Insurance Historical Tables Original Series HI-1. Health Insurance Coverage Status and Type of Coverage – All Persons by Sex, Race and Hispanic Origin: 1987 to 2005 (for 1987–98), www.census.gov/hhes/www/hlthins/data/historical/original.html

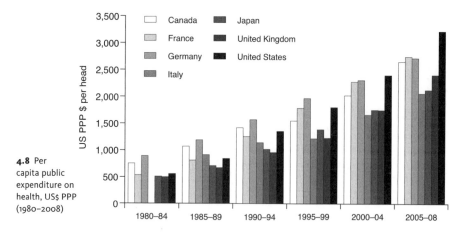

4.8 Per capita public expenditure on health, US$ PPP (1980–2008)

Source: Created by the authors using OECD, *Health Data 2010*, Frequently Requested Data, www.oecd.org/document/16/0,3746,en_2649_37407_2085200_1_1_1_37407,00.html (accessed 18 December 2010)

facilities are privately owned and operated. The private health insurance business benefits from payments that the government makes to provide private health insurance for government employees, and tax breaks for health insurance premiums paid by private sector employers. If these payments are included, the government-financed share of total health spending in 1999 was 59.8 per cent, 25 per cent higher than the Center for Medicare and Medicaid Services (CMS) estimates for the same year (Bitton and Kahn 2003). Private health insurance does not guarantee that health costs will be met; it is estimated that about 700,000 families a year have been going bankrupt as a result of healthcare bills, even though three-quarters of them had health insurance at the onset of illness (Himmelstein et al. 2005).

Around 15 per cent of the population was not covered at all in the period from 1987 to 2009, calling into question the fulfilment of the obligation to ensure that everyone has access to healthcare (see Figure 4.7). Moreover, in 2009 more than 70 per cent of the uninsured had gone without health insurance for more than a year (Kaiser Family Foundation 2010c).

About one quarter of the uninsured go without needed care, including recommended treatments or prescription drugs, because of its cost; and because more than half of the uninsured do not have a regular place to go when they are sick and need medical advice (ibid.). The uninsured are not reimbursed by an insurance scheme for any health expenditures they make. Berk and Monheit (2001) look at the overall private healthcare expenditure of the uninsured compared to those with private insurance; and find that even the very sickest (top 5 per cent in terms of expenditure) of the uninsured spend much less than the comparable group with private insurance. Thus, even the top spenders among the uninsured receive only a small fraction of the care that can be obtained by those with private insurance.

TABLE 4.1 Health expenditure indicators: selected high-income countries

	Total expenditure on health as a % of gross domestic product			General government expenditure on health as a % of total government expenditure			General government expenditure on health as a % of total expenditure on health			Private expenditure on health as a % of total expenditure on health		
	1995	2001	2008	1995	2001	2008	1995	2001	2008	1995	2001	2008
Australia	7.4	8.4	8.8	13.0	15.6	17.6	65.8	66.3	68.0	34.2	33.7	32.0
Canada	9.0	9.3	10.3	13.3	15.5	18.1	71.4	70.0	69.8	28.6	30.0	30.2
France	10.4	10.2	11.1	15.2	15.7	16.6	79.7	79.4	79.0	20.3	20.6	21.0
Germany	10.1	10.4	10.4	15.0	17.4	18.2	81.6	79.3	76.8	18.4	20.7	23.2
Italy	7.3	8.2	9.0	9.8	12.8	14.4	70.8	74.6	77.4	29.2	25.4	22.6
Japan	6.9	7.9	8.1	15.7	16.8	17.9	83.0	81.7	80.9	17.0	18.3	19.1
Netherlands	8.3	8.3	9.1	10.5	11.5	16.4	71.0	62.8	82.1	29.0	37.2	17.9
New Zealand	7.2	7.8	9.0	13.3	15.8	18.0	77.2	76.4	78.7	22.8	23.6	21.3
Norway	7.9	8.8	8.6	13.0	16.7	18.0	84.2	83.6	84.2	15.8	16.4	15.8
Spain	7.4	7.2	8.7	12.1	13.3	15.6	72.2	71.2	72.8	27.8	28.8	27.2
Sweden	8.0	9.0	9.1	10.6	13.2	14.1	86.6	81.7	82.0	13.4	18.2	18.0
Switzerland	9.6	10.6	10.5	14.6	17.3	19.8	53.6	56.9	59.0	46.4	43.1	41.0
UK	6.8	7.3	9.0	13.0	14.5	15.6	83.9	80.0	82.8	16.1	20.0	17.2
US	13.6	14.1	16.0	16.4	17.8	19.2	44.9	44.2	46.5	55.1	55.8	53.5

Source: Created by the authors using World Health Organization Global Health Observatory (GHO) database, apps.who.int/ghodata/# (accessed 18 December 2010)

Despite the exclusion of a substantial minority from health insurance, by the early years of the twenty-first century per capita public expenditure on health was higher than in other leading high-income countries (see Figure 4.8).

Among high-income countries, the United States has by far the highest share of GDP devoted to health expenditure, when both public and private sources are taken into account, as shown in Table 4.1. The greater part of US health expenditure comes from private sources, in contrast to other high-income countries where government expenditure constitutes a high share of total expenditure on health, ranging between 59.0 per cent and 84.2 per cent in 2008.

Although the USA has experienced high and rising health expenditure, there is evidence that the use of this expenditure, both public and private, has not been as effective as in other high-income countries. Peterson and Burton (2008) provide a comprehensive comparison of the US health system with those of other OECD countries. They show that the USA has far fewer doctor visits per person; and a below-average number of hospital beds and practising physicians per person; while the number of nurses per person is roughly the same as the OECD average. However, the USA makes more use of the newest medical technologies. It spends more on prescription drugs per capita than any other OECD country and pays more for brand-name drugs than most OECD countries. Moreover, spending on health administration and insurance was seven times that of the OECD median. Overall, the USA pays significantly higher prices for medical care than other countries (ibid.).

Bitton and Kahn (2003) draw attention to the large overhead costs involved in the US multi-payer system: administration constitutes 20–30 per cent of total US healthcare expenditure. While the average US hospital spends 25 per cent of its budget on billing and administration, Canada's single-payer system has 1 per cent administrative overhead costs. It is estimated that reducing the complexity of the system would save as much as $140 billion annually without reducing the funds spent on care (ibid.).

Obligation of result Have health outcomes improved over time in the USA? Article 12 of ICESCR specifically refers to the requirement for governments to take steps to reduce the infant mortality rate. CEDAW Article 12 states that governments 'shall ensure to women appropriate services in connection with pregnancy, confinement, and the post-natal period'. Figure 4.9 presents the infant mortality rate, measured as number of deaths per 1,000 live births, for the USA over the period 1980–2006. There was a steady decline, especially in the 1980s and early 1990s. However, the infant mortality rate stabilized around 7 deaths per 1,000 live births over the late 1990s and 2000s and did not decline further.

Maternal mortality rate, measured as the number of deaths per 100,000 live births, is presented in Figure 4.10 for the United States over the period 1980–2006. There was a decrease over the 1970s and early 1980s and it stabilized

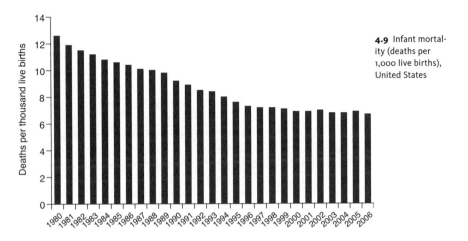

4.9 Infant mortality (deaths per 1,000 live births), United States

Source: Created by the authors using *Health, United States 2009* report, data table for Figure 17, 'Infant, neonatal, and postneonatal mortality rates: United States, 1950–2006', p. 124

at around 7–8 deaths per 100,000 live births on average in the 1990s. However, the maternal mortality rate increased, starting in the 2000s. The data clearly indicate a lack of progressive realization with respect to maternal mortality.

In comparison with other high-income countries, the USA has a high infant mortality rate: among OECD countries, the USA had the fourth-highest infant mortality rate after Turkey, Mexico and Chile in 2006 (OECD Health Data 2010). In terms of the maternal mortality rate, the USA has the sixth-highest rate following Mexico, Turkey, Luxembourg, South Korea and New Zealand, and is above the OECD average (OECD Health Data 2007).

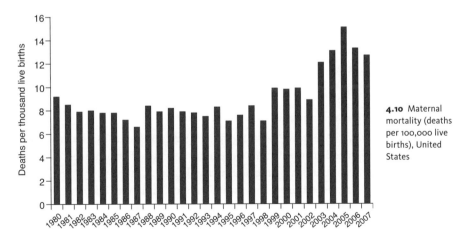

4.10 Maternal mortality (deaths per 100,000 live births), United States

Source: Created by the authors using *Health, United States 2009* report, Table 39, 'Maternal mortality for complications of pregnancy, childbirth, and the puerperium, by race, Hispanic origin, and age: United States, selected years 1950–2006', p. 231

The USA has the lowest life expectancy among major developed nations; and the highest probability of dying before the age of five, as shown in Table 4.2. The probability at birth of not surviving to forty and to sixty years of age is highest in the USA.

TABLE 4.2 Life expectancy indicators: selected high-income countries

	Life expectancy at birth 2004	Probability of dying under age 5 (per 1,000) 2004	Probability at birth of not surviving to age 40 (% of cohort) 2000–05	Probability at birth of not surviving to age 60 (% of cohort) 2000–05
Australia	81.0	5.0	2.3	7.3
Canada	80.0	6.0	2.3	8.1
France	80.0		2.4	8.9
Germany	79.0	5.0	2.0	8.6
Japan	82.0	4.0	1.7	6.9
Italy	81.0	5.0	2.3	7.7
Netherlands	79.0	5.0	2.1	8.3
New Zealand	80.0	6.0	2.4	8.3
Norway	80.0	4.0	2.3	7.9
Spain	80.0	5.0	2.2	7.7
Sweden	80.0	4.0	1.6	6.7
Switzerland	81.0	5.0	2.2	7.2
UK	79.0	6.0	2.2	8.7
US	78.0	8.0	3.5	11.6

Source: *The World Health Report 2006*, Annex Table 1 (pp. 168–77), and *Human Development Report 2007/8*, Table 3 (pp. 238–40) and Table 4 (pp. 241–2)

The high levels of health expenditure in the USA, compared to other high-income countries, are not associated with lower mortality rates and life expectancy rates than in other high-income countries.

Non-discrimination and equality in right to health

Obligation of conduct Are some social groups being excluded by the way that healthcare is organized in the USA? We examine types of insurance coverage for the non-elderly population by race/ethnicity (Figure 4.11); and by citizenship status (Figure 4.12). Hispanics, American Indians and non-Hispanic blacks have higher rates of being uninsured than whites and Asians. Uninsurance rates are significantly higher for non-citizens, with almost half of the non-citizens being uninsured, while only 15 per cent of citizens are uninsured.

The trends in the rate of being uninsured over time (see Figure 4.13) show that Hispanics have persistently higher rates of being uninsured followed by

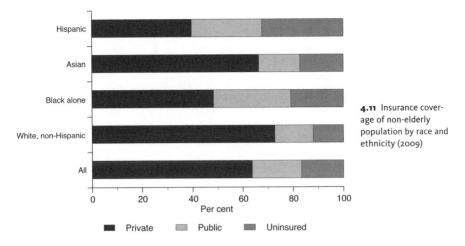

4.11 Insurance coverage of non-elderly population by race and ethnicity (2009)

Source: Created by the authors using data from US Census Bureau, *Income, Poverty and Health Insurance: Coverage in the US*, September 2010, Appendix Table C-2 (pp. 72–5)

blacks. There have been no long-run declines in the percentage of people without insurance; the gaps between different racial/ethnic groups persist over time.

Women have persistently lower rates of being uninsured than men, as shown in Figure 4.14. Low-income people are more likely to be uninsured than high-income people. In 2005, while 34 per cent of persons from households below the poverty level were uninsured, only 12 per cent of those with incomes above 200 per cent of poverty-level income were uninsured. This gap did not narrow over the last two decades (CMS and ASPE 2007). Thus the US health system does not seem to be in compliance with the obligation to guarantee the right to health on an equal basis, without discrimination.

Medicaid was introduced to rectify some of the inequality, by providing

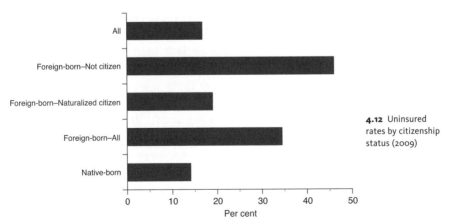

4.12 Uninsured rates by citizenship status (2009)

Source: Created by the authors using data from US Census Bureau, *Income, Poverty and Health Insurance: Coverage in the US*, September 2010, Table 8 (p. 23)

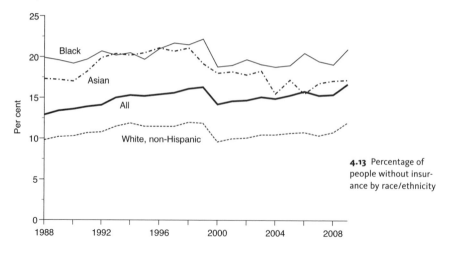

4.13 Percentage of people without insurance by race/ethnicity

Note: The Asian category also includes Pacific Islanders for years before 2002. The survey underwent some changes in 1999, therefore two series are combined to get the full series.

Source: US Census Bureau, Health Insurance Historical Tables (HIA series) HIA-1. Health Insurance Coverage Status and Type of Coverage – All Persons by Sex, Race and Hispanic Origin: 1999 to 2009, www.census.gov/hhes/www/hlthins/data/historical/index.html (accessed 19 December 2010); and Health Insurance Historical Tables Original Series HI-1. Health Insurance Coverage Status and Type of Coverage – All Persons by Sex, Race and Hispanic Origin: 1987 to 2005 (for 1987–2001), www.census.gov/hhes/www/hlthins/data/historical/original.html

health insurance for low-income people, but it does not extend its benefits to all low-income people. Undocumented migrants are not eligible for Medicaid even though they contribute to the economy through their labour. Legal immigrants' eligibility for Medicaid depends on the duration of their residence in the USA. The Personal Responsibility and Work Opportunity Reconciliation Act (PRWORA) of 1996 introduced a five-years-of-residence requirement for eligibility; and introduced new administrative regulations regarding proof of citizenship status that discourage potentially eligible documented immigrants from applying to Medicaid. These changes in policy led to confusion about eligibility and appeared to lead even eligible immigrants to believe that they could not access public programmes. This lack of awareness of eligibility remains a problem even in states that have attempted to continue public insurance for immigrants. Immigrants also have lower access to private insurance owing to their lower chance of getting a job that provides health coverage and the high health insurance premium (King 2007). PRWORA increased the health coverage disparity between immigrants and citizens and contributed to increasing uninsured rates among non-citizens. Not only are uninsured rates among immigrants more than twice that of US-born citizens (as shown in Figure 4.12), the uninsured rates for recent immigrants with fewer than five years of stay are as high as 63 per cent among recent immigrants. Reflecting the large discrepancy in access to coverage, immigrants have greater problems in access to care, obtain less physician care and are significantly less likely

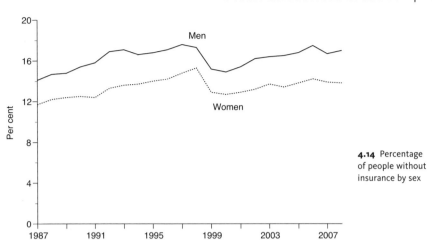

4.14 Percentage of people without insurance by sex

Note: The survey underwent some changes in 1999, therefore two series are combined to get the full series.

Source: US Census Bureau, Health Insurance Historical Tables (HIA series) HIA-1. Health Insurance Coverage Status and Type of Coverage – All Persons by Sex, Race and Hispanic Origin: 1999 to 2009, www.census.gov/hhes/www/hlthins/data/historical/index.html (accessed 19 December 2010); and Health Insurance Historical Tables Original Series HI-1. Health Insurance Coverage Status and Type of Coverage – All Persons by Sex, Race and Hispanic Origin: 1987 to 2005 (for 1987–98), www.census.gov/hhes/www/hlthins/data/historical/original.html

to use emergency rooms at hospitals. These differences are more drastic for recent immigrants owing to language barriers (Kaiser Family Foundation 2009).

Even with public insurance, there are differences between US-born persons and immigrants. Mohanty et al. (2005) found that per capita expenditures of publicly insured immigrants were 44 per cent lower than those of US-born persons with public coverage ($2,774 versus $4,963). In addition, expenditures of higher-income immigrants (those with incomes above or equal to 200 per cent of the poverty line) were 53 per cent lower than those of US-born persons in the same income bracket. Moreover, there was a similar disparity among those with incomes below 200 per cent of the poverty line: migrants' expenditures were 60 per cent lower than those of US-born individuals. This difference in public health expenditure of migrants and US-born persons was also found for emergency care, office-based visits, outpatient visits, inpatient visits and prescription drugs.

Thus immigrants face additional access barriers, including cultural and linguistic barriers, compared with the US-born persons.[7] Moreover, controlling for free care provided by some private institutions does not change the results, showing that lower healthcare expenditure is not due to higher levels of use of free care by immigrants. Also immigrants do not spend less because of less need, since immigrants were found to have slightly worse self-reported health in the survey (ibid.).

The fragmented system of providing access to healthcare results in persistent disparities between different social groups, as reported by the US Department of Health and Human Services, Agency for Healthcare Research and Quality (AHRQ 2008: iv). Lack of insurance is identified as a major barrier to reducing disparities (ibid.: 8–9):

> Uninsured individuals do worse than privately insured individuals on almost 90 per cent of quality measures. Uninsured individuals do worse than privately insured individuals on all access measures. Uninsured individuals are about six times as likely to lack a usual source of care and four times as likely to be without a usual source of care for financial reasons. Uninsured individuals are nearly three times as likely to not get care as soon as wanted for illness or injury, over twice as likely to not have a mammogram (for women over 40), and over twice as likely to have communication problems with their child's provider.

Shi and Stevens (2005), analysing data from the 1996 and 2000 Medical Expenditure Panel Survey, found that Asians, Hispanics and blacks were less likely than whites to have a usual source of care, health professional or doctor visit and dental visit in the past year. These disparities in access to care persisted between 1996 and 2000, even after controlling for health insurance coverage, poverty status, health status and several other factors associated with access to care.

Obligation of result Is inequality in access to health insurance associated with inequality in health outcomes? As noted earlier, Article 12 of ICESCR specifically refers to the requirement for governments to take steps to reduce the infant mortality rate; and CEDAW Article 12 states that governments 'shall ensure

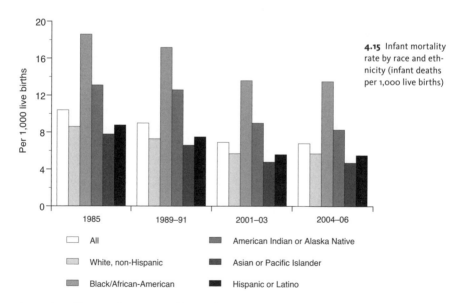

4.15 Infant mortality rate by race and ethnicity (infant deaths per 1,000 live births)

Source: Created by the authors using *Health, United States 2009* report, Table 20 (p. 180), and *Health, United States 2006* report, Table 19 (p. 160)

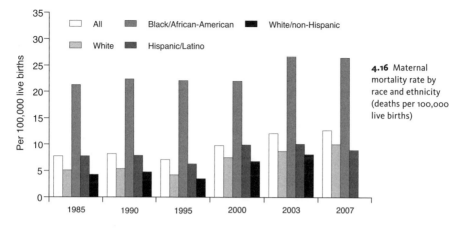

4.16 Maternal mortality rate by race and ethnicity (deaths per 100,000 live births)

Source: Created by the authors using *Health, United States 2009* report, Table 39 (p. 231), and *Health, United States 2006* report, Table 43 (p. 222)

to women appropriate services in connection with pregnancy, confinement, and the post-natal period'. These obligations are subject to the immediate obligation to ensure that all rights are realized without discrimination, on an equal basis for all. Figures 4.15 and 4.16 show infant and maternal mortality rates by race and ethnicity for the period 1985–2007. Although there is decline over time for most of the groups, the gap across racial and ethnic groups does not close. The mortality rates are particularly high for African-Americans.

The age-adjusted death rates by race and ethnicity groups are presented in Figure 4.17. African-Americans have the highest death rate among race/

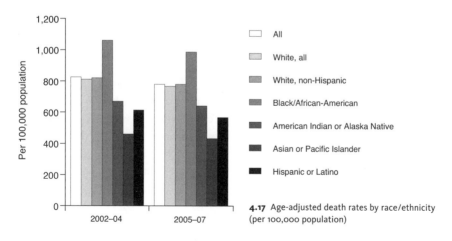

4.17 Age-adjusted death rates by race/ethnicity (per 100,000 population)

Note: Age adjustment is a statistical process to allow communities with different age structures to be compared; www.health.state.ny.us/diseases/chronic/ageadj.htm.

Source: Created by the authors using *Health, United States 2009* report, Table 25 (p. 188), and *Health, United States 2006* report, Table 28 (p. 177)

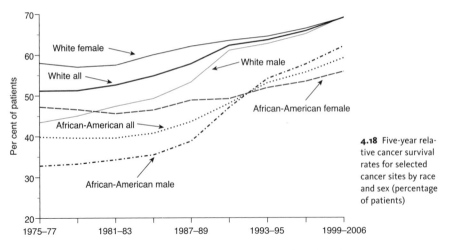

4.18 Five-year relative cancer survival rates for selected cancer sites by race and sex (percentage of patients)

Source: Created by the authors using *Health, United States 2009* report, Table 50 (p. 257)

ethnicity groups. White non-Hispanics have much lower rates than African-Americans but they do worse than American Indians and Hispanics. Asians stand out as the group with the lowest rates.

Woolf et al. (2004) find that the number of deaths averted by improvements in medical technology was 176,633 for the period 1991–2000. Eliminating racial disparities would have saved more lives: had the age-specific mortality rates been comparable across African-Americans and whites during 1991–2000, 886,202 deaths of African-Americans could have been averted.

The relative cancer survival rates by race and sex are presented in Figure 4.18. Both white men and white women have higher survival rates in comparison to their black counterparts, and the gap does not close despite the improvements for both race groups over time.

It is true that racial and ethnic disparities in health outcomes are affected by factors such as socio-economic status and location as well as access to health services. Acevedo-Garcia et al. (2008) show that black and Hispanic children are not only more likely to live in poor families, but are also more likely to live in poor neighbourhoods in comparison to white counterparts. However, health insurance coverage is another important factor that explains racial and ethnic disparities in access to care. For example, Zuvekas and Taliaferro (2003) find that differences in insurance coverage explain up to one third of Hispanic–white disparities and two-fifths of black–white disparities in having a usual source of care.

A list of selected indicators of utilization of health resources by race in 2009 is presented in Figure 4.19. The percentage of Hispanics, followed by African-Americans, who have no usual source of healthcare or reduced access to health care owing to cost is higher than the percentage of whites. Also, the incidence of having no healthcare visits in the past twelve months, or no use

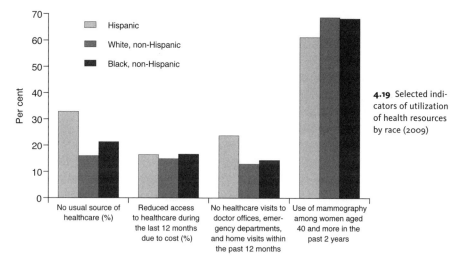

4.19 Selected indicators of utilization of health resources by race (2009)

Source: Created by the authors using *Health, United States 2009* report, Table 76 (p. 310) for 'No usual source of healthcare' measure; Table 77 (p. 312) for 'Reduced access to healthcare' measure; Table 80 (p. 317) for 'No healthcare visits' measure; Table 86 (p. 329) for 'Use of mammography' measure

of mammography among women aged forty or more in the last two years, is much higher among Hispanics.

A study using the Joint Canada/United States Survey of Health (2002/03) shows that income-related health disparities are more severe in the USA than in Canada: Americans in the poorest income quintile are more likely to have poor health, based on general health status and physical mobility limitations, than their Canadian counterparts. In terms of access to healthcare, less affluent, uninsured Americans also had worse access to care such as physician services and higher levels of heathcare need that were unmet. On the other hand, affluent, insured Americans had access to care comparable to that of Canadians (Sanmartin et al. 2006).

Finally, an overview of a number of healthcare quality indicators is presented in Table 4.3 for the USA in comparison to seven industrialized countries. Despite its much higher per capita health spending, the USA has the worst performance in all measures, except breast cancer survival rate, in comparison to Australia, Canada, France, Germany, Japan, New Zealand and the UK; and the second-worst performance in deaths amenable to medical care.

The Obama administration in the USA introduced some healthcare reforms in 2010. However, these did not introduce a social insurance system comparable to that in other high-income countries. The National Economic and Social Rights Initiative comments that:

> The role of the insurance industry, coupled with for-profit hospitals and multinational drug companies, will be consolidated and expanded under the

TABLE 4.3 Healthcare indicators for eight industrialized countries

	Australia	Canada	France	Germany	Japan	New Zealand	United Kingdom	United States
Health expenditure per capita ($)	2,876	3,165	3,159	3,005	2,249	2,083	2,546	6,102
Life expectancy at age 60[1]	18.2	17.7	18.4	17.5	19.6	17.1	16.9	16.6
Deaths amenable to medical care/100,000 population[2]	88	92	75	106	81	109	130	115
Access problems (%)	34	26	n/a	28	n/a	38	13	51
Breast cancer 5 year survival (%)	80.0	82.0	79.7	78.0	79.0	79.0	80.0	88.9
Myocardial infarction 30 day hospital mortality	8.8	12.0	8.0	11.9	10.3	10.9	11.0	14.8
Deaths from surgical or medical mishaps/100,000 population (2004)	0.4	0.5	0.5	0.6	0.2	n/a	0.5	0.7

Notes: 1. Average of male and female healthy life expectancies 2. Percentage of adults with health problems who did not fill prescription or skipped doses, had a medical problem but did not visit a doctor, or skipped test, treatment or follow-up in the past year because of cost.

Source: Davis (2007: 346)

health reform law of March 2101. Rather than transitioning to a social insurance model, access to care will continue to depend on a person's ability to pay rather than health needs. (NESRI 2010: 7)

Minimum core levels of rights: the right to food

As we have acknowledged, health depends upon a number of factors. Among them is a healthy diet, an aspect of the right to food. Thus we consider how far the US government acts to meet its obligation to ensure that people living in the USA enjoy a minimum core level of the right to food.

Obligation of conduct The federal government attempts to ensure a minimum core level of enjoyment of the right to food through the Food Stamps programme.[8] Food Stamps first operated during the Second World War, from 1939 to 1943. It was revived as a pilot programme in 1961 and became nationwide in 1974. The Food Stamps programme provides monthly benefits to eligible low-income families which can be used to purchase food and is operated through the electronic benefit transfer systems.[9] Food Stamps programme eligibility rules are based on gross and net income limits, an asset limit and various non-financial criteria.[10] A household is categorically eligible, and therefore not subject to income and asset standards, if all of its members receive Supplemental Security Income (SSI), cash or in-kind Temporary Assistance to Needy Families (TANF), or in some places General Assistance (GA).

The net income standard states that a household must have a net monthly income at or below 100 per cent of the poverty guideline ($1,767 for a family of four in the contiguous United States in fiscal year 2009).[11] The Personal Responsibility and Work Opportunity Reconciliation Act of 1996 severely restricted eligibility conditions for legal immigrants by introducing the five-year bar. Legal immigrants who have been in the USA for less than five years, and any undocumented immigrants, are ineligible for food stamps. There were 33.5 million people living in 15.2 million households that received food stamps in the United States each month in fiscal year 2009: 47 per cent were children, 44 per cent were non-elderly adults (74 per cent of whom were women) and 8 per cent were elderly adults (USDA 2010).

However, the Food Stamp programme falls short of providing comprehensive food assistance to the hungry. For example, the average benefit of the Food Stamp programme is equivalent to 99 cents per person per meal. Moreover, many people who are eligible do not actually receive food stamps. The United States Department of Agriculture has estimated that only six in ten of those eligible under current rules are participating in the programme (MAHR 2007).

The official poverty measure produced by the US Census Bureau relates to the cost of feeding a family. It is an absolute measure based on an income threshold for each family type (defined in terms of family size and number of children in the family) below which an individual or family is considered to be poor. It considers money income before taxes, including wages, salaries, interest, dividends, self-employment income and welfare cash payments from programmes such as Temporary Assistance for Needy Families, unemployment insurance and social security payments. The thresholds are updated for inflation each year using the Consumer Price Index for All Urban Consumers. Thresholds vary according to the size of the family and ages of the members but do not vary geographically. The poverty threshold concept was first introduced by Social Security analyst Mollie Orshansky in 1963, using an estimate of the cost of feeding an adequate diet to a family, based on the US Department of Agriculture's Economy Food Plan, the cheapest plan developed by the Department of Agriculture and defined as 'designed for temporary or emergency use when funds are low'. Therefore, its adequacy for nutritional needs is highly questionable. Using data for 1955, Orshansky found that families of three or more spent one third of their income on food. She then multiplied the costs of the Economy Food Plan for different family sizes by three to find the poverty line. The Census Bureau adopted these measures to derive the official poverty thresholds (EPI 2001).

The poverty threshold for a single person under age sixty-five was $11,161 in 2009. It was $14,366 for a two-person family unit with no children, and $21,756 for a four-person family unit with two children (US Census Bureau 2010). It is widely accepted that the official poverty measure is not adequate and underestimates the extent of deprivation. The poverty thresholds were developed in the 1960s based on the cost of feeding a family then and have not been redefined to reflect changing economic and social conditions since then (EPI 2001, 2007; Bergman 2000; Frank 2006). For example, while the poverty threshold for a family of four in 1960 was 48 per cent of median family income, it is 30 per cent in 2010 because of the real growth in the median family income. Official poverty thresholds have not kept up with public opinion. For example, the surveys showed that the public believed that families needed an amount that was 1.4 times the poverty threshold in the early 1960s, and almost twice the poverty threshold in 2000.

A government-appointed panel convened by the National Academy of Science (NAS) has produced an alternative system of poverty measurement with thresholds based on actual expenditures on food, clothing and shelter. They also take into account the regional differences in the cost of living (EPI 2001).

Obligation of result Do government measures ensure that everyone has enough to eat? The US Department of Agriculture conducts a regular survey on food security. Food-secure households are those that have access at all times to enough food for an active, healthy life. Food-insecure households are those that do not have access to enough food to fully meet basic needs at all times. Food-insecure households are further classified based on the severity of their circumstances into low food security (food insecurity without hunger) and very

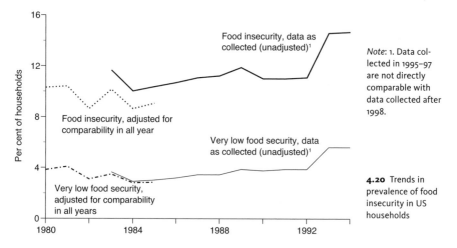

low food security (food insecurity with hunger). USDA explains that adults in food-insecure households are so limited in resources to buy food that they are running out of food, reducing the quality of food their family eats, feeding their children unbalanced diets, skipping meals so their children can eat, or taking other steps that impair the adequacy of the family's diet. Households with very low food security are those in which adults have decreased the quality and quantity of food they consume because of a lack of financial resources, to the point where they are likely to go hungry at times, or in which children's intake has been reduced owing to a lack of family financial resources, to the point that children are likely to go hungry at times. The data are collected through Current Population Survey food security surveys for the years 1995–2009. The 2006 survey covered 46,000 households and was a representative sample of the US civilian population of 118 million households (Nord et al. 2010).

The trends in prevalence of food insecurity in US households over the period 1995–2009 are presented in Figure 4.20. Households affected by food insecurity increased from 10.1 per cent in 1999 to 11.9 per cent in 2004 and to 14.7 per cent (17.4 million households) in 2009. The prevalence of households affected by very low food security (food insecurity with hunger) increased from 3 per cent in 1999 to 3.9 per cent in 2005 and 5.7 per cent in 2009 (6.8 million households). While the households with food insecurity had difficulty providing enough food for all their members owing to a lack of resources, households with very low food security reduced the intake of some household members and disrupted their normal eating patterns. Clearly measures like the Food Stamps programme have been insufficient to guarantee a minimum core level of enjoyment of the right to food in the context of the economic crisis that began in 2008.

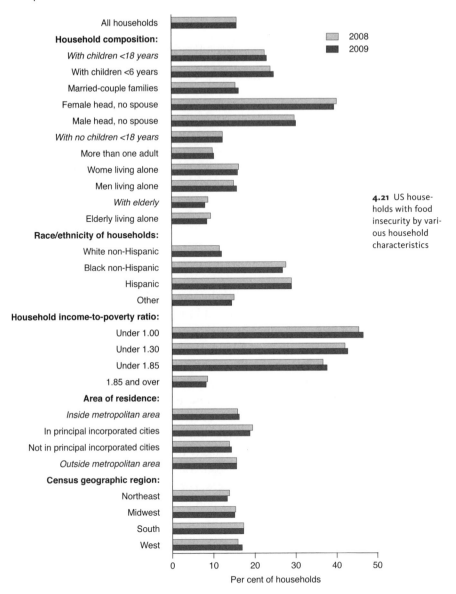

4.21 US households with food insecurity by various household characteristics

Source: US Department of Agriculture, *Household Food Security in the United States*, 2009, Figure 4 (p. 14)

Food insecurity is more common in the most vulnerable segments of society, especially for female-headed single households, families with young children and households of minority race/ethnic groups, as shown by data for 2008 and 2009 in Figure 4.21.[12] The prevalence of food insecurity is particularly high in single-mother families, 36.6 per cent of which suffer from food insecurity, and families with young children, 22.9 per cent of which suffered from food insecurity in 2009. Among the minorities, Hispanic households are the most disadvantaged

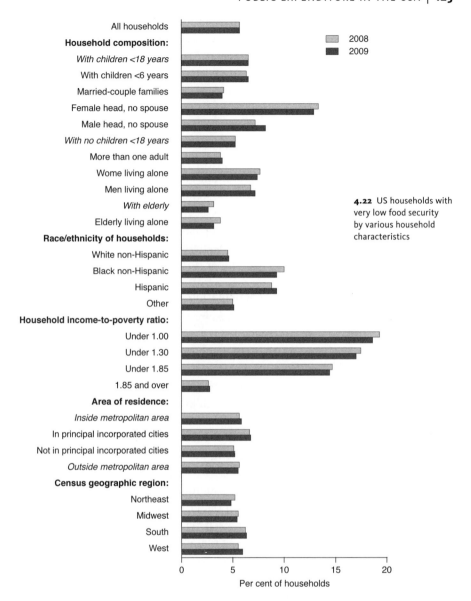

4.22 US households with very low food security by various household characteristics

Source: US Department of Agriculture, *Household Food Security in the United States*, 2009, Figure 5 (p. 15)

group, with 26.9 per cent of them suffering food insecurity in 2009; followed by African-American households, with 24.9 per cent food insecure. Only 11.0 per cent of white, non-Hispanic families suffer from food insecurity, which is below the overall rate of 14.7 per cent for all households. The same disparities also exist with respect to very low food security (food insecurity with hunger). While only 4.6 per cent of white households experience very low food insecurity, the prevalence is 12.9 per cent of female-headed households; and 9.3 per cent of African-American and Hispanic households. The difference is also striking in terms of geographic region, with mostly Southern states having very high food insecurity rates. Arkansas (17.7 per cent), Texas (17.4 per cent), Mississippi (17.1 per cent), Georgia (15.6 per cent), Oklahoma (15.2 per cent), Tennessee (15.1 per cent), Alabama (15 per cent) and Missouri (15 per cent) are among the worst states for food insecurity.[13]

Of all the groups shown in Figure 4.21, food insecurity is highest in households below the poverty line, with 43 per cent of households below the poverty threshold facing food insecurity in 2009. It is clear that food stamps are not ensuring the enjoyment of minimum core levels of the right to food. Indeed, in some states the access to food stamps is being cut. For example, in Idaho the demand for food stamps has been rising, but the state budget is under pressure and the state government has closed nearly a third of the offices where Department of Health and Welfare officials take applications for food stamps (*New York Times*, 10 December 2010, p. 28).

Transparency, accountability and participation

Governments have the obligation to ensure that procedures for the allocation of public expenditure are transparent and accountable, and that there are opportunities for citizens to participate and to exercise their right to information. In the United States the budget is determined through a process that is negotiated by the president and Congress. The Congressional Budget Act of 1974 sets the specific procedures guiding the way in which Congress develops tax and spending legislation in the United States. The key aspect of the Budget Act is the requirement that Congress should develop a budget resolution each year, setting overarching limits on spending and on tax cuts. The federal budget process consists of two steps: the president's budget process and the congressional budget resolution. The president has to ask for funding for 'discretionary' or 'appropriated' programmes such as defence spending, health research and housing each year. The president can propose changes to 'mandatory' or 'entitlement' programmes such as Social Security, Medicare, Medicaid, Food Stamps, unemployment insurance, etc., that are not controlled by annual appropriations. The president can also propose changes to the tax code. In summary, the president's budget must request a specific funding level for appropriated programmes and may also request changes in tax and entitlement laws (Coven and Kogan 2007).

The International Budget Project has recently produced an Open Budget Index, in the first initiative that offers an independent view of budget transparency. It examines the extent of publicly available budget information provided by governments. According to International Budget Partnership (2010), the USA ranked seventh, with a score of 82, following South Africa, New Zealand, the UK, France, Norway and Sweden (the USA ranked sixth in 2006). This group of countries is categorized as providing extensive information to citizens and performing well in terms of ensuring the accountability of government to citizens. However, the USA does not produce a pre-budget statement and citizens' budget statement. The pre-budget statement is important because it is a document setting out the planned overall spending and revenue levels, prior to the submission of the budget to the legislature. It enables discussion of the overall parameters of the budget before the Executive makes more detailed decisions on sectoral or programmatic breakdowns. The absence of this document suggests that the budget drafting process takes place behind closed doors with little public involvement or access to information. France, New Zealand, Sweden and the UK all provide a pre-budget statement. A citizens' budget statement explains the budget in terms a non-expert can readily grasp; thus it helps ordinary people understand the budget process. France, the UK and Sweden produce and distribute such a statement. 'A Citizens' Guide to Federal Budget' was published in the USA for a number of years until 2003; the government no longer publishes this guide.

The detailed survey that underpins the Open Budget Index sheds more light on key aspects of budget transparency in the USA. It reveals that although some information is given on the link between major policy goals and the budget, this information is not fully satisfactory. Although the Government Performance and Results Act of 1993, supplemented by the Programme Assessment Rating Tool, stimulated renewed interest in stating programme goals and evaluating performance as part of the budget process, this link is discussed in a fairly generalized rather than a thorough and comprehensive manner. Performance indicators are presented for programmes representing less than two-thirds of expenditures. Moreover, although the Executive makes available to the public a summary of the budget proposal, it presents all the discretionary policies other than military and homeland security spending as a single category, despite the complexity of programmes. The Executive holds very limited consultations, involving only a few members of the legislature in informal discussions, as part of its process of determining budget priorities. The Executive does not typically consult openly with the public as part of the budget preparation process, but there is a large amount of behind-the-scenes lobbying on behalf of the rich and powerful.

Legislative committees hold public hearings on the macroeconomic and fiscal framework presented in the budget, in which testimony from the executive branch is heard. Hearings on the individual budgets of key agencies are held, in which testimony from the public is heard (International Budget Partnership 2006).

The procurement of goods and services frequently follows an open and competitive process, but there were some reported instances of irregularities. Specific legal authority is sometimes granted that allows an agency in certain circumstances to enter into 'single-source' or other contracts without following the normal open and competitive procedures. Supplementary budgets, such as the ones financing wars, are approved before the funds are expended, but they are not subject to the same deliberate and careful review process as the regular budget. Supplementary budgets have amounted to around 3 per cent of total expenditures in recent years (ibid.).

Although many documents on budget are made available on the Internet, and there is a right-to-information law, there are some problems regarding its implementation, as revealed in the Open Budget Project questionnaire on the United States:[14]

> Although the right has been codified into law, it is sometimes not possible for citizens in practice to obtain access to government information, including budget information. The citizen has access to all the information the government publishes on the budget. However, internal memos detailing assumptions used in preparing estimates, detailed proposals used to prepare the budget and internal decision making memos and information are considered pre-decisional and not available to the public or to the congressional overseers. The detailed *Justification of Estimates* presented by agencies to appropriations committees are also not uniformly available to the public, although this had improved in recent years.

Another issue is related to the availability of detailed data. Highly disaggregated data are available to the public for programmes representing at least two-thirds of, but not all, expenditures.[15]

At the state and local government level, each state has some form of freedom-of-information (FOI) legislation. However, Investigative Reporters and Editors (IRE) in conjunction with the Better Government Association compared the freedom of information laws across states and concluded that the state FOI laws are uniformly weak and easy to undermine, significantly affecting a citizen's ability to monitor even the most fundamental actions of government (IRE 2007).

Conclusion

The level of US real per capita social expenditure has been rising but it is lower than in France, Germany and Italy, while similar to that of Canada and the UK, and higher than in Japan. Per capita public expenditure on healthcare in the USA has been rising in real terms: there has been no retrogression in terms of the allocation of public expenditure to healthcare. However, there is no national health insurance programme providing universal coverage in the USA. Around 15 per cent of the population was not covered at all in the period from 1987 to 2009, calling into question the fulfilment of the obligation to ensure that everyone has access to healthcare.

Among high-income countries, the United States has by far the highest share of GDP devoted to health expenditure, when both public and private sources are taken into account. But this expenditure is not used very effectively:

administration constitutes 20–30 per cent of total US healthcare expenditure. The health outcomes are disappointing: the USA had the fourth-highest infant mortality rate in the OECD after Turkey, Mexico and Chile in 2006. In terms of maternal mortality, the USA has the sixth-highest rate in the OECD. Moreover, the rate has risen since 2000, clearly indicating a lack of progressive realization with respect to maternal health.

There is evidence of a lack of compliance with obligations of non-discrimination and equality with respect to the conduct of public spending on health, with racial/ethnic minorities, women, poor people and migrants being less likely to have access to health insurance. This is matched by evidence of lack of compliance with the obligations of non-discrimination and equality in health outcomes. The healthcare reforms introduced in 2010 did not introduce a comprehensive social insurance system comparable to that of other well-off countries, and there is reason to believe that they will not succeed in addressing all the compliance problems identified.

Though the USA is a rich country, there is evidence that the state is not complying with obligations to provide a minimum core level of enjoyment of the right to food. Despite the Food Stamps programme, a substantial proportion of households lack food security, and this has risen as a result of the economic crisis that began in 2008. Despite increasing needs, access to food stamps is being cut in some places. Single-mother households and those in racial/ethnic minority groups experience higher levels of food insecurity.

The USA has a right-to-information law, and a lot of information is provided about expenditure once budgets have been set, especially at the federal level; but the rich and powerful have much more access to the process of setting budget priorities.

Notes

1 Social security is a programme with automatic entitlements and is therefore outside the discretionary control of the government. Its level is driven mainly by the number of beneficiaries and the retirement of baby boomers is putting pressure on the programme.

2 Defined as 'cash benefits, direct "in-kind" provisions of goods and services, and tax breaks with social purposes'; source: www.oecd-ilibrary.org/sites/factbook-2010-en/10/02/01/index.html?contentType=&itemId=/content/chapter/factbook-2010-75-en&containerItemId=/content/serial/18147364&accessItemIds=&mimeType=text/html. Only federal expenditure is considered in the case of federal countries.

3 Chile, Estonia, Israel and Slovenia joined the OECD in 2010.

4 These figures are in constant prices, thus adjusted for inflation.

5 Medicare is an entitlement programme and Medicaid is a means-tested programme, which explains the difference in the level of spending on these programmes.

6 National Health Expenditures (NHE) is the main source of data on health spending in the USA. Public expenditure on health includes all healthcare expenditures that are channelled through any programme established by public law. It also includes spending on government public health activity such as organizing and delivering publicly provided health services such as epidemiological surveillance, inoculations, immunization/vaccination services, disease prevention programmes, the operation of public health laboratories, and other such

functions. In terms of insurance payments, expenditures under workers' compensation programmes are listed under government expenditures, even though they involve benefits paid by insurers from premiums that have been collected from private as well as public sources. Similarly, premiums paid by enrollees for Medicare Supplementary Medical Insurance are treated as public expenditures since payment of benefits is made by a public programme. However, co-insurance and deductible payments under Medicare are included under out-of-pocket payments and hence private spending. In terms of public programmes, to be included in NHE, a programme must have provision of care or treatment of disease as its primary focus, therefore nutrition, sanitation and anti-pollution programmes are excluded (*National Health Expenditures Accounts: Definitions, Sources, and Methods*, 2008, www.cms.gov/NationalHealthExpendData/02_NationalHealthAccountsHistorical.asp#TopOfPage, accessed 19 December 2010).

7 Mohanty et al. (2005) provide some examples: A study at an inner-city clinic found that one in nine immigrant parents reported that they had not brought their children in for care owing to lack of understanding of Latino culture by the medical staff. Moreover, among the 5–10 million undocumented immigrants residing in the United States, fear of deportation is a barrier to using public programmes.

8 Other important federal programmes related to food include the School Lunch Programme (Free and Reduced-Price Components), the Special Supplemental Nutrition Programme for Women, Infants, and Children (the WIC Programme), the National School Lunch Programme (for free and reduced-price meals only), the School Breakfast Programme (for free and reduced-price meals only), the Child and Adult Care Food Programme (for free and reduced-price meals only) and the Expanded Food and Nutrition Education Programme (CRS 2003).

9 The Food Research and Action Center (FRAC) Food Stamp Programme Overview, www.frac.org/html/federal_food_programmes/programmes/fsp.html.

10 USDA, *Characteristics of the Food Stamp Household, Fiscal Year 2009*, Nutrition Assistance Programme Report Series no. FSP-06-CAR, September 2010.

11 The asset standard indicates that households cannot have more than $2,000 in countable assets, or $3,000 in countable assets if at least one member is age sixty or older or disabled. Countable assets include cash, assets that can easily be converted into cash and some non-liquid resources such as certain vehicles.

12 The following figures are based on Table 2 on p. 10 in Nord et al. (2010).

13 These figures are based on Table 8 on p. 21 in Nord et al. (2010).

14 Comments on Question 64, International Budget Project, Open Budget Questionnaire, United States, October 2005.

15 Question 65/66, International Budget Project, Open Budget Questionnaire, United States, October 2005. It is commented by a peer reviewer that in some cases Congress itself has problems getting this information in a timely manner (a sensitive issue with respect to military spending).

References

Acevedo-Garcia, D., T. L. Osypuk, N. McArdle and D. R. Williams (2008) 'Toward a policy-relevant analysis of geographic and racial/ethnic disparities in child health', *Health Affairs*, 27(2): 321–3.

AHRQ (Agency for Healthcare Research and Quality) (2008) *National Healthcare Disparities Report 2007*, AHRQ Publication no. 08-0041, US Department of Health and Human Services, February.

Ben-Bassat, A. and M. Dahan (2008) 'Social rights in the constitution and in practice', *Journal of Comparative Economics*, 36: 103–19.

Bergman, B. R. (2000) 'Deciding who is poor', *Dollars and Sense Magazine*, March/April.

Berk, M. L. and A. C. Monheit (2001) 'The concentration of health care expenditures, revisited', *Health Affairs*, 20(2): 9–18.

Bitton, A. and J. G. Kahn (2003) 'Government share of health care expenditures', *Journal of the American Medical Association (JAMA)*, 289(9): 1165–6.

CMS (Center for Medicare and Medicaid Services) and ASPE (Office of the Assistant Secretary for Planning and Evaluation) (2007) 'An overview of the US health care system', 31 January.

Coven, M. and R. Kogan (2007) 'Introduction to

Federal Budget Process', Center for Budget and Policy Priorities, August.

CRS (Congressional Research Services) (2003) 'Cash and noncash benefits for persons with limited income: eligibility rules, recipient and expenditure data, FY2000-FY2002', Report # RL32233, Congressional Research Service, Library of Congress, 25 November 2003.

Davis, K. (2007) 'Uninsured in America: problems and possible solutions', *British Medical Journal*, 334: 346–8.

EPI (Economic Policy Institute) (2001) *Poverty and Family Budgets Issue Guides*, Washington, DC: Economic Policy Institute.

— (2007) *The State of Working America 2006/2007*, Washington, DC: Economic Policy Institute.

Frank, E. (2006) 'Dear Dr. Dollar: Can you explain how poverty is defined in government statistics? Is this a realistic definition?', *Dollars and Sense Magazine*, January/February.

Himmelstein, D. U., E. Warren, D. Thorne and S. Woolhandler (2005) 'Illness and injury as contributors to bankruptcy', *Health Affairs*, Market watch web exclusive w5.63-73.

International Budget Partnership (2006) 'More public information needed to hold governments to account', United States Open Budget Index Highlights.

— (2010) 'Open Budget Survey 2010 full report', www.internationalbudget. org/files/2010_Full_Report-English.pdf (accessed 17 December 2010).

IRE (Investigative Reporters and Editors) (2007) 'Freedom of information in the USA', www.ire.org/foi/bga/ (accessed 9 March 2009).

Kaiser Family Foundation (2007) 'Medicare at a glance factsheet', February, www.kff.org/medicare/upload/1066-10.pdf (accessed 2 July 2008).

— (2009) 'Trends in health care costs and spending factsheet, March 2009', www.kff.org/insurance/upload/7692_02.pdf (accessed 19 December 2010).

— (2010a) 'Medicare at a glance factsheet, September 2010', www.kff.org/medicare/upload/1066-13.pdf (accessed 19 December 2010).

— (2010b) 'Medicaid at a glance factsheet, June 2010', www.kff.org/medicaid/

upload/7235-04.pdf (accessed 19 December 2010).

— (2010c) 'The uninsured, a primer: key facts about Americans without health insurance, December 2010', www.kff.org/uninsured/upload/7451-06.pdf (accessed 19 December 2010).

King, M. I. (2007) 'Immigrants in the US health care system – five myths that misinform the American public', Center for American Progress, June, www.americanprogress. org/issues/2007/06/pdf/immigrant_health_report.pdf (accessed 24 January 2009).

MAHR (Minnesota Advocates for Human Rights) (2007) 'Fact sheet on the right to food in the United States'.

Mohanty, S. A., S. Woolhandler, D. U. Himmelstein, S. Pati, O. Carrasquillo and D. H. Bor (2005) 'Health care expenditures of immigrants in the United States: a nationally representative analysis', *American Journal of Public Health*, 95(8): 1431–8.

NESRI (National Economic and Social Rights Initiative) (2006) 'Human rights in the United States', Basic Info Brief, www. nesri.org/sites/default/files/human_rights_basic_info.pdf (accessed 12 May 2008).

— (2010) *Towards Economic and Social Rights in the United States: From Marker Competition to Public Goods*, Joint Submission to the UN Human Rights Council Universal Periodic Review of the United States of America, www.nesri.org (accessed 20 November 2010).

Nord, M., M. Andrews and S. Carlson (2010) 'Measuring food security in the United States – household food security in the United States, 2009', USDA Economic Research Report no. 108, November.

OECD Health Data (2007) http://www. oecd.org/document/16/0,3746,en_2649_37407_2085200_1_1_1_37407,00.html (accessed 24 August 2009).

— (2010) http://www.oecd.org/document/16/0,3746,en_2649_37407_2085200_1_1_1_37407,00.html (accessed 15 August 2010).

Pascal, E. (2008) 'Welfare rights in state constitutions', *Rutgers Law Journal*, 39(4): 863–901.

Peterson, J. L. and R. Burton (2008) *The US Health Care Spending: Comparison with Other OECD Countries*, New York: Nova Science Publishers, Inc.

Sanmartin, C., J. M. Berthelot, E. Ng, K. Murphy, D. L. Blackwell, J. F. Gentleman, M. E. Martinez and C. M. Simile (2006) 'Comparing health and health care use in Canada and the United States', *Health Affairs*, 25(4): 1133–42.

Shi, L. and G. D. Stevens (2005) 'Disparities in access to care and satisfaction among US children: the roles of race/ethnicity and poverty status', *Public Health Reports*, 120, July/August.

US Census Bureau (2010) 'Income, poverty and health insurance: coverage in the US', Current Population Reports, September 2010, www.census.gov/prod/2010pubs/p60-238.pdf.

USDA (United States Department of Agriculture) (2010) 'Characteristics of the Food Stamp household, fiscal year 2009', Nutrition Assistance Programme Report Series no. SNAP-10-CHAR.

Woolf, S. H., R. E. Johnson, G. E. Fryer, G. Rust and D. Satcher (2004) 'The health impact of resolving racial disparities: an analysis of US mortality data', *American Journal of Public Health*, 94(12): 2078–81.

Xu, K. T. (2006) 'State-level variations in income-related inequality in health and health achievement in the US', *Social Science and Medicine*, 63: 457–64.

Zuvekas, S. H. and G. S. Taliaferro (2003) 'Pathways to access: health insurance, the health care delivery system, and racial/ethnic disparities, 1996–1999', *Health Affairs*, 22(2): 139–53.

5 | TAXATION AND ECONOMIC AND SOCIAL RIGHTS IN MEXICO

Lourdes Colinas and Roberto Constantino

Introduction

Tax policy plays an important role in collecting resources for the fulfilment of economic and social rights, and also has a substantial impact on income and wealth distribution.

When studying taxation it is important to raise the following questions: Who pays taxes? Are tax laws and tax administrations capable of generating sufficient revenue for economic and social rights in ways that comply with human rights obligations? Are tax laws and tax collection mechanisms discriminatory? Is tax administration transparent and accountable? Is there any space for public participation in determination of tax policy? This chapter aims at providing an answer for these questions in the case of Mexico. Some examples of Mexico's taxation policy will be discussed, using the following principles inherent to economic and social rights as a framework: maximum available resources, non-discrimination and equality, and transparency, accountability and participation.[1]

Specifically in the case of taxation, the state's obligation of conduct[2] related to the principle of the use of maximum available resources is to introduce and implement tax laws and a tax administration that are capable of generating sufficient revenue for economic and social rights in ways that comply with human rights obligations. The obligation of conduct related to the principle of non-discrimination and equality requires that tax laws and collection measures do not discriminate against particular social groups. Finally, in relation to the principle of transparency, accountability and participation, the obligation of conduct is to ensure that tax administration is transparent and accountable, and opportunities are provided for broad participation in public discussion about appropriate tax policy. In the case of taxation, we consider only the obligation of conduct and not obligation of result,[3] since taxation is not related to any specific right, though it is relevant to all economic and social rights.

As noted by the UN Special Rapporter on economic and social rights, Danilo Türk, 'Taxation, though, remains a key source of finance for public expenditure and, while complex by nature, the system of levying tax should be a criteria [sic] against which compliance with international obligations is measured, as well as a central means of redressing existing imbalances of income distribution' (Türk 1992: para. 83).

Sources of public sector revenue in Mexico

Taxation is not the only major source of public sector revenue in Mexico. Revenue is generated by the federal government itself, through both tax and non-tax measures (70.2 per cent in 2008); but also by state-owned enterprises such as PEMEX (the largest state-owned oil company) and CFE (the Federal Electricity Commission). State-owned enterprises generated 29.8 per cent of public sector revenue in 2007 (see Figure 5.1).

The total revenue of the public sector in 2008 was equal to 24.5 per cent of GDP. Revenue from PEMEX and its subsidiaries is called 'oil revenue' and was equal to 8.3 per cent of GDP in 2008. The high level of dependence on revenue from oil makes public sector revenue highly vulnerable to changes in oil prices and production volumes. Revenue from oil has been increasing over time, but it is subject to fluctuations (see Figure 5.2). Availability of oil revenue has encouraged low tax collection. As a consequence, development priorities such as education, infrastructure, poverty alleviation and basic health do not have long-term stable financing. This implies that the government is at risk of not fulfilling its obligation of progressive realization of human rights, since oil is a natural resource that is becoming depleted and revenues will eventually dwindle.

Revenue generated by the federal government can be divided into tax and non-tax revenue. Non-tax revenue consists mainly of revenue from different types of government fees, penalties and royalties.[4] Oil is a major source of revenue from royalties. Tax revenue is derived from direct and indirect taxes. Direct taxation is applied to income-earners using a progressive scale and its main instruments are income tax (ISR) and the new IETU (*Impuesto Em-*

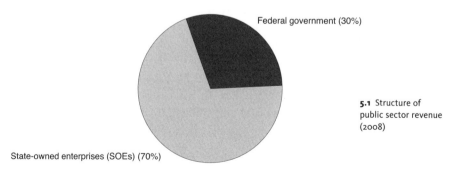

Federal government (30%)

5.1 Structure of public sector revenue (2008)

State-owned enterprises (SOEs) (70%)

Source: Chart generated by the authors with data from the Centre of Studies for Public Finance of the Chamber of Deputies (Centro de Estudios de las Finanzas Públicas de la H. Cámara de Diputados), using estimates from the Federal Income Law 2008 (Ley Ingresos de la Federación para el ejercicio fiscal 2008)

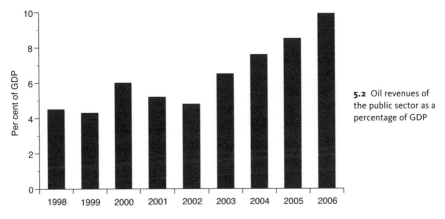

5.2 Oil revenues of the public sector as a percentage of GDP

Note: Excludes excise revenue on gasoline and diesel.

Source: Ministry of Finance, Mexico

presarial a Tasa Única). The IETU is a flat-rate tax on corporate income and came into effect in 2008. It is easier to administer than corporate income tax and provides less scope for preferential treatment in the form of tax allowances and exemptions of various kinds. The new tax is intended to ensure that all companies pay tax on their income and to prevent tax evasion. The main instruments for indirect taxation in Mexico are value added tax (VAT) and IEPS (Special Tax for Production and Services).[5] The Special Tax is an excise tax levied, on top of the VAT, on alcoholic drinks, soft drinks and sports drinks, tobacco, gasoline and diesel fuel. The rates vary according to the product, from 20 to 110 per cent.

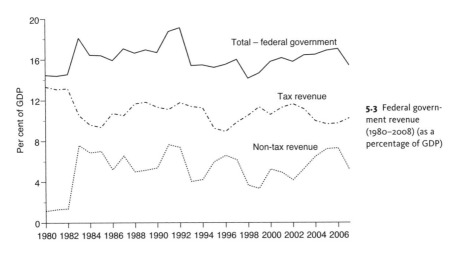

5.3 Federal government revenue (1980–2008) (as a percentage of GDP)

Source: Chart generated by the authors with data from the Centre of Studies for Public Finance of the Chamber of Deputies (Centro de Estudios de las Finanzas Públicas de la H. Cámara de Diputados), using estimates from the Federal Income Law 2008 (Ley Ingresos de la Federación para el ejercicio fiscal 2008)

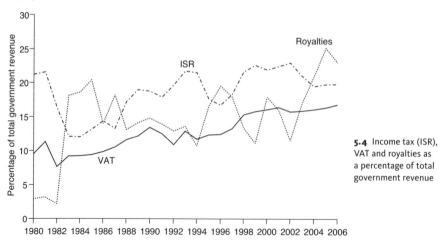

5.4 Income tax (ISR), VAT and royalties as a percentage of total government revenue

Source: Chart generated by the authors with data from the Centre of Studies for Public Finance of the Chamber of Deputies (Centro de Estudios de las Finanzas Públicas de la H. Cámara de Diputados), the Federal Public Account 1981–2006 (Cuenta Pública Federal), the Federal Income Law 2007 and 2008, and the Ministry of Finance

In 1980, 92.1 per cent of revenue came from taxation and 7.9 per cent from non-tax sources, as compared to 2008, when 68.6 per cent came from taxation and 31.4 per cent from non-tax sources.

The trends in federal government revenue as a share of GDP are shown in Figure 5.3. Even though government revenue comes mainly from taxes, non-tax revenue has been increasing, from 1.1 per cent of GDP in 1980 to 5.4 per cent in 2008.

Figure 5.4 shows tax revenue from income tax (ISR) and value added tax

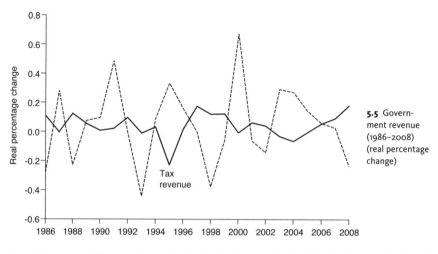

5.5 Government revenue (1986–2008) (real percentage change)

Source: Chart generated by the authors with data from the Centre of Studies for Public Finance of the Chamber of Deputies (Centro de Estudios de las Finanzas Públicas de la H. Cámara de Diputados), the Federal Public Account 1981–2006 (Cuenta Pública Federal), the Federal Income Law 2007, and the Ministry of Finance

(VAT) and revenue from royalties (mainly royalties paid by PEMEX for oil extraction) as a percentage of total government revenue. The share contributed by ISR does not show an upward trend, whereas there is an upward trend in the contribution of VAT and royalties.

Figure 5.5 shows the fluctuations of tax and non-tax revenue. The latter is more variable than tax revenue owing most likely to its vulnerability to changes in the oil industry.

Taxation

In the case of Mexico, it is especially relevant to look at taxation at the federal level; since the principal taxes paid (income tax and value added tax) are collected at this level. In 1980, the fiscal coordination system transferred the responsibility of collecting income and value added tax from local and state governments to the federal government. As a consequence, today around 97 per cent of tax revenue is collected at the federal level and only 3 per cent by states and local governments. State and municipal governments have very limited powers to levy taxes and have their own law for a narrow range of taxes on property, ownership (*tenencia*) and payroll. Property tax is known as *predial*, and it averages 0.1 per cent of the assessed value of the property at the time of sale (immovable property, such as land, located in Mexico is also subject to municipal taxation).

In other western hemisphere countries with federal governments, the proportion of revenue generated by the federal government is lower. In the USA it is 66 per cent and 34 per cent is generated by the state and local governments. In Argentina, the proportion is 64 per cent federal and 36 per cent state and local; and in Brazil, 62 per cent is levied by the federal government and 38 per cent by state and local governments.

Mexico's VAT applies to revenues deriving from the transfer of goods, the granting of temporary rights to use goods, the provision of independent services, and imports (goods and services). Basic foodstuffs such as milk, corn, wheat, meat, agricultural services related to the production of basic foodstuffs, medicines and all exports are subject to the zero rate. The general VAT rate changed in 2010 from 15 per cent to 16 per cent, except in border areas, where the rate has increased from 10 per cent to 11 per cent. Mexico's standard VAT rate is somewhat below the OECD average; some other countries such as Japan (5 per cent), Switzerland (7.6 per cent), Korea (10 per cent) and New Zealand (12.5 per cent) have lower rates. Furthermore, Mexico has the narrowest VAT base among OECD countries.

Income tax is charged using a progressive scale of rates that used to go up to a maximum of 28 per cent (now 30 per cent with the new fiscal reform, which is discussed later in this chapter) and is payable by individuals and corporations. Exemptions for ISR are specified in Article 109 of the income tax law.[6] Some of the most important exemptions are donations; transfers;

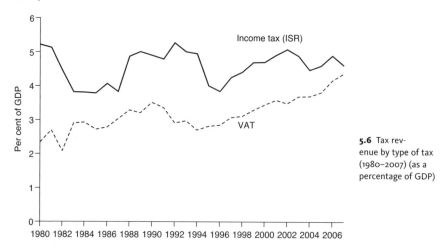

5.6 Tax revenue by type of tax (1980–2007) (as a percentage of GDP)

Source: Chart generated by the authors with data from the Centre of Studies for Public Finance of the Chamber of Deputies (Centro de Estudios de las Finanzas Públicas de la H. Cámara de Diputados), the Federal Public Account 1981–2006 (Cuenta Pública Federal), the Federal Income Law 2007 and 2008, and the Ministry of Finance

sales of some goods such as houses; inheritance; some employment benefits; social security benefits provided by public institutions; and income earned in certain sectors (such as agriculture, livestock and fishing), as long as the amount does not exceed forty times the minimum wage in a year. There is no net wealth tax.

Figure 5.6 shows that VAT revenue as a share of GDP has been increasing

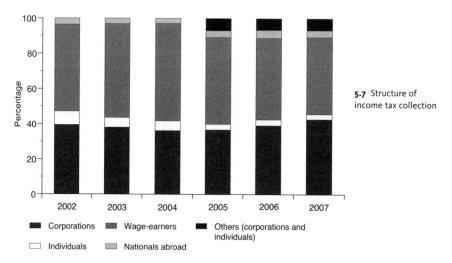

5.7 Structure of income tax collection

Source: Chart generated by the authors with data from the Centre of Studies for Public Finance of the Chamber of Deputies (Centro de Estudios de las Finanzas Públicas de la H. Cámara de Diputados), the Federal Public Account 1981–2006 (Cuenta Pública Federal), the Federal Income Law 2007 and 2008, and the Ministry of Finance

over time, while the share of income tax shows no upward trend. The gap between the shares of income tax and VAT has been narrowing.

Data on corporate income tax in Mexico are difficult to find. The Chamber of Deputies provides information on the shares of income tax revenue generated by tax on corporations, the self-employed, employees and nationals living abroad, and others, for the years 2002 to 2007. The largest share comes from wage-earners, who contribute an average of 49.6 per cent of total income tax revenue for the depicted years (see Figure 5.7).

Even though the maximum rate for income tax was 28 per cent (now 30 per cent), it has been argued that a large number of corporations end up paying substantially less: 13.7 per cent of income on average owing to the vast array of exemptions, deductions and special privileges that are part of the taxation system (Bettinger 2008). Some economic sectors (construction and transportation companies) have special considerations in the taxation scheme.

Taxation and the use of maximum available resources

The International Covenant on Economic, Social and Cultural Rights (Article 2) states the obligation of governments to 'take steps, individually and through international assistance and co-operation, especially economic and technical, to the maximum of its available resources' to bring about the progressive realization of the rights recognized in the Covenant. Furthermore, the Additional Protocol to the American Convention on Human Rights in the area of Economic, Social and Cultural Rights[7] (Article 1), signed by Mexico in 1988 and ratified in 1996, mandates states parties

> to adopt the necessary measures, both domestically and through international cooperation, especially economic and technical, to the extent allowed by their available resources, and taking into account their degree of development, for the purpose of achieving progressively and pursuant to their internal legislations, the full observance of the rights recognized in this Protocol.

The ratio of total tax revenues to gross domestic product (GDP) is a useful indicator to examine to judge whether a country is applying the principle of maximum available resources. The tax-to-GDP ratio in Mexico is shown in Table 5.1, which reveals that Mexico's tax-to-GDP ratio was lower in 2007 than in 1980.

TABLE 5.1 Mexico: tax revenue as percentage of GDP*

1980	1985	1990	1995	2000	2005	2007
13.30	9.40	11.30	9.30	10.60	9.30	10.70

Note: * This figure does not include oil revenue.
Source: Ministry of Finance, Mexico, 2007

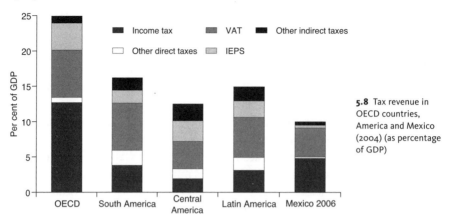

5.8 Tax revenue in OECD countries, America and Mexico (2004) (as percentage of GDP)

Source: Ministry of Finance, Mexico, 2007

The ratio is very low compared to other countries, not only other OECD countries, but also other Latin American countries. As is shown in Figure 5.8, tax revenue as a share of GDP in Mexico is lower than the average for the OECD, South America, Central America and Latin America.

The Economic Commission for Latin America has suggested that in Mexico, as in most Latin American countries, tax revenues have been insufficient to cover public spending needs or to reach the necessary degree of fiscal sustainability. Some countries in the region have implemented structural and administrative changes, but these efforts have been neither 'harmonious nor permanent', and have not been able to reach a more equitable distribution of the tax burden among socio-economic sectors (ECLAC 1998).

The amount of revenue collected depends not only on the rates set out in the tax law, but also on the administration of taxes. In Mexico the Tax Administration Service (SAT) covers each of the four main areas of tax administration: legal interpretation, auditing, collection and customs. But it is far from effective. In Denmark, one kroner spent on tax administration generates 113 kroner of tax revenue. In Mexico, one peso produces only 33 pesos of tax revenue (OECD 2007a).

One example of poor tax management and collection (which compromises the 'use of maximum available resources') can be seen in property tax. As mentioned above, immovable property is subject to municipal taxation and it is usually levied on the cadastral value of the property. The revenue raised by this tax is really low in Mexico compared to similar developing countries (0.2 per cent of GDP; see Figure 5.9). Municipalities do not keep up-to-date land registers and fail to update the cadastral values. The revenue derived from property tax in Mexico could increase if adequate valuation practices were introduced. This would not only strengthen local governments' tax bases, but also ease some concerns over the equity of the tax systems (van den Noord and Heady 2001).

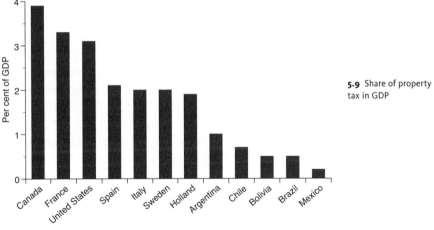

5.9 Share of property tax in GDP

Source: OECD (2007a)

Factors such as loopholes and preferential tax treatments, tax evasion and erosion of the tax base also compromise significantly the mobilization of 'maximum available resources'. People try to pay as little tax as possible. The rich take advantage of legal loopholes in the tax code. Estimates of non-compliance made by tax administration authorities in Mexico suggest that the overall revenue leakage is equivalent to almost half of the statutory revenue base. In addition, the number of individuals registered with the tax administration is equivalent to less than 20 per cent of the labour force (OECD 2006). The tax system is complex, so that the time cost of compliance with tax obligations is high in Mexico (time spent in preparing tax returns, filling out forms and paying taxes is high compared to other countries – 552 hours a year, compared to the OECD average of 202.9 hours). According to the Ministry of Finance, in 2006 an amount equivalent to 33 per cent of tax revenues was returned to taxpayers owing to tax allowances of various kinds. As pointed out by ECLAC, closing legal and corruption-driven illegal loopholes would raise the tax share of GDP by around three percentage points on average in Latin American countries. FUNDAR (2007) shows that preferential tax treatments (not only in income tax but in all taxes) amount to 5.92 per cent of Mexico's GDP. This amount of money is equivalent to sixteen times the resources devoted to the income-transfer programme *Oportunidades*,[8] 1.6 times the entire budget for education in Mexico and 2.2 times the entire budget for health (ibid.).

Tax evasion also remains a central concern. According to the Instituto Tecnológico Autónomo de México (ITAM), tax evasion amounts to around 27 per cent of the potential tax collection (equivalent to 3 per cent of the GDP) (ITAM 2006). Similar calculations have been done by other research institutions. For instance, a study from the Centre for Research and Teaching in Economics (CIDE and ITAM 2003) found that 38 per cent of potential VAT revenue is forgone because of either tax avoidance or tax evasion; this amount is equivalent to 2 per cent of GDP. In terms of the loss of tax revenue from the informal sector, CIDE has estimated how much money the government would collect from VAT if informal sector production were included. The study concludes that this amount would be equivalent to 0.093 per cent of GDP.

There have been some attempts to deal with some of these problems. Fiscal reform was introduced in 2010. The income tax rate has been temporarily increased to 30 per cent (it returns to 28 per cent in 2014). The problem of deferred taxes will be addressed, with the obligation to pay the deferred tax after a period of five years. The first payment will be for 60 per cent of the deferred tax, with 10 per cent being payable in the next four years, requiring payment of 60 per cent of the tax deferred through 2004 in 2010. Fiscal lawyers and tax experts have argued that the implementation of this provision will not be an easy task. For instance, many companies have already prepared requests for constitutional relief (called *amparo*[9]) from this provision of the law. In the case of individuals, the exemption for home sales may be claimed only once every five years, and the deduction of mortgage interest is limited to mortgages related to the acquisition of a single home. The mechanism for withholding of the tax on interest by financial institutions is modified, and now will be a definitive payment.

The tax applicable to the sale and importation of beer has been increased from 25 per cent to 28 per cent. The tax assessed on lotteries and raffles has been increased from 20 per cent to 30 per cent. A new 4 per cent tax on telecommunications has been established, exempting only public and rural telephony and interconnection services.

If a taxpayer has a credit because authorized deductions exceed income, the credit may only be applied against the IETU (the flat tax on corporate income) in the next ten years, without the option to apply the credit against income tax for the same year the credit is generated. The rate of tax on cash deposits has been increased from 2 per cent to 3 per cent, applicable on deposits over $15,000 in each month. This tax is designed to prevent tax evasion through informal cash transactions. The value added tax rate increased from 15 per cent to 16 per cent (from 10 per cent to 11 per cent in the border zone) from 1 January 2010. Certain limited-term transition rules will apply.

As can be seen from the evidence presented here, such as a low tax-to-GDP ratio, inadequate surveillance and enforcement, poor tax management and collection, tax evasion and avoidance, and corruption, the Mexican state has not fulfilled the obligation regarding using its maximum available resources. The 2010 fiscal reform may help in improving compliance – this will require further research to establish.

Non-discrimination and equality

The Mexican Constitution[10] establishes the principles of equity and proportionality in terms of taxation. Article 31, section IV, indicates that taxation practices should be established in terms of the individual's own capacity to pay in accordance with his/her income. Human rights obligations also insist on non-discrimination and equality. Article 2 of the International Covenant on Economic, Social and Cultural Rights (ICESCR) stipulates that 'The States Parties to the present Covenant undertake to guarantee that the rights enunciated in the present Covenant will be exercised without discrimination of any kind as to race, colour, sex, language, religion, political or other opinion, national or social origin, property, birth or other status.'

The Committee on Economic, Social and Cultural Rights (CESCR) has clarified that 'other status' includes 'economic status', understood in terms of wealth/poverty (CESCR 2009). The implication of both the constitution and the International Covenant on Economic, Social and Cultural Rights is that the incidence of tax (i.e. the share of income that is paid in taxes) should be equitable.

Equality in the incidence of taxes is usually assessed by analysing whether taxes are progressive (whether they mean that higher-income people pay a larger share of their income in tax than lower-income people); proportional (whether tax payments represent the same share of income for all taxpayers); or regressive (whether tax payment represents a smaller share of income for higher-income individuals than lower-income ones). As pointed out by Danilo Türk, the Special Rapporteur on economic and social rights:

> Progressive (as opposed to regressive) measures of taxation can, if supported by adequate administrative machinery and enforcement mechanisms, lead to gentle and gradual forms of income redistribution within States without threatening economic stability or patterns of growth, thereby creating conditions that enable a larger proportion of society to enjoy economic, social and cultural rights. (Türk 1992: 16)

Non-discrimination and equality by income status The distribution of personal income between households is very unequal in Mexico, as is confirmed by data from the survey of household income and expenditures.[11] Figure 5.10 shows the unequal distribution of household income in Mexico, from the poorest 10 per cent of households to the richest 10 per cent of households. While inequality fell slightly between 1998 and 2006, it remains very high.

As can be seen from Figure 5.10, which shows the distribution of current income,[12] those households in the highest income decile receive income in excess of 35 per cent of total current income attributed to all households, while the lowest-decile households receive approximately only 2 per cent of total current income. The data from the household survey are likely to underestimate the true extent of inequality, because the higher-income groups do not declare all their income and the really rich evade inclusion in the sample (Cortés 2001). Income inequality is particularly marked between urban and rural areas.

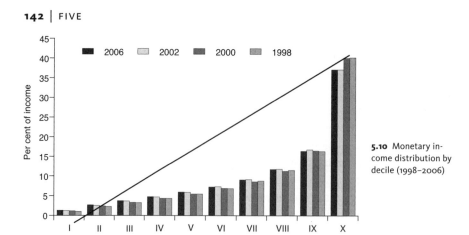

5.10 Monetary income distribution by decile (1998–2006)

Source: INEGI, ENIGH

Income inequalities have remained high even while GDP has been growing. Vargas (2006) establishes (using the *Penn World Tables*[13] for purchasing power parity over the last two decades) that income has grown fastest for the group of households with the greatest income.

This marked distributional inequality prompted the Mexican Congress to incorporate a study of the social impact of taxation as a requirement for the presentation of the Federal Budget by the Executive before the Chamber of Deputies, using the statistical data that were available. In order to comply with this requirement, the executive branch of the Mexican government commissioned a report on taxation incidence using data from the household survey. Figure 5.11 provides an example of this analysis, showing the contribution to income tax revenues that is paid by each income decile, as well as the incidence of taxation (the amount paid in taxes as a share of income) for

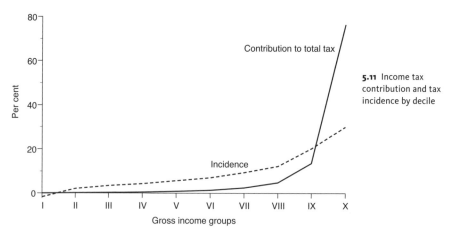

5.11 Income tax contribution and tax incidence by decile

Source: Ministry of Finance, Mexico, 2003

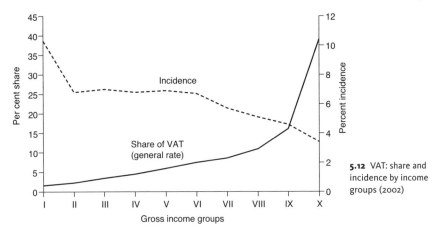

5.12 VAT: share and incidence by income groups (2002)

Source: Ministry of Finance, Mexico, 2003

each income decile. Not surprisingly, individuals and households in deciles 9 and 10 contribute the bulk of tax revenue (about 80 per cent). The incidence of income tax is also highest for these high-income groups, who pay between 20 per cent and 30 per cent of their income in income tax. Income tax is progressive and is in line with the principle of non-discrimination and equality.

The same cannot be said about VAT. In Mexico, basic foodstuffs are zero-rated for VAT. Some government analysts maintain that goods subject to the general VAT rate (15 per cent before the fiscal reform, and now 16 per cent) are normally not part of the consumption basket of the poorest households, and that therefore the impact of VAT on the incomes of the poor is limited. They claim that the incidence of this tax tends to be progressive (SHCP 2003).

This may be the case in terms of incidence on expenditure, but is not the case in terms of incidence on income, as shown by Figure 5.12, produced by the Ministry of Finance. The incidence of VAT in relation to household income is inversely related to the levels of income. Households in lower-income deciles pay a higher share of their total income in VAT, showing that VAT is regressive. It is true that the biggest share of VAT revenue comes from the rich, but as a proportion of their income they pay less than the poorest tenth of households.

The regressive nature of VAT appears to be a structural feature of the Mexican taxation system, as can be seen in Figure 5.13, which shows that the incidence remained regressive in the period 1984–2002.

Unfortunately no data are available on total tax incidence, including both direct and indirect taxes, across the income groups, so it is difficult to come to a definitive conclusion on whether the tax system as a whole meets criteria of non-discrimination and equality between different income groups. It is often suggested that a regressive impact of the tax system may be offset by a progressive incidence of expenditure, with poorer groups benefiting more

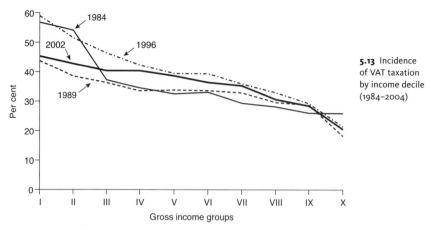

5.13 Incidence of VAT taxation by income decile (1984–2004)

Source: Vargas (2006)

than richer ones from the expenditure that taxation finances. However, the analysis of the incidence of public expenditure by income group in Chapter 3 suggests the opposite. Social expenditure in Mexico benefits the rich more than the poor.

Non-discrimination and equality by gender Stotsky (1996) was one of the first to study the gender inequality of taxation systems. She provides a framework for addressing the concept of gender 'bias' in taxation systems, distinguishing between explicit and implicit bias. She defines explicit bias as occurring when tax legislation treats men and women differently; whereas implicit bias occurs when tax systems contain provisions that have different impacts on men and women because of gender differences in norms and behaviours. A number of countries have taken steps to eliminate explicit gender 'bias' in personal income tax in the past, as presented by Stotsky; for example: France, Ireland, Malaysia, the Netherlands and South Africa (see Box 5.1).

Elson (2006) has argued that Stotsky's analysis has some limitations, because it assumes that an unbiased system would treat women and men the same and have exactly the same impact on them. Thus Stotsky argues that excise taxes on alcoholic drinks are biased against men, because men consume these drinks more than women, and thus these taxes have a higher incidence on the incomes of men than of women. Elson (ibid.) argues that a gender analysis of taxation must go beyond the principle of sameness to recognize that different treatment is not necessarily biased treatment; and differential impact is not necessary biased impact. It all depends whether the differential treatment and impact promote the achievement of equality between women and men, or hinder this achievement. She argues that this is in line with the Convention on the Elimination of All Forms of Discrimination Against Women, which recognizes the case for different treatment if this accelerates the achievement

---

Box 5.1 Eliminating explict gender bias in personal income tax (PIT)

- France (1983) moved from requiring only a husband's signature on family PIT returns to requiring that both spouses sign.
- Ireland (1993) moved from joint filing for PIT in the name of the husband with an option for separate assessment on labour income for the wife, to an option for the wife to be the 'primary taxpayer'.
- Malaysia (1991) moved from a PIT system in which the income of a married woman was attributed to her husband unless she elected separate assessment, to a system in which husbands and wives are treated as separate taxable units with an option for joint treatment.
- The Netherlands (1984) moved from granting a higher tax-free allowance in PIT to a married man than to a married woman, to an equal basic tax allowance.
- South Africa (1995) moved from applying a higher PIT rate schedule to single persons and married women than to married men, to a unified schedule.

Source: Stotsky (1996)

---

of equality between women and men (Article 4); and calls for states to take measures to modify existing patterns of conduct in order to eliminate prejudice and harmful practices (Article 5).

A gender analysis of the Mexican tax system has been conducted by Perez Fragoso and Cota Gonzales (2010) as part of an international project on taxation and gender equity (Grown and Valodia 2010). Personal income tax in Mexico does not have any explicit gender bias, as men and women file their own tax returns. Liability to pay personal income tax is limited to those who earn more than three times the minimum wage. This excludes 64 per cent of the economically active population and 72 per cent of all women in the labour force. Thus more men are liable to pay personal income tax than women; but as well, men are more likely than women to be able to take advantage of tax breaks. For example, the personal income tax law makes provision for tax credits that reduce tax liability for low-income employees; but these are not available for self-employed workers. Since more low-income women than low-income men tend to be self-employed, low-income women are less likely to be able to take advantage of tax credits. This is an implicit bias against women.

Fragoso and Gonzales (2010) also examine the incidence of indirect taxes, including VAT, and the Special Tax on drinks, tobacco and fuel, on both expenditure and income. The incidence of indirect taxes can be examined only on a household basis because income and expenditure data are collected on a household, not on an individual, basis (this is true of all countries). So they use a classification of households by their gender characteristics, including sex of household head; the sex and occupational status of household members (male breadwinner: only men employed, female breadwinner: only women employed, dual breadwinner: both men and women employed, or no one employed); sex and contribution to household income (male-maintained: men contribute 60 per cent or more of household income; female-maintained: women contribute 60 per cent or more, and joint-maintained: neither contributes more than 60 per cent); and gender composition of the household (whether men are in the majority, women are in the majority, or there are equal numbers of women and men).

They found that the incidence on expenditure was progressive, but the incidence on income was regressive. In relation to income, they found that total incidence of all indirect taxes (i.e. VAT plus the Special Taxes) was similar for male- and female-headed households, and for male and female breadwinner households. The incidence was higher for households in which men were in the majority than in those in which women were in the majority. But it was higher for households that were maintained by women, as compared to those maintained by men. We might draw the conclusions that the structure of indirect taxes, taken as a whole, does not have an unequal impact on women as compared to men. However, when we bring children into the picture, there is more cause for concern. The incidence of indirect taxes falls most heavily on female-maintained households with children, irrespective of which income group they are in.

Fragoso and Gonzalez (ibid.: 19) conclude that higher tax incidence among female-earner households with dependants in every income group 'should alert policy-makers to the need to formulate fiscal policy with a gender perspective'.

It is more difficult to analyse the distributional impacts of taxation from a gender perspective than from the perspective of different income groups. While many aspects of the tax system do not discriminate against women, there is cause for concern in the relative inability of women earners to take advantage of tax credits because the credits are available only for employees and not for the self-employed; and in the higher incidence of indirect taxes on households with children in which women contribute most of the earnings.

Transparency, accountability and participation

Transparency, accountability and participation are fundamental human rights principles. They are also reflected in the Mexican Constitution, which was amended in 1977 to include a *right to freedom of information*. Article 6 says in part, 'the right of information shall be guaranteed by the State'. In response to the demand for information, the Federal Law of Transparency and

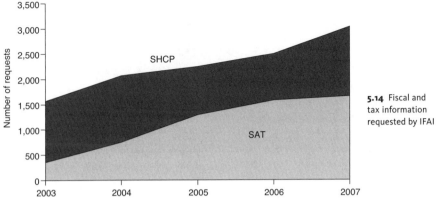

5.14 Fiscal and tax information requested by IFAI

Source: IFAI (2008)

Access to Public Government Information (which will be discussed below) was unanimously approved by parliament in April 2002 and signed by President Fox in June 2002. It went into effect in June 2003. This transparency law allows all persons to demand information in writing from federal government departments, autonomous constitutional bodies and other government bodies. Government agencies must respond to requests within twenty working days. However, accessing data on the tax structure and system is very difficult in Mexico.

The law governing access to public government information states among its broad objectives (Article 4): to 'make public administration transparent', to 'encourage accountability to citizens' so that they may evaluate the performance of government agencies, and to 'contribute to the democratization of Mexican society and the full operation of the Rule of Law'. To implement the law at a national level, the government has created the Federal Institute for Access to Public Information (IFAI), which is now the agency in charge of guaranteeing citizens' right to access public governmental information. There are more than 250 federal agencies and entities that are required to comply with information requirements. The IFAI has played a crucial role in pushing for greater transparency within the Executive.

Using the data that the IFAI produces, it is known that those areas of government activity which receive the most freedom-of-information requests are those overseen by the Ministry of Finance (SHCP) and the Tax Administration Service (SAT) (Figure 5.14).

However, information published by the government in relation to taxation is still neither sufficient nor transparent. In Mexico, the Ministry of Finance does produce a budget document that reports on the amount of revenue forgone as a result of all kinds of tax breaks[14] (*Presupuesto de Gastos Fiscales*); but the document does not provide any detailed and clear explanation about the pros and cons, and the impact on tax collection, of maintaining or eliminating the

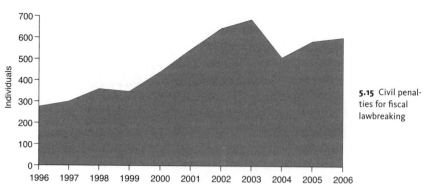

5.15 Civil penalties for fiscal lawbreaking

Source: INEGI (2007)

current preferential tax regimes on taxation (subsidies, exemptions, authorized deductions, differential rates, etc.) (FUNDAR 2007). Full transparency requires such information.

In terms of accountability of the fiscal performance, the ASF (Auditoría Superior de la Federación) is the institution in charge of receiving the public accounts (*Cuenta Pública*) and determining whether public resources were managed according to the law and to national development priorities. The ASF was created by the Chamber of Deputies. The appraisal of the last public accounts published in 2007 shows that several anomalies were detected by the ASF during 2001–05 under the Fox government. Special attention was drawn to *tax arrears* (which consist of tax liabilities that remain unpaid) incurred by Mexican companies and banks. During the period 2001–05, tax arrears increased from 27.9 per cent of ordinary government revenue to 35.1 per cent. The total amount of tax arrears during 2001–05 was 496 billion pesos.[15] In 2005, only 1.7 per cent of arrears were paid. The main debtors are banks, construction companies, sugar mills, national television companies, transport companies, football clubs and one newspaper company. At the end of 2005, banks alone owed the government more than 28 billion pesos in unpaid taxes.

The report for March 2008 from the System for Information Requests (SISI) of the IFAI states that the Tax Administration Service (SAT) has generated the greatest proportion of negative responses to requests for information from the public, arguing that the information is classified. Indeed, this is one of the reasons why in the Federal Tribunal for Fiscal and Administrative Justice during 2005 and 2006, the majority of rulings for protection and revision of tax contributions were related to the Tax Administration Service. On average, these rulings corresponded to a little more than one third of all the rulings.

The search for alternative approaches to strengthen public sector revenues based on the generation of non-oil tax revenues has led the Tax Administration Service to develop strategies that tend to discourage contributors from failing to meet their tax obligations. This strategy is based on the implementation of programmes that impose incremental costs on those who violate the fiscal

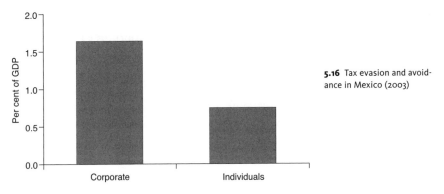

5.16 Tax evasion and avoidance in Mexico (2003)

Source: Bergman et al. (2006); Cantalá et al. (2005)

code. Among the other objectives is also that of increasing the credibility of the tax system by applying such legal sanctions on individuals. Figure 5.15 shows that the numbers that have been sanctioned have grown over time; however, the number of individuals subject to penalties or sanctions for fiscal lawbreaking is less than the numbers of individuals estimated to have not met their tax obligations.

It is important to differentiate between fiscal evasion, which is considered a crime because the individual or entity evades paying their tax obligations, and fiscal avoidance, which in the strictest sense consists of taking advantage of the legal loopholes to reduce the tax burden paid. Studies by Cantalá et al. (2005) and Bergman et al. (2006) establish that the complexity of tax legislation and the presence of exceptions in the treatment of tax obligations according to sector of production can create incentives for contributors to fail to meet their fiscal obligations. It is most likely that individuals engage in evasion while corporations engage in avoidance. The response by the tax authorities to both types of failure to meet tax obligations is also differentiated. Indeed, the damage to the public purse estimated as a result of corporate avoidance is greater than that of individual evasion (see Figure 5.16): corporate avoidance is estimated, for 2003, at 1.5 per cent of GDP while individual evasion is estimated at a little over 0.5 per cent of GDP.

The approval of the law governing access to public information facilitates greater social participation and oversight of taxation. Unfortunately, it is not sufficient to guarantee a greater voice for ordinary citizens in the design of tax policy, despite the existence of the Democratic Planning Law. The central problem concerning tax policy is how to devise the incentives and mechanisms to ensure that corporations and the rich contribute effectively to financing the production of those public goods and services required for the realization of economic and social rights. There needs to be a more effective mechanism for holding corporations and rich people to account in respect of paying taxes.

Conclusions

In order to raise money for financing development priorities such as education, health, water and sanitation, taxation remains a key source of government revenue.

Taxation policies have been examined here using the principles of maximum available resources, non-discrimination and equality, and transparency, accountability and participation. In Mexico, a high proportion of government revenue comes from revenues and royalties from PEMEX, the state-owned oil company. Since oil is a depleting natural resource, PEMEX will eventually no longer be able to sustain these revenues. In the absence of a comprehensive tax reform, the exhaustion of this oil revenue will significantly deplete the resources available to realize economic and social rights.

Tax revenue in Mexico is low compared to other Latin American countries; and tax administration is marred by inadequate surveillance and enforcement, poor tax management and collection, loopholes and preferential tax treatments. There is significant tax evasion and avoidance.

In terms of non-discrimination and equality, tax incidence analysis indicates that the impact of the general rate of VAT on the income of the lowest deciles is proportionally greater than the impact on higher deciles. This contrasts with the case of income tax, in which incidence is progressive. It is more difficult to analyse the distributional impacts of taxation from a gender perspective than from the perspective of different income groups. While many aspects of the tax system do not discriminate against women, there is cause for concern in the relative inability of women earners to take advantage of tax credits because the credits are available only for employees and not for the self-employed; and in the higher incidence of indirect taxes on households with children in which women contribute most of the earnings.

Finally, in terms of transparency, the Federal Law of Transparency and Access to Public Information in Mexico constitutes a significant improvement. However, the tax information that is available is still not sufficient, nor is it transparent, even though taxation and tax policy generate the most freedom-of-information requests. There have been improvements in mechanisms to hold those who break the tax law to account, but tax evasion and avoidance remain high.

In light of this analysis, we conclude that in order to meet its obligations to use maximum available resources, further reform of the design and administration of the tax system is required. Should this be realized, there will be a greater likelihood that economic and social rights can be progressively realized.

Notes

1 *Maximum available resources*: this principle recognizes that the resources at the disposition of a government are not unlimited. The definition has not yet been further elaborated by the UN Committee on Economic, Social and Cultural Rights (CESCR) in a General Comment, though the human rights community is beginning to pay more attention to this issue.

There is widespread agreement that maximum available resources does not just depend on the size and structure of the economy and its rate of growth. It also depends on how the state mobilizes resources to fund its obligations; *no discrimination and equality*: emphasizes the fact that everyone is entitled to the enjoyment of human rights irrespective of gender, religion, ethnic, social or national origin, political or other opinion, property, birth or other status; *transparency, accountability and participation*: the CESCR emphasizes that: 'rights and obligation demand accountability ... whatever the mechanisms of accountability, they must be accessible, transparent and effective' (United Nations, Committee on Economic, Social and Cultural Rights, 2001, para. 14, UN Doc. E/C.12.2001/10).

2 The obligation of *conduct* requires action reasonably calculated to realize the enjoyment of a particular right (see Maastricht Guidelines and CESRC General Comment 3, 'The Nature of States Parties' Obligations', 1999).

3 The obligation of *result* requires the states to achieve specific targets to satisfy a detailed substantive standard (see Maastricht Guidelines and CESRC General Comment 3, 'The Nature of States Parties' Obligations', 1999).

4 Called in Spanish *derechos, productos y aprovechamientos*.

5 Special Tax for Production and Services (*Impuesto Especial por Producción y Servicios*).

6 See Ley del Impuesto Sobre la Renta (Article 109), www.sat.gob.mx/.

7 Known as the 'Protocol of San Salvador'.

8 Mexico's conditional cash transfer programme and principal anti-poverty initiative.

9 There is no exact equivalent in English for the word *amparo*, which embraces the concept of appealing a law decision and legal protection. In this case, it refers to avoiding payment of taxes on the basis of the law's gaps. See Clagett and Valderrama (1973) and Merryman and Clark (1978).

10 *Constitución Política de los Estados Unidos Mexicanos*, www.constitucion.gob.mx/.

11 The Survey of Income and Expenditure (ENIGH) is a statistical instrument which is sampled probabilistically and is nationally representative. Unfortunately, given the size of the sample, the analysis cannot be dis-

aggregated by region, state, municipality or community.

12 Current monetary income, without adjustment for under-declaration or exclusion of the rich, using the National Accounts. Current income consists of earnings, salaries and other remuneration.

13 The *Penn World Tables* provide purchasing power parity and national income accounts converted to international prices for 188 countries for some or all of the years 1950–2004.

14 Economists call these forgone revenues tax expenditures. In economic terms they are equivalent to collecting revenue and then distributing it as subsidies.

15 $45 billion approximately.

References

Bergman, M., V. Carreón and F. Hernández Trillo (2006) *Evasión fiscal del impuesto sobre la renta de personas morales*, Mexico: CIDE.

Bettinger, H. (2008). Ernst & Young, www.cnnexpansion.com/economia/2007/8/8/las-empresas-pagan-13-del-isr.

Cantalá, D., J. Sempere and H. Sobrazo (2005) *Evasión fiscal en el impuesto sobre la renta de personas físicas*, Mexico: El Colegio de México.

Centro de Estudios de las Finanzas Públicas (2007) *Tendencias del Sistema Tributario Mexicano*, CEPF/007/2007, Mexico: Cámara de Diputados LX legislatura.

CESCR (Committee on Economic, Social and Cultural Rights) (2009) General Comment 20, 'Non-Discrimination in Economic, Social and Cultural Rights' (Article 2, para. 2), UN Doc. no. E/C.12/GC/20.

CIDE (Centro de Investigación y Docencia Económicas) and ITAM (Instituto Tecnológico Autónomo de México (2003) *Análisis de las Finanzas Públicas en México*, ed. Foro Consultivo de la Ciencia y el Consejo de Ciencia y Tecnología, Mexico.

Clagett, H. and D. M. Valderrama (1973) *Writ of Amparo, Judicial Review, and Protection of Individual Rights: A revised guide to the law and legal literature of Mexico*, Washington, DC: Library of Congress.

Constitución Política de los Estados Unidos Mexicanos (n.d.) www.constitucion.gob.mx/.

Cortés, F. (2001) 'El cálculo de la pobreza en

México a partir de la encuesta de ingresos y gastos', *Comercio Exterior*, 51(10), Mexico.

ECLAC (Economic Commission for Latin America and the Caribbean) (1998) *The Fiscal Covenant. Strengths, Weaknesses, Challenges*, LC/G.2024/I, Santiago de Chile, April.

Elson, D. (2006) *Budgeting for Women's Rights: Monitoring Government Budgets for Compliance with CEDAW*, New York: UNIFEM.

Fragoso, P. L. and C. Gonzalez (2010) 'Gender and taxation in Mexico', in C. Grown and I. Valodia (eds), *Taxation and Gender Equity. A comparative analysis of direct and indirect taxes in developing and developed countries*, London: Routledge.

FUNDAR Centro de Análisis e Investigación (2007) *Opacidad en la política de ingresos*, Working paper, Mexico DF, October.

Grown, C. and I. Valodia (eds) (2010) *Taxation and Gender Equity. A comparative analysis of direct and indirect taxes in developing and developed countries*, London: Routledge.

IFAI (2008) *Estadísticas del Sistema de Solicitudes de Información al 20 de marzo de 2008*, Mexico.

INEGI (2004) *Sistema de Cuentas Nacionales de México (1999–2004)*, Cuentas por Sectores Institucionales, vol. 1, Mexico.

— (2007) *Anuario estadístico de los Estados Unidos Mexicanos*, Mexico.

ITAM (Instituto Tecnológico Autónomo de México) (2006) *Medición de la Evasión Fiscal en México*, Mexico: Centro de Economía Aplicada y Políticas Públicas.

Merryman, J. and D. S. Clark (1978) *Comparative Law: Western European and Latin American Systems*, Indianapolis, IN/New York/Charlotesville, VA: Bobbs-Merrill.

Mexico, Secretaría de Hacienda y Crédito Público (2005) *Presupuesto de Gastos Fiscales 2005 and 2007*, Mexico.

OECD (Organisation for Economic Co-operation and Development) (2006) *Statistical Chart 2006*, Paris: OECD.

— (2007a) *Revenue Statistics 1965–2006*, 2007 edn.

— (2007b) *Getting It Right. OECD Perspectives on policy challenges in Mexico*, Paris: OECD.

— (2009) *Revenue Statistics 1965–2008*, Paris: OECD.

SHCP (2003) *Estudio sobre la distribución del pago de impuestos*, Mexico: Secretaría de Hacienda y Crédito Público.

Stotsky, J. G. (1996) *Gender Bias in Tax Systems. How tax systems treat men and women differently*, WP/96/99, Washington, DC: International Monetary Fund.

Türk, D. (1992) *The realization of economic, social and cultural rights*, Special Rapporteur on Economic and Social Rights, Final report submitted to the UN Commission on Human Rights, E/CN.4/Sub.2/1992/16.

Van den Noord, P. and C. Heady (2001) *Surveillance of Tax Policies: A Synthesis of Findings in Economic Surveys*, OECD Economics Department Working Papers

Vargas, C. (2006) 'Incidencia fiscal y del gasto sobre la renta familiar: un enfoque de microdatos para México 1984–2002', Doctoral thesis, Universitat Autónoma de Barcelona.

6 | TAXATION AND ECONOMIC AND SOCIAL RIGHTS IN THE USA

Radhika Balakrishnan

Introduction

Taxation is one of the most important ways available to a government to raise revenues to fulfil its human rights obligations. This chapter examines the conduct of tax policy in the US in light of human rights principles of (i) the requirement to use the maximum resources for realizing economic and social rights as specified in ICESR Article 2, (ii) non-discrimination and equality, and (iii) transparency, accountability and participation in tax policy. This chapter does not examine obligation of result in relation to taxation, since the relation between tax revenue and the realization of economic and social rights depends on expenditure policy.

US tax policy

The United States system of taxation is comprised of seven main sources of revenue: (i) income tax; (ii) corporate tax; (iii) excise tax; (iv) estate tax; (v) social insurance tax; (vi) sales tax; and (vii) property tax. While some of these taxes are levied at both the federal and state levels, others are levied only at the state and/or local levels.

Types of taxation in the USA Personal *income taxes* are levied at both the state and local levels on income from wages and salaries, as well as interest, dividends, capital gains, self-employment, alimony and prizes. Most state income tax systems are modelled after the federal equivalent, though some state systems differ. *Corporate taxable income* is defined as total revenues minus the cost of goods sold, wages and salaries, depreciation, repairs, interest paid, and other deductions at both the federal and state levels.

An *excise tax* is a tax on the production, sale or use of a particular commodity. Excise taxes are levied at both the federal and state levels, and are normally incorporated into the price of a product (such as alcohol or tobacco) such that the amount of tax actually being paid by the consumer is not immediately evident. In contrast, the *sales taxes* are levied only at the state and local levels, and are most often shown on purchase receipts as an addition to the selling price of a product.

The *estate tax* can be assessed at both the federal and state levels and is applied to transfers of large estates and gifts to beneficiaries, one of the principal ways to tax inherited wealth, while *social insurance taxes* (also known as payroll taxes or Social Security taxes) are applied only at the federal level and actually comprise two separate taxes: a tax primarily used to fund Social Security and a tax used to maintain the Medicare programme.[1] Finally, *property tax* is a tax on real estate, including land, private residences and commercial properties, and is levied at the local level (Roach 2003: 5–8).

Obligation of conduct

Maximum available resources The International Convention on Economic, Social and Cultural Rights (ICESCR) calls on each state 'to take steps ... to the maximum of its available resources, with a view to achieving progressively the full realization of ... rights ... by all appropriate means'.[2] The Committee on Economic and Social Rights (CESR) has clarified that 'such steps should be deliberate, concrete and targeted as clearly as possible',[3] and that 'the phrase "to the maximum of its available resources" was intended ... to refer to both the resources existing within a state and those available from the international community'.[4] Since it is impossible to take steps toward the progressive realization of human rights without resources, the maximum available resources obligation is 'both a protect- and fulfil-bound obligation' (Kunnemann 1995).

There has been some literature on the issue of maximum available resources but on the whole it takes as given the amount of financial resources available to government and does not examine the ways in which such resources are generated. Robertson (1994) suggests that there are five resources that are instrumental to the steps referred to in the ICESCR: (i) money; (ii) natural resources; (iii) human resources; (iv) technology; and (v) information. Capital resources facilitate social welfare in areas such as health, shelter and education. Natural resources, such as land, seeds and animals, provide for physical welfare, such as food and clothing. Human resources ensure the capacity to take steps and fulfil obligations. Technology promotes efficiency and innovation, enabling entities to take newer and better steps. Information provides insight into what, and by which means, steps are necessary to fulfil human rights. Robertson sees taxes on wealth such as taxes on inheritance, property and net wealth as an infringement on the right to property and the use of privately held resources for public purposes (ibid.: 695–7). This chapter argues that taxes of all kinds facilitate realization of economic and social rights and taxes on wealth are not an infringement of human rights.

The concept of maximum available resources which the government should utilize for progressive realization of human rights has not yet been fully developed. The UN Committee on Economic, Social and Cultural Rights made a statement in 2007 entitled 'An Evaluation of the Obligation to Take Steps to the "Maximum of Available Resources" under an Optional Protocol to the

Covenant'. However, the statement did not define what constitutes available resources beyond stating that it refers to 'both the resources existing within a state as well as those available from the international community through international cooperation and assistance'. However, it has used the following indicators in assessing a government's compliance with this obligation: comparing economic, social and cultural rights (ESCR-) related expenditures versus expenditures for non-ESCR-related areas; comparing expenditures in an area (e.g. education, health) with expenditures in the same area by countries at a comparable level of development; comparing allocations and expenditures against international indicators, such as UNDP's indicator that 5 per cent of GDP should go to human expenditures (which for poor countries are specified as basic education, primary healthcare, basic water; UNDP 1991). We note that these indicators focus only on expenditure and on international assistance.

Several UN Special Rapporteurs and Independent Experts have also addressed the meaning of 'maximum available resources'. The Special Rapporteur on economic and social rights noted that:

> Progressive (as opposed to regressive) measures of taxation can, if supported by adequate administrative machinery and enforcement mechanisms, lead to gentle and gradual forms of income redistribution within states without threatening economic stability or patterns of growth, thereby creating conditions that enable a larger proportion of society to enjoy economic, social and cultural rights. (Türk 1992)

Magdalena Sepulveda, the Independent Expert on the question of human rights and extreme poverty, has drawn the following conclusions with regard to the obligation of governments to use the 'maximum of available resources' to realize ESCR (Sepulveda 2003). Governments must mobilize resources within the country to their utmost ability.

- Government expenditures must be efficient (the 'efficiency criterion' could also be applied to revenue collection).
- Government expenditures must be effective (impact).
- Failure to curb corruption is a failure to comply with the obligation.
- Funds earmarked in the budget for ESCR must not be diverted to non-ESCR areas.
- Funds earmarked for ESCR must be fully expended for that purpose.
- Governments that introduce regressive measures, such as cuts in expenditure on ESCR, must show that they have used the maximum of available resources to avoid taking such a step.
- Governments must do all they can to secure international assistance where national resources are inadequate to realize ESCR.

Her conclusion points to the importance of resource mobilization, as well as of expenditure policy and international assistance.

Olivier de Schutter, the Special Rapporteur on the right to food, in his 2009 report on Brazil, draws attention to the role of taxes in fulfilling the obligation to use the maximum available resources:

> The tax structure in Brazil remains highly regressive. Tax rates are high for goods and services and low for income and property, bringing about very inequitable outcomes. ... while the social programmes developed under the 'zero Hunger' strategy are impressive in scope. They are essentially funded by the very persons whom they seek to benefit, as the regressive system of taxation seriously limits the redistributive aspect of the programmes. Only by introducing a tax reform that would reverse the current situation could Brazil claim to be seeking to realize the right to adequate food by taking steps to the maximum of its available resources. (De Schutter 2009: para. 36)

In the United States taxes are the primary way in which government gets revenue and the tax policy has an enormous impact on the availability of resources.

The Maastricht Guidelines suggest that 'States enjoy a margin of discretion in selecting the means for implementing their respective obligations'.[5] As Diane Elson (Elson 2006) notes, one benefit of the margin of discretion rule is the avoidance of one size fits all, as seen in measures implemented by the International Monetary Fund and the World Bank. However, the absence of a specific model for raising revenues means that those monitoring compliance will need a means of evaluating the efficacy of government policies. Elson (ibid.) points out that states must justify the bases of their plans to raise and utilize resources. This approach makes it possible not only to evaluate the rationale behind specific policies, but to compare them to those of other states that are proving more successful at realizing human rights.

One of the difficult issues when it comes to examining maximum available resources is that there is no agreement in the human rights treaties or other literature as to how to assess compliance. We therefore use indicators such as tax rates comparable to those of economically similar countries; in other words, does the United States collect a larger or smaller proportion of tax as a percentage of GDP than other economically equivalent countries, and how has that percentage changed over time, comparatively speaking? Other relevant indicators include shares of revenue generated by direct taxes, e.g. corporate and individual taxes, and indirect taxes, e.g. sales, VAT and excise, taxes. Does the tax burden fall disproportionately on those with the least ability to pay? How much revenue is forgone owing to unnecessary tax breaks for the wealthy and corporations?

In the period between 1975 and 2007, nominal GDP rose continuously from less than $1.63 trillion to more than $14.07 trillion in 2007;[6] during the same period, however, total tax revenues as a percentage of US GDP did not rise as consistently. Though there was a steady increase in the tax-to-GDP ratio

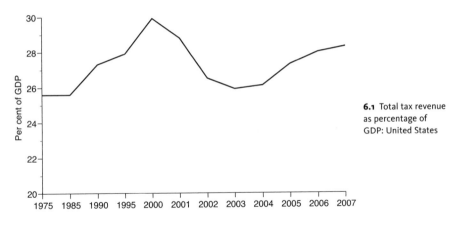

6.1 Total tax revenue as percentage of GDP: United States

Source: OECD (2009)

till about 2000, we see a huge decline in 2000. As Figure 6.1 shows, between 2000 and 2004 total tax revenue as a percentage of GDP plummeted from nearly 30 per cent to around 25 per cent. This means that in a mere four-year period tax revenues fell to a thirty-year low. The causes of the quick decline are difficult to isolate, but the tax cuts for the very wealthy in 2000 certainly had an impact on the ratio. After 2004 we see again an increase in the ratio, but we also find that both corporate profits as a percentage of GDP and tax revenue as a percentage of GDP rose in that time. From 2003 to 2007, corporate tax revenue as a part of total tax receipts increased from 7.5 per cent to 14.4 per cent owing to the very high increase in profits. Though the increase in profits made the tax-to-GDP ratio go up from 2004 to 2007, it has not reached the 29.9 per cent it recorded in 2000. It can also be argued that if not for the tax cuts the potential resources available for meeting economic and social rights obligations would have been far greater.

This trend is not unique to the United States. As Figure 6.2 illustrates, many comparable countries also saw a decline in tax revenues beginning in 2000. However, the decline in the USA is much sharper and the percentage of total tax revenue to GDP in the United States was already significantly lower than that of other OECD countries at almost every given time.[7]

The composition of federal tax receipts by source between 1960 and 2006 is shown in Figure 6.3. While the percentage of revenue from personal income tax remained in the 40–50 per cent range during this forty-six-year period, the percentage of revenue coming from corporate income tax shrank considerably. Dependence on social insurance taxes increased while the share of excise taxes declined. The overall trend is an increased share of revenue from progressive individual income taxes as well as flat, regressive social insurance taxes, both of which offset the reduced share generated by corporations and luxury goods (excise taxes).

Corporate income tax receipts as a fraction of GDP have fallen by half,

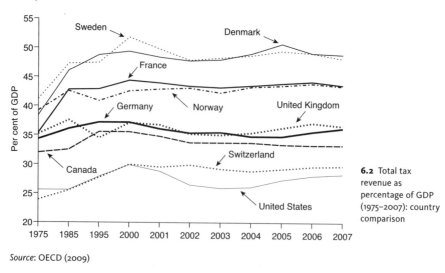

6.2 Total tax revenue as percentage of GDP (1975–2007): country comparison

Source: OECD (2009)

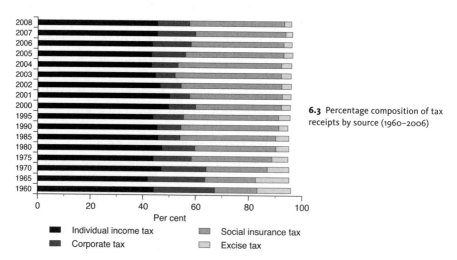

6.3 Percentage composition of tax receipts by source (1960–2006)

Source: Executive Office of the President of the United States, Office of Management and Budget (2009), *Budget of the US Government FY 2009, Historical Tables*, Table 2.1: 'Receipts by Source: 1934–2014', www.whitehouse.gov/omb/budget/Historicals/

from 3.5–4 per cent to less than 2 per cent, while corporate profits as a share of GDP rose (Piketty and Saez 2007). Corporate income tax revenues have declined, in terms of their share of federal taxes (see Figure 6.4) and their share of the economy. Corporate tax revenues averaged approximately 5 per cent of GDP in the 1950s and 4 per cent in the 1960s, but fell sharply to nearly 1 per cent in 1983. This fall reflects a combination of tax cuts and poor economic conditions. After rising slightly above 2 per cent of GDP during part of the 1990s, corporate receipts fell again after 2000: the lowest was observed in 2000, at 1.8 per cent, when the economy slowed. By 2003,

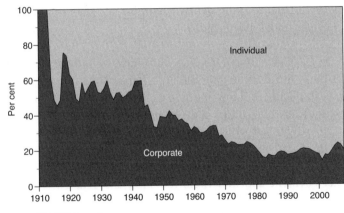

6.4 Corporate versus personal share of federal income tax

Source: TRAC IRS (2009)

corporate revenues had dropped to 1.2 per cent of GDP, the lowest level since 1937, except for 1983 (Friedman 2003). History has shown that economic slowdowns do not necessarily call for a reduction of corporate income taxes in order to ignite growth.

Just as the corporate income tax rate has decreased over time,[8] there has also been a great decrease in the top marginal tax rate on individual income. In the 1960s, the statutory individual tax rate applied to the marginal dollar of the highest income level was 91 per cent; by 1988 the rate had declined to 28 per cent; it increased to 39.6 per cent in 1993, but fell again to 35 per cent by 2003. As Lee Price of the Economic Policy Institute notes about the enormous costs of such decreases, 'over the last five fiscal years ... tax cuts have had a direct cost of $860 billion and (with interest costs) a total effect on the deficit of $929 billion' (Price 2006).

In examining the trend in tax structure in the United States it is clear that the changes in tax policy have decreased the amount of revenue generated and therefore the USA has not met its obligation to use the maximum available resources. For those people who have not been able to meet their basic needs, such as health and food, from the market, the state has to make sure that there is some provision to meet their basic needs through the use of its resources. In particular at a time of crisis, there has to be a need to at least keep the ratio of tax to GDP at a rate that is consistent with human rights obligations. The debate in 2011 in the United States regarding whether to make the tax cuts on the wealthy permanent should have been conducted in the context of the revenue that would be forgone and the inability of the state to meet its economic and social rights obligations. According to the Centre for American Progress, without the loss of revenue due to the tax cuts and the spending on the two wars in Iraq and Afghanistan, the budget deficit would have been only 4.7 per cent of gross domestic product in 2009, instead of the eye-catching 11.2 per cent – despite the weak economy and the costly efforts taken to restore it. In 2010, the deficit would be 3.2 per cent instead of 9.6 per cent (Ettlinger and Linden 2009).

Non-discrimination and equality States have an obligation to 'ensure that tax laws and collection measures do not discriminate' (Balakrishnan et al. 2007: 13) either explicitly or implicitly. It is important to note that non-discrimination and equality are immediate obligations that states have to fulfil. One may evaluate the extent to which this obligation is fulfilled by analysing the tax code, its implementation and scope for tax avoidance.

It is also possible to investigate (through tax incidence studies) the relationship between tax payment and household incomes; and link this to race and gender.

In looking at the tax code one may look at the incentives and disincentives that tax policies create for different groups of people. As Elson (2006) notes, 'taxes not only raise revenue, they also provide incentives and disincentives to certain forms of behaviour'. These incentives and disincentives can lead to implicit discrimination; e.g., as discussed below, married women may decide to leave, or not to enter, the formal labour market owing to their higher marginal tax burden. Leaving the labour market decreases their skills and experience levels and further marginalizes them in terms of future employment opportunities.

States' obligations to respect, protect and fulfil involve obligations of conduct. According to the Committee on Economic, Social and Cultural Rights,

> The obligation to respect requires States Parties to refrain from discriminatory actions that directly or indirectly result in the denial of the equal right of men and women to their enjoyment of economic, social, and cultural rights. Respecting this right obliges States Parties to not adopt, and to repeal laws and rescind policies, administrative measures, and programmes that do not conform to the right protected by Article 3.[9]

In terms of taxation, states are required to not only respect gender equality through the abandonment of laws that *explicitly* discriminate against women, but also take into consideration gender analyses that reveal current and potential *implicit* discrimination against women. Such analyses must include, *inter alia*, the effects of individual and joint filing schemes on women, especially the marriage penalty; the effects of regressive tax measures such as value added tax (VAT) and sales tax; and the incentives and disincentives that certain tax policies create for women.

Part II(B)(2) of General Comment 16 specifies states' obligations to protect women from gender discrimination and inequality: 'The obligation to protect requires States Parties to take steps aimed directly at the elimination of prejudices, customary and all other practices that perpetuate the notion of inferiority or superiority of either of the sexes, and stereotyped roles for men and women.' While tax policy in the United States does not contain any explicit discrimination against women, it may contain implicit class and gender bias. For example, rent and childcare expenses are not tax deductible, but some tax relief is allowed against interest paid on mortgages. As a result, single mothers, who tend to have lower incomes, rent their accommodation, and have to pay childcare costs if they undertake paid work, face a greater tax burden in relation to their incomes than married heterosexual couples with children and stay-at-home mothers who buy their own homes and do not have to pay childcare costs. Thus the tax system discriminates against single mothers, as compared to male-breadwinner families, perpetuating the stereotype of the superiority of male-breadwinner families.

Finally, the Committee clarifies various components of state obligations to fulfil the economic, social and cultural human rights of women. 'The obligation to fulfil requires States Parties to take steps to ensure that in practice, men and women enjoy their economic, social, and cultural rights on a basis of equality. Such steps should include', *inter alia*, designing and implementing policies and programmes to give long-term effect to the economic, social and cultural rights of both men and women on the basis of equality. These may include the adoption of temporary special measures to accelerate women's equal enjoyment of their rights, gender audits, and gender-specific allocation of resources.[10]

Thus, not only do states have the obligation to overcome stereotypes and implicit/explicit gender bias in tax policy as a means of protecting women's rights to equality and non-discrimination, they also have the obligation to ensure that adequate and immediate legislation is passed to end all such discrimination and inequality.

In the United States, unlike in most other countries, married couples file a joint tax return as a family rather than individual tax returns. Joint filing systems evolved from a household model where men were the income earners and women the dependent homemakers. In this system, the income of a married woman is added to that of her husband, and the amount of tax that the couple pays is higher than if they were not married – this is often referred to as the marriage tax (UNDP 2010: 5). Though married women earn on average less than their husbands, their income is in fact taxed at a higher marginal tax rate. As Elson notes, 'joint tax filing by married couples in the progressive tax system results in the lower-earning spouse, who is usually the woman, facing a higher marginal tax rate on her first dollar earned than she would have as an individual and than her husband' (Anderson 1999, cited in Elson 2006: 79). This higher marginal tax rate faced by married women resulting from the joint filing system serves as a disincentive for women to engage in the formal labour economy.

The disincentives that higher marginal rates create for married women 'are further exacerbated by their responsibilities in the unpaid care economy during their reproductive years' (Barnett and Grown 2004).

In the USA, married women who participate in the unpaid care economy instead of the paid labour economy are rewarded for their 'choice'. As Elson (2006: 81) notes:

> In the US, the tax contribution of a married couple in which one spouse participates in the labour market and one spouse stays at home and does unpaid domestic work is lower than that of a married couple in which both partners participate in the labour market. This is criticized by feminists ... as a system that favours traditional, patriarchal marriage in which there is a male breadwinner and a dependent wife.

Economist Julie Nelson notes, 'If household labour does indeed significantly contribute to household economic welfare, then the application of standards of horizontal equity to the tax system should take this into account' (Nelson 1996: 100). In other words, when judging the fairness of a tax system one should take into account the value of household labour in determining the fairness of the tax system.

Personal income taxes are not the only realm of taxation in which women face implicit discrimination and resulting inequality. As International Monetary Fund economist Janet Stotsky (1996: iii) notes, 'Commodity taxes, trade taxes, and corporate income taxes may lead to implicit gender bias through changes in household consumption, household income, or patterns of industrial development.' Commodity taxes include the value added tax used in the state of Michigan under the name of a Single Business Tax (SBT) and state sales taxes which are applied by all states except six.[11] Sales taxes are likely to be regressive because they tax consumers without taking into consideration consumers' income and therefore their ability to pay taxes depends on what goods are included. Groups with little to no disposable income invariably pay a higher percentage of their incomes in sales and value added taxes than do richer households. Elson (2006: 91) points out that because women tend to be more concentrated in lower-income households than are men, and female-headed households on average tend to have lower incomes than male-headed households, VAT not only has a higher incidence on poor households, it also has a higher incidence on women than on men. It results in substantive inequality between women and men.

The higher incidence on women is not solely due to the fact that women are concentrated in poorer households. Female spending habits are also a factor in the analysis of how and why women face a higher incidence of sales tax. Barnett and Grown (2004: 40) observe that 'women tend to consume goods and services that benefit family health, education, and nutrition, while men consume more of their income on personal items. Thus, women may bear a disproportionately larger burden of indirect taxation.'

General Comment 16 specifies state obligations of conduct to respect, protect and fulfil women's rights to non-discrimination and equality according to gender. While this General Comment did not clarify obligations of conduct concerning race and discrimination/inequality, it can be assumed that the spirit of the Committee's clarifications was intended to provide a basis for protection for all groups subject to discrimination and inequality. Therefore, one may claim that the obligations of conduct with respect to discrimination based on gender are also obligations of conduct with respect to discrimination based on race. Therefore, the obligation to respect requires states parties to refrain from discriminatory actions that directly or indirectly result in the denial of the equal right of all races, ethnicities and indigenous groups to their enjoyment of economic, social and cultural rights. States parties are obliged not to adopt and to repeal laws and rescind policies, administrative measures and programmes that do not conform to the right protected by Article 3.[12]

In this section we examine the incidence of taxation on household income, and the extent to which it reveals patterns of discrimination.

The obligation with respect to non-discrimination and equality in taxation can be considered in terms of the obligation to facilitate, provide and promote 'policies and programmes to give long-term effect to the economic, social and cultural rights of [all racial and ethnic groups] on the basis of equality'.[13] In terms of taxation, states must not only respect the right to non-discrimination and equality by eliminating policies and laws that explicitly harm racial and ethnic groups, they must also take into consideration analyses that show existing and potential implicit discrimination. Such analyses must include, *inter alia*, the effects of regressive tax measures such as VAT and sales tax, the effects of under-representation and participation in tax policy-making, the impact of high property taxation on lower-income groups, and the incentives/disincentives that tax policies create for different racial and ethnic groups. States are also obliged to ensure that tax policies do not have the intent or effect of discriminating against the poor by conferring benefits to the rich at the expense of the poor or by conferring benefits to the rich that are not also conferred to the poor.

In order for various racial and ethnic groups to achieve the equal enjoyment of economic, social and cultural rights, states must adopt temporary measures that offset implicit racial- and ethnic-oriented discrimination and promote legislation that aims to provide an even playing field for disadvantaged groups.[14] Although federal law strictly forbids explicit discrimination in US government policy, implicit discrimination has yet to be overcome.

To examine taxation in terms of discrimination, we focus on the incidence of tax on household income, by income quintile. (This is often known as the effective rate of tax.) The federal income tax incidence per income quintile is generally more progressive, although it has become less so over time. In addition, we examine the impact of state and local taxes, both of which are generally more regressive. The change in the incidence of taxation from 1960 to 2004 (Piketty and Saez 2007) is illustrated in Figure 6.5. The horizontal axis displays groups according to the percentile of household income, ranging from the second quintile (20–40), the lowest level of income included in these graphs, to the top 0.01 per cent (99.9–100.0), the highest income level. The bottom quintile (0–20) is excluded from the analysis because many low-income earners have zero market income, receive only government transfers and do not file income tax returns. There were cuts in the tax rates at all levels between 1960 and 2004, but the contribution from estate and corporate taxes decreased the most. Those at the top end of the income distribution decreased their share of the tax revenue the most while shifting the burden to those lower down on the scale, primarily through payroll taxes.[15] What these two graphs illustrate is that the largest change from 1960 to 2004 is the decrease in the amount of tax paid by the top quintile in terms of estate tax and corporate tax, with the effective tax rate going from about 70 per cent to 30 per cent; the incidence of income tax has stayed somewhat the same while the incidence of payroll tax has increased for the middle quintile.

Economic status is specifically mentioned in relation to discrimination in the 1969 American Convention on Human Rights, also known as the Pact San Jose. Article 1(1) of the Pact ensures the 'free and full exercise of ... rights and freedoms, without any discrimination for reasons of ... national or social origin, economic status, birth, or any other social condition'. McNaughton (2007) argues that non-discrimination with respect to economic status is also implied in the ICESCR, as Article 2 specifies 'property', along with 'race, colour, sex, language, religion, political or other opinion, national or social origin', in its list of the distinctions that are not permitted to be a base for discrimination. She suggests that 'property' has generally been interpreted to mean 'wealth'.

State and local, sales and excise taxes are regressive (see Figure 6.6). An Institute on Taxation and Economic Policy study (ITEP 2009) looked at the tax incidence in all fifty states of the United States in 2002. This study found that the average state and local tax incidence on the best-off 1 per cent of families is 6.4 per cent before accounting for the tax savings from federal item-ized deductions. After the federal offset, the effective tax rate on the best-off 1 per cent is a mere 5.2 per cent. The average effective tax rate on families in the middle 20 per cent of the income spectrum is 9.7 per cent before the federal offset and 9.4 per cent after – almost twice the effective rate that the richest people pay. The average effective tax rate on the poorest 20 per cent of families is the highest of all. At 10.9 per cent, it is more than double the effective rate on the very wealthy (ibid.: 2). (See Figure 6.7.) Changes to these taxes have been regressive (see Figure 6.8).

The above data indicate the regressive nature of state and local taxes. Those with the least wealth and thus the lowest economic status pay a bigger share of their income in taxes than do those with the most wealth and the highest economic status. Below, we provide some data on the composition of the groups

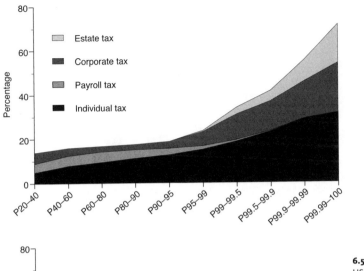

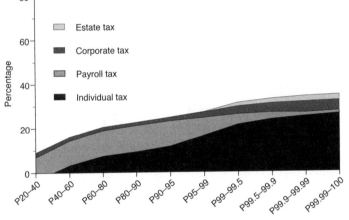

6.5 Incidence of US federal taxes by household income group

Source: Piketty and Saez (2007: Fig. 1)

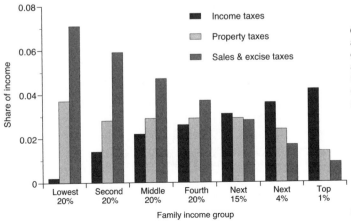

6.6 Comparing average incidence of different state and local taxes on household income of different household groups

Source: ITEP (2009)

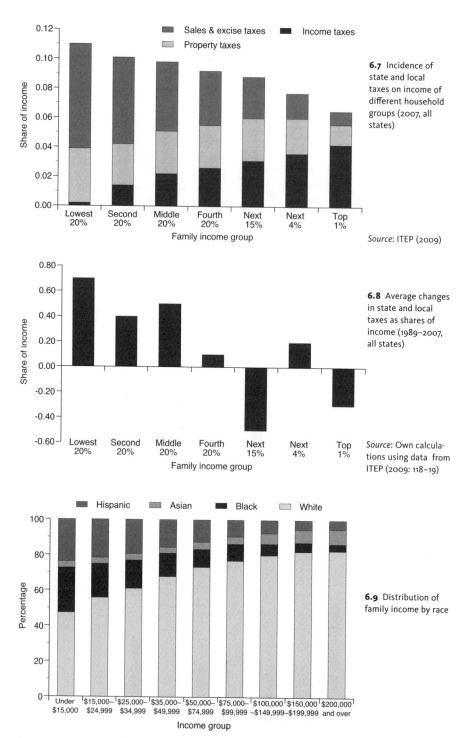

6.7 Incidence of state and local taxes on income of different household groups (2007, all states)

Source: ITEP (2009)

6.8 Average changes in state and local taxes as shares of income (1989–2007, all states)

Source: Own calculations using data from ITEP (2009: 118–19)

6.9 Distribution of family income by race

Source: US Census Bureau, Current Population Survey, Annual Social and Economic Supplements. Income: Historical Tables: Families: Table F-23: Families by Total Money Income, Race, and Hispanic Origin of Householder, www.census.gov/hhes/www/income/data/historical/families/index.html

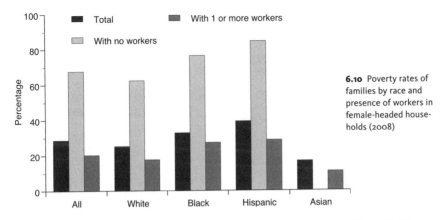

6.10 Poverty rates of families by race and presence of workers in female-headed households (2008)

Source: US Census Bureau, Current Population Survey, Table POV41: Region, Division and Type of Residence – Poverty Status for All People, Family Members and Unrelated Individuals by Family Structure: 2008

with the lowest economic status (see Figure 6.9). As shown in Figure 6.10, poverty rates in the USA are the highest among female-headed households. Comparing different groups by race, black and Latino median family income levels are lower than those of white families. We can therefore infer that the tax policy has imposed an undue burden on those with the lowest economic status – in other words, women and people of colour.

Transparency, accountability and participation The obligation of conduct for the achievement of transparency, accountability and participation in taxation is 'to ensure that tax codes and administration are transparent and accountable, and opportunities are provided for broad participation in public discussion about appropriate tax policy' (Balakrishnan et al. 2007: 14). As a result, states must design and construct tax policies and legislation that are understandable to the common citizen. In other words, the tax structure must be navigable by all, as opposed to only the technocrats who are charged with its development. States must also be held accountable for violations of civil, political, economic, social and cultural rights that are caused by tax policies that discriminate, are corrupt, non-participatory and do not foster the realization of rights through revenue generation. States are obligated to consider the opinions and needs of all subject to and/or affected by taxation, and to allow them to participate openly, freely and without hindrance. The following section attempts to situation the discussion in the context of US tax policy.

In the context of the US tax policy, relevant indicators relate to the provision of information on, scope of consultation about and implementation of tax law. Ordinary citizens must be able to realize their right to information about, and voice in, tax policy. Governments must ensure that the public's ideas and needs are actually taken into account when, for example, discussing changes to tax policy or structure.

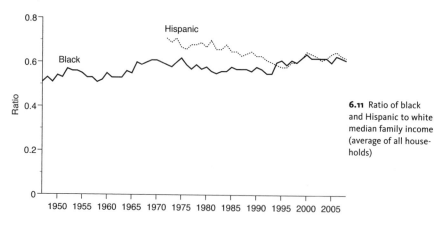

6.11 Ratio of black and Hispanic to white median family income (average of all households)

Source: Data elaborated from US Census Bureau, Current Population Survey, Annual Social and Economic Supplements, Table F-5: Race and Hispanic Origin of Householder – Families by Median and Mean Income: 1947 to 2008 (families as of March of the following year. Income in current and 2008 CPI-U-RS adjusted dollars)

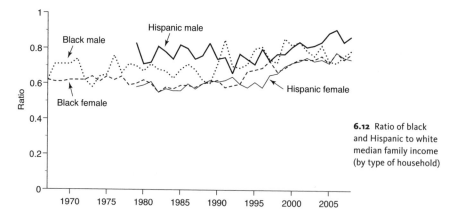

6.12 Ratio of black and Hispanic to white median family income (by type of household)

Source: Data elaborated from US Census Bureau, Current Population Survey, Annual Social and Economic Supplements, Table F-5: Race and Hispanic Origin of Householder – Families by Median and Mean Income: 1947 to 2008 (families as of March of the following year. Income in current and 2008 CPI-U-RS adjusted dollars)

Congress and the executive branch are jointly charged with setting tax policy. The IRS, according to the Freedom of Information Act, is charged with providing information about tax policy to the public. The Congressional Budget Office (CBO) and the IRS together produce annual statistics, particularly on tax progressivity, that are available to the public, but do not include information about corporate income, estate tax or payroll taxes. Other than Congress, there exists the IRS Oversight Board as well as National Taxpayer Advocate, an independent federal agency which acts as a watchdog over the IRS. The Advocate reports to Congress twice a year on significant issues affecting taxpayers, the IRS and complications in the tax code.

In her report to Congress, National Taxpayer Advocate Nina Olson focused on issues of transparency. In addressing the complexity and opaque nature of US tax codes, Olson juxtaposed the difficulty of ordinary taxpayers in navigating tax provisions with the ease with which those who are able to afford accountants – particularly corporations – are able to reduce their tax contributions. Olson (2007: 2–3) notes:

> The complexity of the tax code is a driver of noncompliance because it creates loopholes that aggressive taxpayers can exploit. Corporate tax shelters and abusive schemes pursued by individual taxpayers exist largely because of ambiguities in the law. Tax law or procedural complexity is also responsible for the significant majority of taxpayer reporting errors. For taxpayers seeking to exploit loopholes, complexity presents countless opportunities. Many law firms, accounting firms, and investment banking firms have made tens of millions of dollars by scouring the Code for ambiguities and then advising taxpayers to enter into transactions, with differing levels of business purpose or economic substance, to take advantage of those ambiguities.
>
> The IRS devotes significant resources to identifying these transactions and challenging them, where appropriate, but many are legitimate under existing law and many more fall into a grey area. A simpler tax code could reduce these administrative challenges enormously. Moreover, traditional economic analysis focuses on the goals of equity and efficiency in writing the tax laws. To those, one should add transparency. To the extent revision of the Code [is] to provide greater transparency of payments of income without imposing undue burden on taxpayers, the higher compliance rates associated with third party information reporting can be more readily achieved in a broader array of transactions.

Olson argues for changes in tax law that would ensure that the tax payment is more evenly shared. As Figure 6.8 indicates, there has been a serious decrease in tax revenue owing primarily to the reduction in the share of tax contributions of the wealthiest individuals. Avi-Yonah and Clausing (2007: 1) note that:

> [t]he current system of taxing the income of multinational firms in the United States is flawed across multiple dimensions. The system provides an artificial tax incentive to earn income in low tax countries, rewards aggressive tax planning, and is not compatible with any common metrics of efficiency. The US system is also notoriously complex; observers are nearly unanimous in lamenting the heavy compliance burdens and the impracticality of coherent enforcement. Further, despite a corporate tax rate one standard deviation above that of other OECD countries, the US corporate tax system raises relatively little revenue, due in part to the shifting of income outside the US tax base.

In Figure 6.13, we see the ability of business to avoid paying their share of

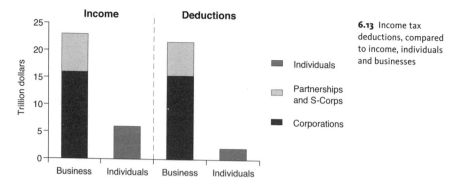

6.13 Income tax deductions, compared to income, individuals and businesses

Source: TRAC IRS (2007) *Graphical Highlights: Income and Deductions on Federal Federal Returns Tax Year 2002,* trac.syr.edu/tracirs/trends/v10/corpvsindreceipts.html

tax contribution by availing themselves of tax loopholes. Corporate deductions are 96.8 per cent of income versus only 26.6 per cent for individuals.

In addition, the audits of corporations have reduced dramatically over time and there has been a decrease in the penalties levied against corporations for negligence and fraud. Though there has been a slight increase in audits since 2004, it is not at all near the levels of the 1990s.

There is certainly citizen participation in setting tax policy to the extent that members of Congress are citizens themselves. In addition, there is a degree of public accountability in tax policy to the extent that there is congressional and independent oversight of the IRS. Yet the relatively few members of Congress who create and oversee tax policy do not alone satisfy the principle of public participation and accountability. In addition, while independent oversight organizations are a step in the right direction, such principles cannot be satisfied without the broader participation of average citizens. Perhaps the

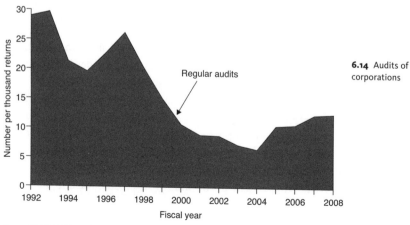

6.14 Audits of corporations

Source: TRAC IRS (2009)

Negligence

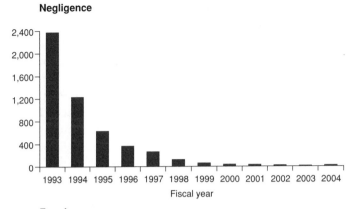

Fraud

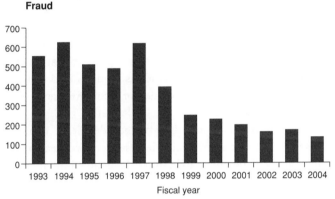

6.15 Number of civil penalties against corporations

Source: TRAC IRS (2007) *Civil Penalties Assessed to Corporations against Tax Fraud and Negligence of the IRS*, trac.syr.edu/tracirs/trends/v10/corpfraud.html

biggest barrier to broad public participation in the development of tax policy is the lack of transparency in the tax system.

The data and reports that are made available by Congress and the IRS are often overly complex and extremely difficult for the common citizen to comprehend. While there are several civil society tax justice groups and policy think tanks that analyse and report on such data in accessible language, they are neither founded nor funded by the government in an effort to meet its obligations of transparency, accountability and participation to taxpaying residents. Indeed, without such groups, the legal mechanisms made possible by the tax structure would likely go unnoticed, allowing corporations and the very wealthy to continue to gain from a system that is tilted to their benefit, while the lower income groups continue to foot the bill and enable the government to fulfil its economic and social obligations towards its citizens.

Conclusions/recommendations

States must ensure non-discrimination and equality in taxation by prohibiting state and local governments from, for example, placing high rates of taxation on sales of items that are disproportionately consumed by the poor. States must recompense for past instances of discrimination and inequality through programmes that advantage the poor until they have achieved economic and social equality. States must eliminate tax loopholes and credits that benefit the richer echelons of society.

In the case of personal income taxes, non-discrimination requires that a higher share of revenue should come from men than from women. Elson (2006: 81) notes that 'the principle of "ability to pay" in taxation implies that men's share should be higher because their share of total taxable income is higher than that of women'. Temporary tax policies should include VAT and sales tax exemptions on items that are disproportionately consumed by poor racial and ethnic minorities; a lower personal income tax for poorer racial and ethnic minorities.

States should hold on to tax revenues in times of boom in order to better respond in time of crisis by expanding expenditure to provide for minimum essential rights for poor people. The state's human rights obligation with respect to taxation at the national, state and local levels requires it to maintain maximum available resources in order to provide for economic and social rights in times of both boom and bust.

In the current debate on reducing the US budget deficit, a focus on taxation to support use of the maximum available resources will lead to the design of a tax policy that will be more effective at meeting human rights obligations.

Notes

1 For an explanation of Medicare, see Chapter 4.

2 See ICESCR Part II, Article 2, para. 1.

3 Committee on ESCR, General Comment 3, para. 2.

4 Ibid., para. 13.

5 In Maastricht Guidelines, Part II, para. 8.

6 Data available at www.bea.gov/national/nipaweb/TableView.asp?SelectedTable=5&ViewSeries=NO&Java=no&Request3Place=N&3Place=N&FromView=YES&Freq=Year&FirstYear=1975&LastYear=2007&3Place=N&Update=Update&JavaBox=no#Mid.

7 The US percentage was 28.3 in 2007 compared to 48.2 in Sweden.

8 Tax rates have gone from 52 per cent in 1969 to 35 per cent by 2010; www.taxpolicycenter.org/taxfacts/content/pdf/corporate_historical_bracket.pdf.

9 Committee on ESCR, General Comment 16, Part II(B)(1).

10 Ibid., Part II(B)(3).

11 Alaska, Delaware, Hawaii, Montana, New Hampshire and Oregon do not apply sales taxes.

12 International Committee on ESCR, General Comment 16, Part II(B)(1).

13 Ibid., Part II(B)(3).

14 Ibid., Part II(B)(2).

15 The data used in the graph include individual and corporate income, estate and payroll taxes.

References

American Convention on Human Rights (1969) 'Pact San Jose', Inter-American Specialized Conference on Human Rights, Organization of American States, November.

Avi-Yonah, R. S. and K. Clausing (2007) 'A proposal to adopt formulary apportionment for corporate income taxation: the Hamilton Project', University of Michigan John M. Olin Center for Law and Economics Working Paper, April.

Balakrishnan, R. et al. (2007) 'Realizing economic and social rights: a comparative country study', Concept Paper, Cuernavaca, Mexico, January.

Barnett, K. and C. Grown (2004) 'Gender impacts of government revenue collection: the case of taxation', Commonwealth Secretariat.

Budget of the US Government FY 2006 (2006) *Historical Tables*, Executive Office of the President of the United States, Office of Management and Budget, www.white-house.gov/omb/budget/fy2006/sheets/hist02z3.xls.

— (2009) *Historical Tables*, Executive Office of the President of the United States, Office of Management and Budget, www.white-house.gov/omb/budget/Historicals/.

Bureau of Economic Analysis (2010) *National Income and Product Accounts Tables*, www.bea.gov/national/index.htm.

CESCR (Committee on Economic, Social and Cultural Rights) (1966) International Convention on Civil and Political Rights, Resolution 2200A (XXI) of December 1966, entry into force March 1976, in accordance with Article 49, www.escr-net.org/resources_more/resources_more_show.htm?doc_id=425510.

— (2005a) General Comment 3, www.escr-net.org/resources_more/resources_more_show.htm?doc_id=425215.

— (2005b) General Comment 16, www.unhchr.ch/tbs/doc.nsf/(Symbol)/E.C.12.2005.4.En?Opendocument.

De Schutter, O. (2009) 'Report of the Social Rapporteur on the Right to Food', Human Rights Council, 13th Session, Agenda item 3, United Nations (A//HRC/13/33/Add.6).

Elson, D. (2006) *Budgeting for Women's Rights: Monitoring Government Budgets for Compliance with CEDAW*, UNIFEM.

Ettlinger, M. and M. Linden (2009) 'Who is to blame for the deficit number?', Mimeo, Centre for American Progress, 25 August.

Friedman, J. (2003) 'The decline of corporate income tax revenues', Center on Budget and Policy Priorities, October.

ITEP (Institute on Taxation and Economic Policy) (2003) 'Who pays? A distributional analysis of the tax systems in all 50 states', 2nd edn, November, www.gacurb.org/reports/revenue_itepstudy.pdf.

— (2009) 'Who pays? A distributional analysis of the tax systems in all 50 states', 3rd edn, November, www.itepnet.org/whopays3.pdf.

Kunnemann, R. (1995) 'A coherent approach to human rights', *Human Rights Quarterly*, 17(2), May.

Maastricht Guidelines (1997) *Maastricht Guidelines on Violations of Economic, Social and Cultural Rights*, Maastricht, 22–26 January, www1.umn.edu/humanrts/instree/Maastrichtguidelines_.html.

McNaughton, G. (2007) *Concepts of Equality in Law*, Mimeo.

Nelson, J. (1996) *Feminism, Objectivity, and Economics*, London: Routledge.

OECD (2009) *Factbook 2009: Economic, Environmental and Social Statistics*, www.oecd-ilibrary.org/economics/oecd-factbook-2009_factbook-2009-en.

Olson, N. (2007) *Written Statement of Nina E. Olson, National Taxpayer Advocate, before the Committee on the Budget, US House of Representatives, on the IRS and the Tax Gap*, February.

Piketty, T. and E. Saez (2007) 'How progressive is the US federal tax system? A historical and international perspective', *Journal of Economic Perspectives*, 21(1): 3–24.

Price, L. (2006) 'The boom that wasn't', Economic Policy Institute (EPI) Briefing Paper, March.

Roach, B. (2003) 'Progressive and regressive taxation in the United States: who's really paying (and not paying) their fair share?', Global Development and Environment Institute Working Paper no. 03-10, October.

Robertson, R. E. (1994) 'Measuring state compliance with the obligation to devote the "maximum available resources" to realizing economic, social, and cultural rights', *Human Rights Quarterly*, 16(4).

Sepulveda, M. (2003) *The Nature of Obligations under the International Covenant on Economic Social and Cultural Rights*, Intersentia.

Stotsky, J. G. (1996) 'Gender bias in tax systems', IMF Working Paper WP/96/99, September.

TRAC IRS (2009) *Graphical Highlights*, TRAC Reports, Inc., trac.syr.edu/tracirs/highlights/current/.

Türk, D. (1992) 'The realization of economic,

social and cultural rights, Special Rapporteur on Economic and Social Rights', Final report submitted to the UN Commission on Human Rights (E/CN.4/Sub.2/1992/16).

UNDP (1991) *Human Development Report*, New York: Oxford University Press for the United Nations Development Programme.

— (2010) 'Gender equality and poverty reduction: taxation', *Issues Brief*, 1, United Nations Development Programme, April.

US Census Bureau (2008) Current Population Survey 2008, Annual Social and Economic Supplement, Poverty Tables, www.census.gov/hhes/www/cpstables/032010/pov/toc.htm.

7 | TRADE POLICY AND HUMAN RIGHTS: MEXICO

Alberto Serdan-Rosales and Carlos Salas

Introduction

Comprehensive trade liberalization began in Mexico with accession to the General Agreement on Tariffs and Trade in January 1986. Prior to that Mexico had in 1965 instituted special trade rules to promote labour-intensive assembly plants that imported most of their inputs and exported all of their output (the maquiladora or maquila factories).[1] Initially the maquilas (which are mainly foreign owned) were confined to the northern states that border the USA, under the Border Industrialization Program. They were allowed to import inputs duty free from the USA, and when the final products were then exported to the USA, US import duties were levied only on the value added.[2] In the early 1970s, some of the location restrictions on the maquila were relaxed and they could expand to other states. All location restrictions had disappeared by the early 1990s.

In 1994 the Mexican government embarked on a policy of intensive trade liberalization for the whole economy, with the signing of the North American Free Trade Agreement with the USA and Canada, and by 2005 had twelve international free trade agreements with forty-two countries. Mexico is also a member of the World Trade Organization. NAFTA eliminated import duties and import quotas[3] on trade between the three countries. More than one half of the value of the trade between the three countries was already exempt from tariffs when NAFTA took effect; and other tariffs and quotas were scheduled to be phased out immediately or over five, ten or fifteen years. The last remaining trade restrictions on a handful of agricultural commodities, such as US exports to Mexico of corn, dry edible beans, non-fat dry milk and high-fructose corn syrup, and Mexican exports to the United States of sugar and certain horticultural products, were removed as of 1 January 2008 (USDA 2008).

NAFTA also included a number of side agreements, relating to the rights of business and labour, and the scope of domestic policy. In this it was in line with many other recent international trade agreements, which have broadened the scope of such agreements to include many other things besides import controls. NAFTA has hundreds of pages referring to non-trade policies to which all signatory parties must conform. For that reason, it is as much a cross-border investment agreement as a trade agreement. For example, Chapter

11, dealing with rights of cross-border investors, puts limits on environmental protections, service sector regulation, investment and development policy, and government procurement preferences. NAFTA also required Mexico to change its Constitution to permit foreign investors to purchase land.

According to Moreno-Brid et al. (2005), the Mexican government had the following aims in signing NAFTA:

> NAFTA was seen as a vehicle to achieve two goals. The first was to set the Mexican economy on a non-inflationary, export-led growth path driven by sales of manufactured goods, mainly to the United States. The underlying assumption was that NAFTA ... would encourage local and foreign investment in the production of tradable goods to exploit Mexico's potential as an export platform to the United States. The rapid expansion of Mexico's manufacturing sector – which would allegedly occur, stimulated by exports of labour-intensive products – would then pull the rest of the domestic economy onto a trajectory of high and persistent growth ... The second – and politically decisive – objective was to guarantee the lock-in of Mexico's macroeconomic reform process. Indeed, the government of President Salinas (1988–94) claimed that NAFTA imposed international legal and extra-legal constraints that would deter any attempt by subsequent governments in Mexico to return to trade protectionism.

The text of NAFTA claims that all three countries and the people who live in them will benefit, as the agreement will:

> strengthen the special bonds of friendship and cooperation among their nations; contribute to the harmonious development and expansion of world trade and provide a catalyst to broader international cooperation; ... create new employment opportunities and improve working conditions and living standards in their respective territories; ... preserve their flexibility to safeguard the public welfare; promote sustainable development; and protect, enhance and enforce basic workers' rights. (NAFTA 1993)

Mainstream economic theory certainly promotes the idea that there are gains from trade liberalization based on specialization according to comparative advantage. A country is assumed to have a comparative advantage in the production of products that more intensively use the factor of production with which it is relatively richly endowed. Thus Mexico is assumed to have a comparative advantage in the production of labour-intensive goods (that is, Mexico can produce them relatively cheaply), and the USA and Canada in the production of capital-intensive goods (that is, the USA and Canada can produce them relatively cheaply). Countries should reduce barriers to trade that protect relatively high-cost industries, and import at lower prices from the international market. Deraniyagala (2005: 99–105) summarizes the theory as consisting of the following propositions:

free trade optimizes global resource allocation; free trade maximizes consumer welfare; free trade leads to increased productivity growth and promotes economic growth; government intervention on trade policies is generally distortionary, reducing welfare and growth; countries with liberal trade regimes grow faster than countries with closed regimes; trade liberalization, by lowering tariffs and non-tariff barriers should be the focus of trade policy.

It is acknowledged that trade liberalization produces losers as well as winners, and that the gains from trade are not equally shared, neither within nor between countries. For instance, the gains consist of cheaper goods (if imports are cheaper than home production) and more employment in production of exports (if exports expand). The losses consist of loss of employment in production that can no longer compete with imports, and loss of tax revenue to fund public services, since trade liberalization implies cutting taxes on trade (i.e. import tariffs). The theory of trade liberalization assumes that in the long run full employment prevails, and that resources, including labour, will be reallocated from non-competitive sectors to competitive sectors.

This theory does recognize that in the short run there will be costs in restructuring the economy and reallocating resources to more competitive industries; as argued by Bhaduri (2005: 71–3), these costs are likely to be greater when trade is liberalized between developed and developing countries. Action by the state is fundamental to reducing the adjustment costs, and the claim that ultimately everyone can gain from free trade depends on the state acting to compensate the losses of any who are adversely impacted by restructuring.

According to mainstream economists, NAFTA should have led to an overall improvement in employment and the general standard of living in Mexico, by giving incentives to produce more efficiently and promoting faster economic growth. Mexico would be able to reap these gains because of its geographical position as a neighbour of the USA and its lower costs in manufacturing industries, owing to its cheaper labour.

In this chapter, we examine the maquila industries and NAFTA in particular, and trade liberalization in general, in the light of the human rights principles of progressive realization, equality and non-discrimination, and minimum core obligations to secure essential levels of economic and social rights. Trade policy has implications for the whole range of economic and social rights; in this chapter we consider trade policy in relation to the right to work (ICESCR Article 6); the right to just and favourable conditions of work (ICESCR Article 7); and the right to an adequate standard of living (ICESCR Article 11), with a particular focus on the right to food. The chapter does not aim to present a comprehensive study of the impact of NAFTA. We examine results in the realization of the rights to work and to food that can reasonably be considered related to NAFTA as a way of cross-checking the conduct of trade policy. If NAFTA had been followed by improvements in the enjoyment of these (and other) rights, there would not be the degree of concern about its impact that now exists in all three countries that are party to it.

Progressive realization, with respect to the right to work and to just and favourable conditions of work

Obligation of conduct Mainstream economic theory suggests that trade liberalization will in general promote the progressive realization of these rights, but recognizes that some workers may lose jobs as an immediate effect of trade liberalization, and that there may be pressure in a period of restructuring on terms and conditions of work. NAFTA does include a side agreement, the North American Agreement on Labour Cooperation (NAALC), which is supposed to safeguard labour rights. Its main provisions are shown in Table 7.1, together with the enforcement mechanisms. The text of NAALC claims it is intended to 'improve working conditions and living standards in each Party's territory; promote, to the maximum extent possible, the labour principles set out in [this agreement] ...' (NAALC 1993). As Bolle (2001: 2) notes: 'This was the first labour side agreement ever attached to a trade agreement [and] marked the first time that workers' rights considerations were ever linked to a trade agreement in more than just a passing manner.'

However, as Bolle (ibid.: 8) points out, for some groups 'NAALC falls short of the original plan ... they argue that NAALC does not go nearly far enough in protecting workers: If workers were granted status equal to that of the goods they produce, the workers' rights provisions would be in NAFTA and enforceable under it.' The enforcement mechanisms of NAALC are weak. Since 1994,

> under the labour side agreement, [only] 34 petitions have been submitted alleging noncompliance by one of the NAFTA countries with existing labour legislation, and 22 of these have been against Mexico, although some of the cases against the United States involve working conditions and compensation for migrant workers ... Eleven submissions against Mexico were advanced to the next stage of ministerial consultations. (Cook 2006: 5–6)

Unlike that of the USA, the government of Mexico did not conduct any official assessment of the likely impact of free trade on different social groups before signing NAFTA. It was expected that more jobs would be created in manufacturing; but there was a concern that Mexican small farmers would not be able to compete with the capital-intensive large-scale US farmers, who could produce staple crops like maize (corn) at considerably lower unit costs. Before the introduction of NAFTA, small farmers were receiving subsidized water and other inputs in maize production as well as benefiting from measures to support prices paid to Mexican farmers at levels higher than the world price of maize. US producers were selling maize at about half the price paid to farmers in Mexico. After NAFTA was introduced, there were sharp cuts in the farm subsidy programme for maize. The PROCAMPO programme

TABLE 7.1 NAALC's labour principles

Group and principles	Extent of enforceability
Group I 1. Freedom of association and protection of the right to organize; 2. The right to bargain collectively; and 3. The right to strike.	Enforceable by discussion of National Administrative Offices, Secretariat, and Ministerial Council.
Group II 1. Prohibition of forced labour; 2. Minimum employment standards pertaining to overtime pay; 3. Elimination of employment discrimination; 4. Equal pay for women and men; 5. Compensation in cases of occupational injuries and illnesses; and 6. Protection of migrant workers.	Enforceable by discussion as indicated for Group I plus evaluation by an Evaluation Committee of Experts.
Group III 1. Labour protections for children and young persons; 2. Minimum employment standards pertaining to minimum wages; and 3. Prevention of occupational injuries and illnesses.	Enforceable by discussion as for Group I, evaluation as for Group II, and sanctions determined by an Arbitral Panel.

Source: Bolle (2001: 4)

was created to mitigate some of the distributional effects of NAFTA reform. It was intended to provide a compensatory income transfer to producers of basic crops, including maize, beans, rice, wheat, sorghum, barley, soybeans and cotton. According to Saudalet and de Janvry (2001), '… the objectives were political (to manage the political acceptability of the free trade agreement among farmers), economic (to provide farmers with liquidity to adjust production to the new set of relative prices), and social (to prevent an increase in already extensive levels of poverty among smallholders and a rapid process of out-migration to the cities and the border in the North)'. The programme was designed to last for fifteen years, during which time transfers were to be given on a per-hectare basis, but could not be used to support the production of particular crops (King 2006: 9).

However, it was never adequately funded. During Zedillo's administration (1995–2000) the budget for PROCAMPO fell 6.2 per cent annually in real terms; and during Fox's presidency (2001–06), the budget for PROCAMPO decreased by 0.1 per cent annually on average. Under Zedillo, the subsidy

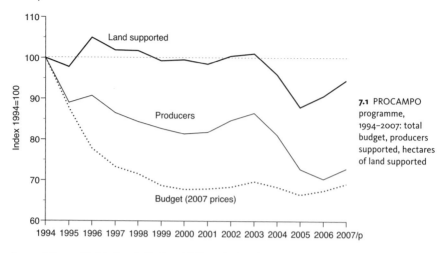

7.1 PROCAMPO programme, 1994–2007: total budget, producers supported, hectares of land supported

Source: Authors, with data from Calderón and Tykhonenko (2007) and Fox (2006)

per producer decreased by 2.9 per cent in real terms; under Fox it increased by 2.4 per cent, but the number of producers benefiting decreased by 2.3 per cent (Figures 7.1 and 7.2).

Not only was the PROCAMPO programme underfunded, in addition the Mexican government unilaterally decided to liberalize trade in maize (corn) faster than NAFTA required. NAFTA allowed for a gradual transition towards full liberalization of trade in maize, setting a quota for the amount that could be imported into Mexico duty free. Imports above this quota were to be subject to import duty that would gradually decrease over fifteen years and be eliminated in 2008, when free trade in maize would come into operation (King 2006: 9). Nevertheless, according to ANEC (2008), Mexican govern-

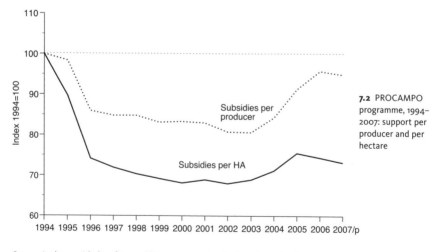

7.2 PROCAMPO programme, 1994–2007: support per producer and per hectare

Source: Authors, with data from Calderón and Tykhonenko (2007) and Fox (2006)

ments allowed duty-free imports from the USA well above the quota. ANEC estimates that not charging duty on all the imports above the quota meant that about $US3.8 billion tax revenue was lost by the Mexican governments over the period 1995–2006, reducing the capacity to compensate farmers.

Though not directly linked to NAFTA, there were some other programmes that helped low-income farmers. An example is the 'Support to Peasants Programme – *Programa de Jornaleros Agricolas*'. In 1995, this programme reached 309,238 peasants, rising to 558,946 peasants in 2006 (an increase of 80.7 per cent). However, in the same period, the budget for this programme decreased by 7.5 per cent in real terms. In 2006, its budget of $US12.8 million provided on average only $US1.9 per peasant each month, compared to $US3.7 per peasant each month in 1995.

The limited support available to those adversely affected by trade liberalization was noted in 1999 by the Committee on Economic, Social and Cultural Rights, in its comments on the Mexican *Third Periodic Report* on compliance with ICESCR:

> The Committee calls upon the State party, when negotiating with international financial institutions and implementing structural adjustment programs and macroeconomic policies affecting foreign debt servicing, integration into the global free market economy, etc., to take into account their effect on the enjoyment of economic, social and cultural rights, in particular for the most vulnerable groups of society. (CESCR 1999: para. 34)
>
> The Committee recommends that the State party continue to strengthen its efforts to alleviate any negative effects that the implementation of NAFTA might have on certain vulnerable sectors of the population. (Ibid.: para. 35)

In 2005, in their *Fourth Periodic Report*, the Mexican government stated:

> As is well known, notwithstanding the economic growth which has been observed following the entry into force of the North American Free Trade Agreement (NAFTA), there are still some inequalities between zones. NAFTA has succeeded in creating major poles of development, principally in border zones and in the center of the country; but other regions have remained marginalized from this growth. With a view to countering the negative effects of the free trade agreement, which in some regions of the country have become aggravated, the government of Mexico has taken measures consisting of the framing of comprehensive territorial development policies focusing on the combat against poverty and inequality. (CESCR 2005: para. 1140).

The government said it had created 'a regional development [section] in the National Development Plan 2001–2006'; an 'Office of Strategic Planning and Regional Development in the Office of the President of the Republic'; and the Puebla-Panama Plan, and the National Urban Development and Territorial Planning Programme (ibid.: paras 1141–2). However, by 2008 the

Office no longer existed, and the Puebla-Panama Plan had been replaced by the Mesoamérica Project, which did not mention anything about compensation schemes related to trade effects. There were no targeted programmes directed to those likely to be adversely affected by trade liberalization: Mexican medium and small producers of textiles, electronics, toys, metal goods, rice and wheat.

A North American Development Bank (NADB) had been brought into operation at the same time as NAFTA was signed. The NADB was created under the November 1993 Agreement between the Government of the United States of America and the Government of the United Mexican States Concerning the Establishment of a Border Environment Cooperation Commission and a North American Development Bank. The NADB included the US Community Adjustment and Investment Program (USCAIP) and the *Programa Complementario de Apoyo a Comunidades y Empresas* (Mexican CAIP) in order to assist US communities and the private sector in creating new jobs and preserving existing jobs in areas adjusting to changes in their economies as a result of NAFTA (USCAIP); and to support basic infrastructure development throughout Mexico, as well as to help communities and businesses benefit from NAFTA (Mexican CAIP). However, NADB operated only in Mexico's northern border states, while the need for infrastructure, and probably most of the negative impacts of trade liberalization, is in the southern states of Mexico.

In 1999 the Mexican CAIP was transferred from the NADB to the Banco Nacional de Obras y Servicios Públicos (Banobras – the Mexican development bank). According to the Office of Supreme Audit in Mexico (ASF 2007: 176–81), this programme was dissolved by the Mexican government on 26 March 2001 and replaced by the '*Programa de Operaciones de Apoyo para el Ajuste de Comunidades e Inversiones*'.[4] Neither programme appears in any of the annual reports of Banobras from 2003 to 2007 that are available on its web page (Banobras 2008). Moreover, neither the NADB nor Banobras has the resources of other development banks in the region. For instance, in 2006 the Banco Nacional de Desenvolvimento Econômico e Social (BNDES) of Brazil disbursed $24.1 billion while NADB and Banobras combined disbursed only $US1.8 billion. The NADB has failed to serve as a development bank and provider of adjustment assistance.

Obligation of result Gallagher and Zarsky (2004) summarize the results of the Mexican trade liberalization strategy thus:

> First, the integration strategy achieved many of its goals, including increasing FDI inflows, productivity and manufactured exports. However, the large growth of the manufacturing sector has generated a persistent – and growing – trade deficit. Exports grew fast but imports grew faster. Unbalanced import-dependence and the trade deficit it generates suggest that the integration strategy as currently constituted may not be financially or economically

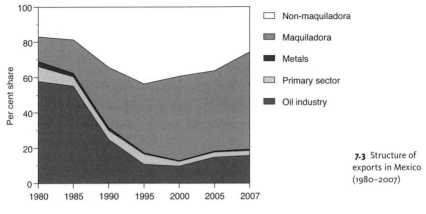

7.3 Structure of exports in Mexico (1980–2007)

Legend:
- Non-maquiladora
- Maquiladora
- Metals
- Primary sector
- Oil industry

Source: Banxico (2007)

sustainable in the long term ... Second, FDI-led integration with the regional and global economy has done little to promote sustainable industrial development in Mexico. Domestic growth and investment were stagnant and, except for a few 'bright spots', hoped-for spillovers, industrial restructuring, job growth, and environmental improvements did not materialize. Relying heavily on cheap labour and imports for productive inputs, the foreign manufacturing sector remains largely disconnected from the domestic Mexican economy.

While in 1980 the manufacturing sector represented just 30.8 per cent of total exports, in 2007 it represented 80.8 per cent. This growth was powered by the maquila sector, which accounts for a growing proportion of exports, as shown in Figure 7.3.

The manufacturing sector became more export-oriented after NAFTA; while in 1994 exports represented 11.8 per cent of the entire manufacturing production in Mexico, in 2002 they represented 20 per cent. The domination of the maquilas means that the net value of manufacturing exports is much less than the gross value. The value added to the total export maquila production has decreased over time: while in 1990 the value added represented 20 per cent of the total production in the export maquila sector, in 2004 it was only 8 per cent. In the same period, the usage of goods produced in Mexico by the maquila sector did not increase much; while in 1990 the national supplies represented 1.7 of the total production of the export maquila sector, in 2004 they represented only 3.6 per cent (BIE–INEGI 2008, in Esquinca 2008).

In the period 1995–2000, there was a rapid increase in manufacturing jobs, especially in automobiles, clothing and electronics. Automobiles benefited from the creation of a single market for auto assembly and auto parts, comprising all three partner countries. NAFTA gave a particular boost to maquila production of clothing, because it ended tariffs on the export of clothing from Mexico to the USA if all components were of NAFTA country origin, and it also relaxed or eliminated many quota restrictions on clothing imports, while exports of clothing from other low-wage countries remained subject to tariffs and limited by quotas until the end of the Multi Fibre Arrangement (MFA) in 2005. Clothing sector companies from around the world relocated some of their operations to Mexico to take advantage of entry to the US market (Canas and Gilmer 2009). In electronics, jobs increased despite the provisions of NAFTA Article 303, which required Mexico to charge import duties on components from non-NAFTA countries. Mexico countered Article 303 by selectively lowering the duty on import components that came mainly from Asia (ibid.).

The growth of jobs was not sustained into the twenty-first century, and by 2008 manufacturing employment had fallen to more or less the level achieved in 1997. Since its peak in 2000, manufacturing had lost 1.04 million permanent jobs by March 2009, 25 per cent of the total (Peters 2009: 27–8). This was not the result of trade policy in itself; among the factors responsible were the overvalued exchange rate (the result of central bank policy, as discussed in Chapter 1); and competition from China. After China became a member of the WTO in 2001, Chinese exports to the USA were subject to lower import duties; and the ending of the MFA in 2005 meant that there were no longer quota restrictions on imports of clothing from China into the USA. Chinese exports displaced Mexican exports in the US market, and Mexico's share of manufacturing imports into the USA fell from around 80 per cent in the 1990s to 45 per cent in November 2008 (ibid.: 29). This shows that trade liberalization by itself cannot be relied upon to create employment on a sustainable basis. There needs to be investment in technical innovations and productivity improvements. Had NADB been able to play the role of a real development bank, it might have been able to support the creation of more sustainable manufacturing employment.

In agriculture, as had been expected, imports of some major staple crops increased, as Mexican smallholders were unable to compete with large-scale US farmers using modern technology. Maize imports accounted for 9.8 per cent of domestic consumption in the period 1990–93 and 28.3 per cent in the period 2002–05. Wheat imports amounted to 18.8 per cent of domestic consumption in the period 1990–93 and 55.3 per cent in the period 2002–05. Imports of rice and soya also rose as a share of domestic consumption; in contrast, the share of imports in consumption of bean stayed much the same, and for sorghum and barley the share of imports fell (see Table 7.2).

Agricultural productivity fell. According to Calva, Schwentesius and Gómez-Cruz (cited in Pacheco 2005: 335), agricultural GDP per capita in the period 2000–02 was 1.5 per cent less than in the period 1991–93 and 13.1 per cent less than in the period 1980–82. Furthermore, per capita production of the eight most important grains in the period 2000–02 was 4.2 per cent less than in the period 1991–93 and 14.8 per cent less than in the period 1980–82. Some Mexican farmers were able to increase exports of fruit and vegetables

TABLE 7.2 Imports as a share of the domestic consumption of staple foods, Mexico (1990–2005) (%)

Period	Beans	Wheat	Maize	Rice	Sorghum	Soya	Barley	Average
90–93	5.90	18.80	9.80	34.90	45.30	71.90	14.20	28.70
94–97	5.90	30.80	15.10	42.10	33.20	92.20	33.10	36.10
98–01	10.90	46.10	24.00	62.30	41.80	96.90	26.00	44.00
02–05	6.00	55.30	28.30	72.80	36.90	96.70	7.00	43.30

Source: Authors, with data from Bancomext and SIAP/SAGARPA in ANEC (2008)

to the USA, but these were better-off farmers located in a small number of states with relatively good infrastructure and used to modern technology. Their success did not outweigh the adverse impact of NAFTA on smallholder maize farmers. Two million jobs were lost in agriculture: in 1995 the agricultural sector employed 7.8 million people while in 2007 it employed only 5.8 million (STPS 2008, in Esquinca 2008).

The failure of NAFTA to support progressive realization of the right to work on a sustainable basis is demonstrated by the increase in migration from Mexico to the USA. One of the arguments put forward by proponents of NAFTA was that it would create jobs in Mexico and reduce migration. But the reverse happened. CONAPO (2007) estimates that migration from Mexico to the USA increased by 133 per cent between the periods 1987–92 and 1997–2002. Passel (2005: 16) estimates that the number of unauthorized Mexican migrants to the USA increased from 40,000 every year on average between 1980 and 1984 to 485,000 between 2000 and 2004. According to Passel, the total Mexican-born population in the USA dramatically increased from 760,000 in 1970, to 2.2 million in 1980, to 10.6 million in 2004. According to the American Community Survey, in 2006 this figure reached 11.5 million, of which 28.1 per cent had entered the USA after 2000 and 34 per cent had entered between 1990 and 1999. An increasing number of migrants came from states that had not historically had high rates of migration, but which had been hard hit by NAFTA's impact on small farmers.

Not only did trade liberalization fail to support progressive realization of the right to work, it also failed to support progressive realization of the right to just and favourable conditions of work. Real wages in the manufacturing sector fell, on average, 8.1 per cent between 1994 and 2006. The financial crisis (the so-called Tequila Crisis) in 1995 is likely to have been mainly responsible for the sharp fall, but even after the economy had recovered, by 2004 manufacturing real wages had not recovered to the levels of the 1994. The case of the clothing and auto parts industries is enlightening. Those sectors experienced job creation between 1995 and 2000, but wages did not

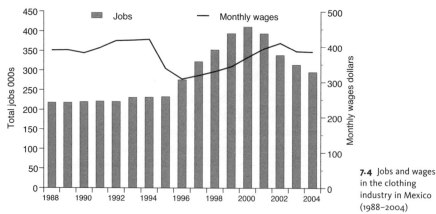

7.4 Jobs and wages in the clothing industry in Mexico (1988–2004)

Source: Authors, using data from BIE–INEGI (2007)

recover to the levels they had enjoyed before the Tequila Crisis, as shown in Figures 7.4 and 7.5.

As Sandra Polaski (2004: 9) states: 'It is striking that a free-trade agreement that dramatically increased exports and foreign direct investment has not done more to increase wages and living standards for average Mexican workers – or even for workers in most export firms – relative to pre-NAFTA levels.' The fall in real wages in the manufacturing sector cannot be explained by a drop in the manufacturing sector's productivity. On the contrary, the productivity of this sector has been increasing over time (see Figure 7.6). Between 1994 and 2004 productivity grew 25.6 per cent and real wages dropped 8.2 per cent in the same period. This phenomenon of productivity growing faster than wages occurs in sixty-two (89 per cent) of the seventy economic sectors into which the Mexican economy is divided. In contrast, wages grew more than

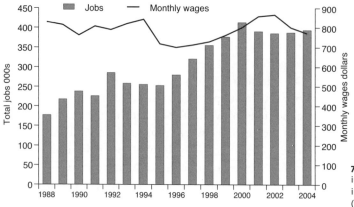

7.5 Jobs and wages in the auto parts industry in Mexico (1988–2004)

Source: Authors, using data from BIE–INEGI (2007)

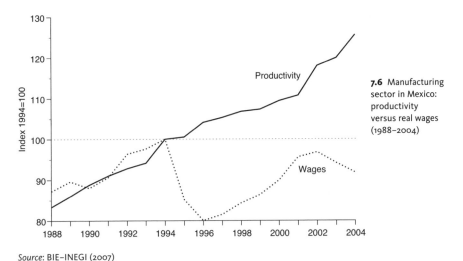

7.6 Manufacturing sector in Mexico: productivity versus real wages (1988–2004)

Source: BIE–INEGI (2007)

productivity in eight sectors (11 per cent), including public administration and defence, which are shielded from world markets.

It seems likely that this is the result of a deliberate policy to maintain labour costs in order to attract more investment and to compete in international markets. The result for the blue-collar workers is that they have not seen a progressive realization of their right to just and favourable conditions of work.

Non-discrimination and equality, with respect to the right to work and to just and favourable conditions of work

Obligations of conduct The principle of no discrimination is stated in Article 2 of the ICESCR: 'The States Parties to the present Covenant undertake to guarantee that the rights enunciated in the present Covenant will be exercised without discrimination of any kind as to race, colour, sex, language, religion, political or other opinion, national or social origin, property, birth or other status.'

According to the International Labour Organization (ILO 2007: 7):

There is consensus that discrimination at work is a violation of a human right that entails a waste of human talents, with detrimental effects on productivity and economic growth, and generates socioeconomic inequalities that undermine social cohesion and solidarity and act as a brake on the reduction of poverty. There is also agreement that promoting equality of opportunity and equality of treatment is necessary in order to move towards the elimination of discrimination in law and in practice.

Consequently, equality is not just about prohibiting discrimination; it is about transforming labour policy to make it more inclusive and fair.

Most of the trade liberalization measures that were introduced in Mexico from 1986 onwards had no mention of non-discrimination and equality. However, NAFTA was an exception. On the surface it might seem that NAFTA does comply with the principle of non-discrimination and equality between different social groups. As shown in Table 7.1, the side agreement on labour (NAALC) did mention elimination of employment discrimination and equal pay for women and men. However, to ensure non-discrimination, governments must carry out policies not only to protect and respect but also to fulfil the human rights of specific social groups that have been traditionally left behind. Consequently, equality is not just about prohibiting formal discrimination; it is about transforming labour policy to make it more inclusive and fair. There is no provision in NAALC requiring this kind of proactive policy and no powerful enforcement mechanism for the provisions on non-discrimination and equality.

Moreover, it was foreseen that NAFTA would have an adverse impact on the livelihoods of rural people (among whom indigenous groups are over-represented), whose wages already lagged behind those of manufacturing workers.

There would be less reason for concern at the lack attention to non-discrimination if gaps between wages and employment of different social groups most affected by NAFTA had narrowed. For that reason we examine evidence on some relevant gaps.

Obligations of result This gap between the average wages of manufacturing and agricultural workers has historically been increasing, and the trend has deepened since trade liberalization. In 1988 average monthly real wages in the manufacturing sector were 13.2 times higher than in agriculture. In 1994, manufacturing wages were 20.8 times higher than in agriculture, and in 2004 they were 25.7 times higher. In other words, in 1994, on average, every worker in the manufacturing sector received US$822 in real terms every month, while

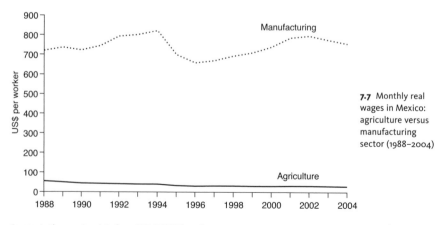

7.7 Monthly real wages in Mexico: agriculture versus manufacturing sector (1988–2004)

Source: Authors, using data from BIE–INEGI (2007)

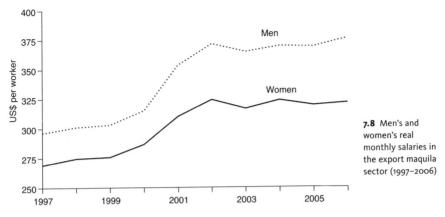

7.8 Men's and women's real monthly salaries in the export maquila sector (1997–2006)

Source: Authors, using data from BIE-INEGI (2007)

an agricultural worker received US$40 ($1.3 a day) on average. In 2004 every worker in the manufacturing sector received on average US$755 monthly while an agriculture worker received only $US29, which is less than a dollar per day (see Figure 7.7).

But even within the manufacturing sector, social inequalities have deepened. For instance, the gender wage gap among blue-collar workers (*obreros*) in the maquila factories has grown, as shown in Figure 7.8. In real terms, in 1997[5] monthly salaries of blue-collar men in the maquila factories were $US27 higher than the monthly salaries of blue-collar women. In 2006, they were $US55 higher. The salaries of both men and women have increased since 1997 in real terms, but men's salaries increased by 27 per cent and women's salaries by only 19 per cent.

Regional inequalities have also grown in monthly wages in the maquila export sector, as shown in Figure 7.9. On average, during the period 1981–93

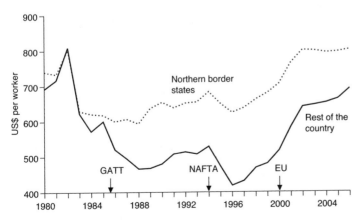

7.9 Monthly real wages in the export maquila sector (1980–2006)

Source: Authors, using data from BIE–INEGI (2007)

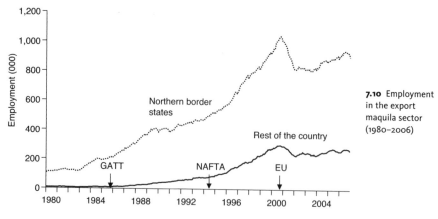

7.10 Employment in the export maquila sector (1980–2006)

Source: Authors, with data from BIE–INEGI (2007)

the monthly real wage of a worker in the maquila factories in the northern border states was $US89 higher than that of the worker in the maquila factories in the rest of the country. In the period 1994–2006, the average real monthly wage of a maquila worker in the northern border states was $US169 higher than that of a maquila worker in the rest of the country. The number of maquila jobs in the rest of the country increased more rapidly after the introduction of NAFTA, but still remains well below the number in the northern border states (as shown in Figure 7.10).

On average, in every year during the period 1981–93 there were 261,415 more jobs in the northern border states than in the rest of the country. In the period 1994–2006, the difference between the northern border states and the rest of the country had grown to 580,298 jobs.

We should note that wages in the maquila sector are lower than in the manufacturing sector as a whole. In 1990 each worker earned $US722 per month in the manufacturing sector, 1.5 times the value of the monthly earnings of a worker in the export maquila sector ($US497). By 2004 the gap had shrunk only slightly despite expansion of jobs in the maquila sector: the average monthly wages of a worker in the manufacturing sector were 1.4 times the wage of an export maquila sector worker.

The non-discrimination provisions in NAFTA have not been matched by a reduction in wage inequalities by sector, gender and location, in sectors most closely related to international trade.

Minimum core obligations to ensure a minimum level of enjoyment of key rights: the right to food

Obligation of conduct The state has an obligation to ensure a minimum level of enjoyment of key rights, such as the right to food. The right to food is mentioned in the Universal Declaration of Human Rights (UDHR) Article 25: 'Everyone has the right to a standard of living adequate for the health and well-being of himself and his family, including food, clothing, housing and medical care.' The International Covenant on Economic, Social and Cultural Rights (ICESCR) identifies the right to food as part of the right to an adequate standard of living.

The UN has appointed a Special Rapporteur on the right to food who has further clarified its meaning:

> The right to food is the right to have regular, permanent and unrestricted access, either directly or by means of financial purchases, to quantitatively and qualitatively adequate and sufficient food corresponding to the cultural traditions of the people to which the consumer belongs, and which ensures physical and mental, individual and collective, fulfilling and dignified life free of fear. (Ziegler 2006: 4)

NAFTA might be expected to help realize the right by lowering the price of food through imports of lower-cost food from the USA, thus improving financial access; but we also have to ask whether there were any other provisions in NAFTA that might jeopardize the safety and nutritional content of food.[6]

Obligations of result While the general level of inflation fell in the period after the introduction of NAFTA, the rate of increase in the prices of the staple foods, tortilla, bread and cereals, was higher than the general level of inflation. For example, in the month of December 1995, the Consumer Price Index (CPI) rose by 52 per cent, but the prices of tortilla, bread and cereals increased by 79 per cent. In the period January 1994 to June 2008, prices of tortilla, bread and cereals rose faster than the CPI in 127 months out of 174 (73 per cent of the time); while between January 1974 and June 1988, the prices of tortilla, bread and cereals rose at a faster rate than the CPI only 38 per cent of the time. This happened despite a substantial increase in imports of maize and wheat (Figure 7.11). We should note that many US agribusiness

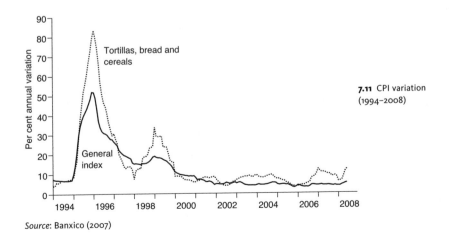

7.11 CPI variation (1994–2008)

Source: Banxico (2007)

TABLE 7.3 Average CPI of selected products with reference to the general index (1980–2008)

	1980–84	1985–89	1990–94	1995–99	2000–04	2005–08
All foods	115.1	114.1	105.7	106.2	101.5	106.5
Tortillas, bread and cereals	75.3	85.2	82.7	93.9	102	114.8
Fruits and vegetables	78.4	69.5	82.8	89.7	97.8	100.1
Tomatoes	62.6	56	68	81.7	101.5	104.3
Processed soups	117.8	116.8	122.9	123.1	101.7	95.4
Meat	170.8	170.3	147	122.9	103.5	107.3
Junk food	126.4	143.2	113	110.8	103.2	102.8
Medicines	56.1	66.2	54.6	81.9	101.6	111.5
Education	67.5	65.7	84.9	90	100.6	111.4
Shoes and clothing	140.3	142.6	110	101	98.7	87.2
Electric and electronic equipment	260.5	219	136.3	126.4	100.8	78.8
Automobiles	147.8	190.7	130.4	127.3	101.2	86.5
Furniture	157.5	152.9	119.2	108.7	100.7	90.8
Entertainment: toys, photographic equipment, sports supplies, music	152.3	154.7	118.3	111.5	100.5	85.4

Source: Authors, using data from Banxico 2008, and BIE–INEGI (2007)

multinationals bought corn-processing or tortilla-making factories in Mexico after the signing of NAFTA.

A more detailed view of trends in relative prices is provided by Table 7.3. Whereas the average levels of consumer prices of tortillas, bread and cereals, and of fruits and vegetables, have increased relative to the general level of consumer prices, the average prices of meat and 'junk' food have declined relative to the general level of prices. The average levels of prices of medicines and educational products have also risen relative to the general level of prices, whereas the prices of shoes and clothing, electric and electronic equipment, automobiles and entertainment goods have all fallen relative to the general level of prices.

Rises in the prices of staple foods hit poor Mexicans particularly hard. In 2000, the poorest 10 per cent of households allocated 73 per cent of their current income to buying food; by 2006 this figure had grown to 79 per cent, as shown in Figure 7.12. In contrast, the households in the rest of the deciles reduced the share of the income that goes to food, up to five percentage points in some cases. By 2006, Deciles II to IV still allocated 40 per cent or more of their income to food.

The relative increases in the prices of staples and fruit and vegetables,

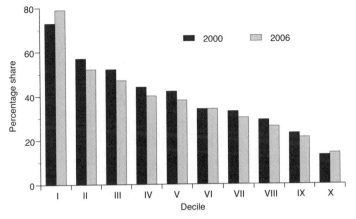

7.12 Food expenditure as a share of monetary current income of households, by deciles (2000–06)

Source: Authors, with data from ENIGH–INEGHI (2000, 2006)

and decreases in the prices of meat and junk food, have not surprisingly led low-income Mexicans to change their diet. In her study of how nutrition, obesity and diet are linked to globalization, Hawkes (2006) argues that the three major processes of market integration (production and trade of agricultural goods; foreign direct investment in food processing and retailing; and global food advertising and promotion) have led to health problems in Mexico owing to changing patterns of consumption. In commenting on food consumption, obesity and diet-related chronic diseases in Mexico, Hawkes (ibid.) notes that:

> Between 1988 and 1999, percentage of total energy intake from fat increased from 23.5 per cent to 30.3 per cent and between 1984 and 1998, purchases of refined carbohydrates increased by 37.2 per cent. Although the absolute increases of fat were higher in the wealthier north and Mexico City (30–32 per cent), the poorer southern region also experienced a significant increase (22 per cent). At the same time, trends in obesity and diabetes are reaching 'epidemic' proportions. Overweight/obesity increased 78 per cent between 1988 and 1998, from 33 per cent to 59 per cent. Obesity is now quite high in some poor rural communities: the greatest relative changes occurred in the poorer southern region (81 per cent) compared to the wealthier north (46 per cent). More recent figures estimated overweight/obesity at 62.5 per cent in 2004. While the obese clearly consume sufficient energy, the same cannot be said of micronutrients: women who are underweight, normal weight or overweight/obese are equally likely to suffer from anemia. Obesity is also giving rise to an epidemic of diabetes which is rising fastest in the poor regions. Over 8 per cent of Mexicans now have diabetes, which the W[orld] H[ealth] O[rganization] estimates costs the country US$15 billion a year.

Greater reliance on imports to meet basic food needs has also made poor Mexicans more vulnerable to rapid surges in food prices on world markets, as

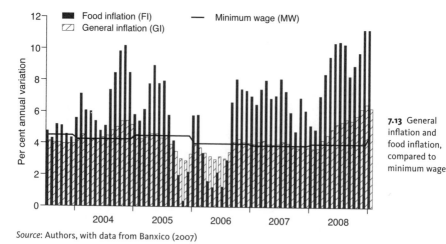

7.13 General inflation and food inflation, compared to minimum wage

Source: Authors, with data from Banxico (2007)

the experience of 2008/09 demonstrated. Figure 7.13 shows how much faster food prices rose than the general prices index and the minimum wage in the period July 2003 to January 2009.

The evidence discussed here suggests that trade liberalization in general, and NAFTA in particular, have not assisted in securing a minimum level of enjoyment of the right to food for low-income Mexicans.

Conclusions

The Mexican government stresses the importance of higher exports in evaluating the success of trade liberalization. Many progressive economists as well as civil society organizations have argued that there are other relevant indicators for assessing trade policies: such as employment (and the quality of such employment), inequality and the standard of living. This chapter has built upon their efforts.[7]

The analysis presented in this chapter has shown that trade liberalization failed to support progressive realization of the right to work, and progressive realization of the right to just and favourable conditions of work. The conduct of trade policy could have been more compliant with human rights obligations even within the NAFTA framework: for instance, free trade in maize could have been phased in more slowly; more extensive support could have been offered to small farmers to develop exports of fruits and vegetables; instead of NADB, a well-resourced and well-functioning development bank could have been set up to support innovation in production. These measures would have helped to support progressive realization of the right to work and to just and favourable conditions of work.

Trade liberalization also failed to support non-discrimination and equality in the labour market; even though NAFTA had a side agreement on labour (NAALC) that did mention elimination of employment discrimination and equal pay for women and men. But there were no effective enforcement mechanisms and no proactive policy. In the absence of these, pay inequalities between different social groups widened.

On the face of it, NAFTA might have supported securing a minimum level of enjoyment of the right to food for low-income Mexicans, as it facilitated imports of maize and other key staples from lower-cost US farmers. But this did not result in lower prices of tortillas, bread and cereals for Mexican consumers. Moreover, the relative prices of less nutritious food, likely to be injurious to health, fell, and the diet of low-income Mexicans worsened.

Notes

1 Both terms are used for these factories. The information on the maquila in this paragraph comes from Canas and Gilmer (2009).

2 The value added is the price of the export minus the value of the imported inputs.

3 Import duties are also called tariffs. They are typically levied as a percentage of the value of the import. Import quotas are quantitative restrictions on the amount of a particular good that can be imported.

4 The ASF (2007: 182) found that during the transference of resources from one programme to the other, 7,393,000 pesos went missing.

5 Unfortunately, this is the first year for which sex-disaggregated data are available, which reveals another type of gender blindness and discrimination in national statistics.

6 See also Chapter 8 on trade policy and economic and social rights in the USA.

7 In Mexico, among many others: DECA–Equipo Pueblo; Red Mexicana de Acción frente al Libre Comercio (RMALC); Centro de Derechos Humanos Miguel Agustín Pro Juárez (PRODH); INCIDE Social; Centro de Derechos Humanos Fray Bartolomé de las Casas; Centro de Derechos Humanos Fray Francisco de Vitoria; Academia Mexicana de Derechos Humanos; Alianza Mexicana por la Autodeterminación de los Pueblos (AMAP); Campo de Política Social de Convergencia de Organismos Civiles por la Democracia; Casa y Ciudad de la Coalición Hábitat México; Cátedra UNESCO de Derechos Humanos de la Universidad Nacional Autónoma de México; Centro de Capacitación en Ecología y Salud para Campesinos–Defensoría del Derecho a la Salud (CCESC-DDS); Centro de Derechos Humanos Tepeyac del Istmo de Tehuantepec (CDHTT); Centro de Estudios Ecuménicos

(CEE); Centro de Estudios para el Desarrollo Rural (CESDER); Centro de Estudios Sociales y Culturales Antonio de Montesinos (CAM); Centro de Formación e Investigación Municipal (CEFIMAC); Centro Fray Julián Garcés de Derechos Humanos y Desarrollo Local; Centro de Reflexión y Acción Laboral de Fomento Cultural y Educativo (CEREAL); Centro Mexicano de Derecho Ambiental (CEMDA); Comisión Ciudadana de Derechos Humanos del Noroeste; Comisión Mexicana de Defensa y Promoción de los Derechos Humanos (CMDPDH); Comité de América Latina y El Caribe para la Defensa de los Derechos de la Mujer–México (CLADEM México); Comité de Superación de Jóvenes de Tabasco; Consejo de Ejidos y Comunidades Opositores a la Presa la Parota (CECOP); Consorcio para el Diálogo Parlamentario y la Equidad; Convergencia de Organismos Civiles por la Democracia; Coordinadora Comunitaria Miravalle (COCOMI); El Barzón Movimiento Jurídico Nacional; Elige–Red de Jóvenes por los Derechos Sexuales y Reproductivos (ELIGE); Enlace, Comunicación y Capacitación (Enlace–Chiapas); Espacio de Coordinación de Organizaciones Civiles sobre DESC (Espacio DESC–capítulo mexicano de la Plataforma Interamericana de Derechos Humanos, Democracia y Desarrollo); FIAN Sección México; Foro para el Desarrollo Sustentable – Chiapas; FUNDAR Centro de Análisis e Investigación (FUNDAR); Iniciativas para la Identidad y la Inclusión (INICIA); Instituto Mexicano para el Desarrollo Comunitario (IMDEC); Liga Mexicana de Defensa de los Derechos Humanos (LIMEDDH); Movimiento Ciudadano por la Democracia (MCD); Oficina para América Latina de la Coalición Internacional para el Hábitat (HICAL); Podemos; Promoción y Capacitación en los Derechos Económicos y Sociales de las

Mujeres (PROCADESC); Radar – Colectivo de Estudios Alternativos en Derecho; Red Mexicana de Investigadores sobre Sociedad Civil (REMISOC); Red por los Derechos de la Infancia en México; Red Puentes Sociales; Salud Integral para la Mujer (SIPAM); Servicios para una Educación Alternativa (EDUCA); Sin Fronteras; Unión Campesina Emiliano Zapata Vive (UCEZ VIVE). See PRODH et al. (2006: 3–5) for other organizations that are committed to the human rights perspective.

References

ANEC (2008) *Special Report on Agriculture*, Asociación Nacional de Empresas Comercializadoras de Productores del Campo.

ASF (2007) *Informe del Resultado de la Revisión y Fiscalización Superior de la Cuenta Pública 2005.* Sector Hacienda y Crédito Público, Auditoría Superior de la Federación, Mexico: Congreso de la Unión.

Banobras (2008) *Informe Anual 2003, 2004, 2005, 2006, 2007.* Mexico: Banco Nacional de Obras y Servicios Públicos, www. banobras.gob.mx/GuiaseInformacion-Complementaria/InformacionFinanciera/InformesAnuales/Pages/informe_anual. aspx (accessed July 2008).

Banxico (2007) *Estadísticas*, Mexico: Banco de México.

— Exchange rates, www.banxico.org.mx/SieInternet/consultar DirectorioInternet Action.do? accion=consultarCuadro&id Cuadro=CF86& sector=6&locale=es (accessed June 2008)

— Inflation www.banxico.org.mx/SieInternet/consultarDirectorioInternetAction.do? accion=consultarCuadroAnalitico&idCuadro =CA55&sector=8&locale=es (accessed June 2008)

— Minimum wages www.banxico.gob.mx/polmoneinflacion/estadisticas/laboural/laboural.html (accessed June 2008)

— Wages in the manufacturing sector www. banxico.gob.mx/polmoneinflacion/estadisticas/laboural/laboural.html (accessed June 2008)

Bhaduri, A. (2005) 'Toward the optimum degree of openness', in K. Gallagher (ed.), *Putting Development First: The Importance of Policy Space in the WTO and IFIs*, London: Zed Books.

BIE–INEGI (2007) *Sistema de Cuentas Nacionales de México*, Banco de Información Económica/Instituto Nacional de Geografía, Estadística e Informática

— Wages in the manufacturing sector, dgcnesyp.inegi.gob.mx/cgi-win/bdieintsi. exe/NIVM10000200070020050#ARBOL (accessed June 2008)

— Productivity in the manufacturing sector, dgcnesyp.inegi.gob.mx/cgi-win/bdieintsi. exe/NIVM10000200070020050#ARBOL (accessed June 2008)

— Salaries and social benefits in the manufacturing sector: dgcnesyp.inegi.gob.mx/cgi-win/bdieintsi. exe/NIVA050080040#ARBOL; dgcnesyp.inegi.gob.mx/cgi-win/bdieintsi. exe/NIVA05008000100010#ARBOL; dgcnesyp.inegi.gob.mx/cgi-win/bdieintsi. exe/NIVA05008000300010# ARBOL (accessed June 2008)

— Wages and employment in the maquila sector: dgcnesyp.inegi.gob.mx/cgi-win/bdieintsi. exe/NIVA0500600010#ARBOL; dgcnesyp.inegi.gob.mx/cgi-win/bdieintsi. exe/NIVA0500600200010#ARBOL; dgcnesyp.inegi.gob.mx/cgi-win/bdieintsi. exe/NIVA0500600300010#ARBOL; dgcnesyp.inegi.gob.mx/cgi-win/bdieintsi. exe/NIVA0500600400010#ARBOL; dgcnesyp.inegi.gob.mx/cgi-win/bdieintsi. exe/NIVJ15000200030005000050005# ARBOL; dgcnesyp.inegi.gob.mx/cgi-win/bdieintsi. exe/NIVJ15000200030005000050010# ARBOL; dgcnesyp.inegi.gob.mx/cgi-win/bdieintsi. exe/NIVJ15000200030005000050015# ARBOL; dgcnesyp.inegi.gob.mx/cgi-win/bdieintsi. exe/NIVJ15000200030005000050020# ARBOL; dgcnesyp.inegi.gob.mx/cgi-win/bdieintsi. exe/NIVJ1500020003000500100100010# ARBOL (accessed June 2008)

Bolle, M. J. (2001) *NAFTA Labour Side Agreement: Lessons for Workers' Rights and Fast-Track Debate*, Report 97–861E, Congressional Research Service, Washington, DC.

Calderón, H. F. (2007) 'Primer informe de gobierno', *Anexos Estadísticos*, Mexico: Presidencia de la República.

Calderón, C. and A. Tykhonenko (2007) 'Convergencia regional e inversión extranjera directa en México en el contexto del TLCAN, 1994–2002', *Investigación Económica*, LXVI(257): 15–41.

Canas, J. and R. Gilmer (2009) 'The maquiladora's changing geography', *Southwest Economy*, vol. 10, 2nd quarter.

CESCR (1999) *Final Observations on the Third Periodic Report: Mexico*, Committee on Economic, Social and Cultural Rights (E/C.12/1/Add.41).

— (2005) *Fourth Periodic Reports Submitted by States Parties under Articles 16 and 17 of the Covenant: Mexico*, Committee on Economic, Social and Cultural Rights (E/C.12/4/Add.16).

CONAPO – Consejo Nacional de Población. (2007). Series sobre Migración Internacional (consulted in June 2008): http://www.conapo.gob.mx/mig_int/s2008/01.htm

Cook, C. (2006) *Mexico–U.S. Relations: Issues for the 109th Congress*, RL32724, Congressional Research Service, Washington, DC.

Deraniyagala, S. (2005) 'Neoliberalism in international trade: sound economics and/or a question of faith?', in A. Saad-Filho and D. Johnston (eds), *Neoliberalism: A critical reader*, London: Pluto, pp. 99–105.

ENIGH–INEGI (2000, 2002, 2004, 2005, 2006) *Encuesta Nacional de Ingresos y Gastos de los Hogares*, Instituto Nacional de Geografía, Estadística e Informática.

Esquinca, M. T. (2008) *Special Report on Labour.*

Fox, Q. V. (2006) 'Sexto informe de gobierno', *Anexos Estadísticos*, Mexico: Presidencia de la República.

Gallagher, K. and L. Zarsky (2004) *Sustainable Industrial Development? The Performance of Mexico's FDI-led Integration Strategy*, G-DAE Working Papers, Global Development and Environment Institute, Fletcher School of Law and Diplomacy, Tufts University.

Hawkes, C. (2006) 'Uneven dietary development: linking the policies and processes of globalization with the nutrition transition, obesity and diet-related chronic diseases', in *Globalization and Health 2006*, Food Consumption and Nutrition Division, International Food Policy Research Institute, Washington, DC, globalizationandhealth.com/content/2/1/4 (accessed July 2008).

ILO (International Labour Organization) (2007) *Equality at Work: Tackling the challenges: Global Report under the follow-up to the ILO Declaration on Fundamental Principles and Rights at Work*, Report I (B) of the Director-General, 96th Session, International Labour Conference, Geneva.

King, A. (2006) *Ten Years with NAFTA: A Review of the Literature and an Analysis of Farmer Responses in Sonora and Veracruz, Mexico*, Mexico: CIMMYT Special Report 06–01.

Moreno-Brid, J. C., J. Santamaría and V. Rivas (2005) 'Industrialization and economic growth in Mexico after NAFTA: the road travelled', *Development and Change*, 36(6): 1095–119.

NAALC (North American Agreement on Labor Cooperation) (1993) 13 September. Available at http://www.naalc.org/naalc/naalc-full-text.htm.

NAFTA (North American Free Trade Agreement) (1993) *Legal Text*, www.nafta–sec–alena.org/DefaultSite/index_e.aspx?DetailID=79 (accessed June 2007).

Pacheco, E. (2005) 'El trabajo agropecuario en México: 1991–2003', in C. Salas (ed.), *La Situación del Trabajo en México, 2006*, Mexico: Plaza y Valdés, pp. 331–54.

Passel, J. (2005) 'Background briefing prepared for Task Force on Immigration and America's Future', in *Unauthorized Migrants: Numbers and Characteristics*, Pew Hispanic Center, 14 June, pewhispanic.org/files/reports/46.pdf.

Peters, E. D. (2009) 'Manufacturing competitiveness: toward a regional development agenda', in *The Future of North American Trade Policy: Lessons from NAFTA*, Frederick S. Pardee Center, Boston University.

Polaski, S. (2004) 'Mexican employment, productivity and income a decade after NAFTA', Brief submitted to the Canadian Standing Senate Committee on Foreign Affairs, 25 February.

PRODH et al. (2006) *Report of Civil Society Organisations on the Situation of Economic, Social, Cultural and Environmental Rights in Mexico (1997–2006): Alternative Report to the IV Periodic Report of the Mexican State on the Implementation of the ICESCR*, Mexico: Centro de Derechos Humanos Miguel Agustín Pro Juárez.

Saudalet, E. and A. de Janvry (2001) 'Cash transfer programs with income multipliers:

PROCAMPO in Mexico', *World Development*, 29(6): 1043–56.

USDA (United States Department of Agriculture) (2008) 'North American Free Trade Agreement (NAFTA)', Fact sheet, US Department of Agriculture – Foreign Agricultural Service, January.

Ziegler, J. (2006) 'Economic, Social and Cultural Rights: The right to food', Report of the Special Rapporteur on the right to food, United Nations Commission on Human Rights, 62nd Session, Item 10 of the provisional agenda, E/CN.4/2006/44, 16 March.

Nursel Aydiner-Avsar and Diane Elson

Introduction

Human rights advocates have only recently begun to work on trade policy. In 1998 the International NGO Committee for Human Rights in Trade and Investment was formed to promote the positive integration of human rights into international economic policy and practice. This advocacy led to a May 1998 statement by the Committee on Economic, Social and Cultural Rights (CESCR) which insisted that trade, finance and investment are in no way exempt from human rights principles.[1] It was followed in August 1999 by a resolution of the UN Sub-Commission on Protection and Promotion of Human Rights calling for the full integration of human rights principles into economic policy processes at the international level.[2] The CESCR endorsed the August 1999 resolution, and issued a statement urging WTO members to review all international trade and investment agreements and policies in order to ensure their consistency with human rights obligations. These developments led the way to a series of resolutions in 2000 and 2001 that addressed issues such as intellectual property, trade in services and globalization, and were followed by studies and reports by Sub-Commission members or by the Office of the UN High Commissioner for Human Rights (Prove 2007). It is important to note that states have human rights obligations with respect not only to people living in their own territories but to those in other territories. Kunnemann (2007) gives an outline of the key aspects of these extraterritorial obligations that arise from the ICESCR. Such obligations are particularly relevant to the trade policies of large, rich countries which have important impacts on people in other countries.

However, governments continue to compartmentalize human rights and trade commitments in different ministries, and lack understanding of the binding nature of human rights treaties. Moreover, advocates of trade liberalization fail to see the risk of conflict between trade liberalization and human rights, and indeed sometimes argue that international trade by itself promotes human rights by opening up countries to Western influence.

Particularly important is the issue that trade treaties and human rights treaties have different understandings of the concept of 'non-discrimination', as pointed out by Khor (2007). While in a human rights context 'non-discrimination' allows for positive discrimination in favour of those who are most vulnerable, in trade agreements it is considered as requiring most-favoured-nation treatment and national treatment. Under most-favoured-nation treatment, every partner to the agreement must be treated in the same way as any other.[3] Under national treatment countries are required to treat foreign products at least as well as local products[4] (thus a country can even treat a foreign product more favourably than the local product). This rule does not allow positive discrimination in favour of the most vulnerable – such as small local businesses and small farms – by their governments, especially when extended to services, intellectual property, investment, procurement and competition rules, which today are all covered by many trade agreements.

Concerns have been expressed by De Schutter (2007) that human rights are threatened by some aspects of the World Trade Organization agreements; for instance, that the right to health is threatened by intellectual property rights protection under the Trade Related Intellectual Property Rights agreement; and that the General Agreement on Trade in Services may threaten the rights to water and education; and that the Agreement on Agriculture jeopardizes the right to food by limiting the policies governments can use to ensure food security. Trade liberalization has also been argued to have implications for the right to work, by increasing inequalities between skilled and low-skilled workers and changing the overall structure of the economy (ibid.).

The risks of conflict between trade treaties and human rights treaties are obscured by neoclassical trade theory, because it has such an entrenched view of the benefits of free trade. Human rights advocates are often unaware that not all economists share that view, and that significant groups are critical of trade liberalization. Neoclassical economists have long argued that trade liberalization raises the general standard of living within a country by giving incentives for countries to specialize in the production of the goods that they can produce relatively cheaply in comparison with trading partners. This favourable impact, however, depends on there being mechanisms that keep imports and exports in balance. Critical economists point to the lack of such mechanisms; and to evidence that trade liberalization in poor countries has been followed by persistent trade deficits (i.e. the volume of imports is greater than that of exports) leading to indebtedness, as countries have to borrow to pay for their imports (e.g. Milberg 1994; McCombie and Thirlwall 1994). Both neoclassical and critical economists agree that trade liberalization produces losers as well as winners, and that the gains from trade are not necessarily equally shared either within or between countries. The gains include cheaper goods for consumption (if imports are cheaper than home production) and more employment in production of exports (if exports expand). The losses include loss of employment in production that can no longer compete with imports, and loss of tax revenue to fund public services, since trade liberalization implies cutting taxes on trade (i.e. import tariffs). According to neoclassical trade theory, there will be sufficient benefits for the winners to compensate the losers for their losses. The question of whether losers actually are compensated is rarely emphasized. Progressive economists examine this question, but also have a broader view of gains and losses, which includes gains and losses in power. They ask whose power is strengthened by trade liberalization and whose power is weakened, and see trade liberalization as a strategy through which powerful corporations seek access to new markets to gain a competitive advantage through use of new technology and/or cheap labour (Milberg 1994; Shaikh 2007).

The human rights dimensions of US trade policy will be discussed here primarily in relation to the North American Free Trade Agreement (NAFTA), which was negotiated in the early 1990s by the administration of President George Bush and brought into force in 1994, by the Clinton administration. The governments of the USA, Mexico and Canada all argued that NAFTA would increase international trade and foreign investment; improve efficiency and lead to faster economic growth. Through these mechanisms, it was argued, the general prosperity of all three countries would be improved. NAFTA required all three nations to eliminate controls on imports, scheduled to be phased out immediately or over five, ten or fifteen years. More than one half of the trade value was already exempt from tariffs when the agreement took effect. The last remaining trade restrictions on a handful of agricultural commodities, such as US exports to Mexico of corn, dry edible beans, non-fat dry milk and high-fructose corn syrup, and Mexican exports to the United States of sugar and certain horticultural products, were removed on 1 January 2008 (USDA 2008).

NAFTA also included a number of side agreements, relating to the rights of business and labour, and the scope of domestic policy. In this it was in line with many other recent international trade agreements, which have broadened the scope of such agreements to include many other things besides import controls. NAFTA has hundreds of pages referring to non-trade policies to which all signatory parties must conform. For that reason, it is as much a cross-border investment agreement as a trade agreement. For example, Chapter 11, dealing with rights of cross-border investors, put limits on environmental protections, service sector regulation, investment and development policy, and government procurement preferences. NAFTA also required Mexico to change its Constitution to permit foreign investors to purchase land.

When first introduced, NAFTA promoters promised it would create many new jobs, raise living standards in all three countries, improve environmental conditions and transform Mexico from a poor developing country into a booming new market for US exports. On the other hand, NAFTA opponents argued that it would launch a race to the bottom in wages, destroy hundreds of thousands of good-quality jobs, undermine democratic control of domestic policy-making and threaten environmental and food safety standards.

Here we examine NAFTA in the light of the human rights principles of non-discrimination and equality, with a particular focus on the right to work and to just and favourable conditions of work; and in light of the extra-territorial obligations of the government of the USA, with respect to minimum core obligations to secure minimum levels of enjoyment of the right to food in Mexico. Finally, NAFTA will be examined in light of the principles of transparency, accountability and participation, with a particular focus on its dispute settlement mechanism.

Non-discrimination and equality

Article 2 of the International Covenant on Economic, Social and Cultural Rights (ICESCR) stipulates that:

> The States Parties to the present Covenant undertake to guarantee that the rights enunciated in the present Covenant will be exercised without discrimination of any kind as to race, colour, sex, language, religion, political or other opinion, national or social origin, property, birth or other status.

The Committee on Economic, Social and Cultural Rights (CESCR) has clarified that 'other status' includes 'economic status', understood in terms of wealth/poverty (CESCR 2009). Here we will pay particular attention to the obligation to ensure that human rights are exercised without discrimination on grounds of race/ethnicity, gender, property and economic status,[5] with a focus on the right to work (Article 6) and the right to just and favourable conditions of work (Article 7).

Obligation of conduct It is agreed among economists that trade liberalization has different impacts on different groups. From a human rights perspective we are particularly interested in the possibility of adverse impacts on groups that have been relatively deprived of enjoyment of human rights, such as low-income workers, a group in which racial/ethnic minorities and women are over-represented; and whether measures were taken to avert an adverse impact. Therefore we consider whether the US government conducted studies of the likely impact of NAFTA on employment and conditions of work of these relatively deprived social groups, before concluding the NAFTA agreement; whether the US government put in place adequate measures to compensate any deprived social groups likely to lose employment and/or just and remunerative conditions of work; and whether the US government ensured equal treatment of different social groups in the construction of the side agreements relating to labour rights and business rights.

The US International Trade Commission (USITC) did produce a report, *The Likely Impact on the United States of a Free Trade Agreement with Mexico*, in February 1991. While it offers no estimates regarding overall job or income gains or losses, it suggests that unskilled workers in the USA would suffer a slight fall in their real income, while skilled workers and owners of capital services would benefit from the decline in prices of imports and as a result enjoy an increase in their real income (USITC 1991).

The USA already had a Trade Adjustment Assistance (TAA) programme,[6] established in 1974 as a mechanism to provide those low-income workers affected by trade-related employment loss with temporary aid and retraining. Workers had to show that they had lost their jobs owing to an increase in imports; or a shift in production to another country with which the USA had a preferential trade agreement, or from which there was a prospect of a rise in imports. When NAFTA was passed, a new TAA programme – known as NAFTA-Transitional Adjustment Assistance (NAFTA-TAA) – was established, targeting only the workers affected by NAFTA-related employment loss. The Trade Act of 2002 consolidated both programmes into a single expanded programme and extended it to the end of 2007. On 17 February 2009, the Trade and Globalization Adjustment Assistance Act of 2009 was signed into law by President Obama as part of the American Recovery and Reinvestment Act of 2009 (Recovery Act), extending the TAA programme until 31 December 2010; and improving some of its provisions.

The NAFTA-TAA programme was underfunded. President George H. W. Bush had mentioned an allocation of $4 billion a year for NAFTA-TAA in 1992 during the congressional debate. However, the NAFTA-TAA and the general TAA programmes were together allocated only $3.08 billion in total for the seven-year period of 1994–2002. Only a fraction of these funds went to NAFTA-TAA, while the general TAA programme received the lion's share of them. Over the course of NAFTA-TAA's existence, it was allocated a total of $464 million, compared to $2.67 billion that was appropriated for the general TAA programme (Tucker et al. 2005). Amounts appropriated for the consolidated Trade Adjustment Assistance Programme totalled $5.33 billion (in constant 2000 dollars) for the six years 2003–08.[7] But this had to cover workers displaced by Chinese imports after China's accession to the World Trade Organization in 2001, as well as those whose job loss was related to NAFTA.

Besides the issue of funding, there are also issues regarding access to the programme. To obtain TAA services and benefits, a group of workers (at least three) must file a petition with both the US Department of Labour and the trade coordinator or dislocated worker unit in the state in which they live. Each worker in the group may then apply for the individual services and benefits separately if the petition is approved and certified. According to the Department of Labour TAA programme database, in relation to all TAA programmes, there were 36,131 petitions filed and 21,215 of them were certified between the end of 1994 and the end of 2009. The estimated number of workers covered by certified petitions is 2,184,641 while 811,517 workers are estimated to be covered by petitions that were denied.[8] Tucker et al. (ibid.) report that fewer than 60 per cent of the estimated number of workers who lost their jobs after NAFTA was certified were eligible under NAFTA-TAA.[9] A report by the Congressional Government Accountability Office found that many workers are not aware of the TAA assistance for which they are eligible (GAO 2006). Moreover, only a fraction of those workers certified eligible for TAA received the benefits to which they were entitled; for example, only 244,552 out of 406,051 workers received any of the benefits of training, trade adjustment allowances, relocation or job search allowances between the end of 2006 and 2009.[10] The annual number of workers certified for the programme also decreased from 197,748 in 2003 to 126,606 in 2008.[11]

Prior to the latest changes introduced by the Obama administration in 2009, NAFTA-TAA and its successor covered only the manufacturing sector; service sector workers who lost their jobs as a result of trade liberalization were not eligible. Workers who were eligible for NAFTA-TAA could receive benefits, including training, job search allowances, relocation allowances and income support for up to fifty-two weeks after their unemployment insurance had run out. The expanded and consolidated TAA programme introduced in 2002 supposedly provided more assistance for eligible workers, including measures supposed to enable them to maintain their health insurance, and subsidies to protect them against loss of income through moving to new jobs that pay lower wages. However, these measures were implemented in ways that exclude most workers who lose their jobs from benefiting.

For instance, only 6 per cent of eligible workers had actually used the Health Care Tax Credit (HCTC) that was supposed to give displaced workers a form of portable healthcare insurance. This was because a three- to six-month waiting period was required before eligible workers were certified for participation in the programme. Because of the programme's design, trade-displaced workers would have to pay full healthcare premiums prior to their certification. This represents a cost which most recently displaced workers simply cannot afford (Tucker et al. 2005). The Congressional Government Accountability Office conducted a survey of workers involved in five plant closings, and found that only 3–12 per cent of eligible workers used the HCTC; 39–60 per cent of workers were not aware of the credit; and about 80 per cent of those workers without health insurance reported that HCTC was not high enough for them to afford to maintain their health insurance (GAO 2006).

Similarly, the wage subsidy programme,[12] established in the 2002 TAA bill, has very stringent eligibility conditions. Eligible workers must not have 'easily transferable skills' in order to qualify for the wage subsidy programme – a provision which discriminates against workers who are re-employed doing similar kinds of work but at lower pay than in their previous job. A related provision also discriminates against workers who do not have transferable skills, but who worked in firms in which the majority of employees did have transferable skills. These workers were not eligible for wage subsidies under the new TAA rules (Tucker et al. 2005). The inability to enrol in training is another problem with the programme. Moreover, the programme is restricted to workers over the age of fifty (Rosen 2008).

Some changes in the TAA programme were introduced by the Obama administration under the 2009 Recovery Act.[13] The programme now includes workers and firms in the service sector, makes benefits available to workers whose jobs have been offshored to any country (earlier it was covering jobs lost owing to a free trade agreement between a country and the United States); and aims to improve workers' training opportunities and opportunities for health insurance coverage. Moreover, the statutory cap on funds that may be allocated to the states for training is increased from $220,000,000 to $575,000,000 per year; and the maximum amount of Trade Readjustment Allowance (TRA) income support a worker may receive was increased. The deadlines to enrol in training were extended. The HCTC was made more generous. Although these measures are important, they will be in place only until 31 December 2010; and it is not clear whether there will be any improvement in the implementation of the programme.

In short, while programmes were introduced that supposedly provided assistance to compensate workers who lose their jobs as a result of NAFTA, and other trade liberalization measures, the programmes do not seem to be very effective in assisting low-income workers who lose their jobs.

We now turn to the issue of side agreements and whether they treated different social groups differently, with a focus on labour rights as compared to intellectual property rights, bearing in mind that the owners of intellectual property rights tend to have much more wealth than employees. As initially negotiated, NAFTA included no provisions to protect labour rights. They were later introduced through a side agreement, the North American Agreement on Labour Cooperation (NAALC). One of the key structural weaknesses of NAALC is its lack of an independent oversight body. Instead, weak bilateral and trilateral mechanisms form the basis for enforcement. As a result, its potential as a means for promoting respect for, and improvements in, labour rights is very limited. Moreover, the lack of an independent body gives complete discretion to each country's National Administrative Office in dealing with complaints (Solomon 2001). Another major weakness is related to the limited coverage of the accord. For instance, non-compliance with the laws related to three key labour rights – namely freedom of association and the right to organize, the right to bargain collectively, and the right to strike – cannot be brought before the enforcement bodies (ibid.). In their overview of NAALC cases related to workplace health and safety issues, Delp et al. (2004) conclude that it failed to protect the right to safe jobs.

The weakness of NAALC is in contrast to the strength of the side agreement on Intellectual Property Rights, which gives much greater protection to the rights of property owners than the former does to the rights of labour, as the following extract shows (CTC 2001):

Which of my rights are protected?

If you're a businessman:

NAFTA protection for Intellectual Property Rights

The agreement contains 14 pages of fine print spelling out detailed standards for protecting video and cassette recordings, films, literary and artistic works, industrial property, new varieties of plants, copyrights, trademarks, patents, satellite signals, semiconductor designs, geographical indicators, industrial designs and trade secrets.

If you're a worker:

NAFTA Side Agreement protection for Worker Rights

The Side Agreement contains no specified labour standards. Moreover, only the persistent failure of a government to enforce its own labour laws in three areas – minimum wage, child labour, worker health and safety – may be subject to sanction. A government's persistent non-enforcement of the most fundamental labour rights – the right to strike, the right to organize and collective bargaining rights – is specifically excluded from the reach of sanctions. Thus the victimization of workers seeking to organize is not eligible for redress through sanctions, only through voluntary consultation between governments. Nothing in the NAFTA prevents a government from lowering its labour standards. Moreover, a government cannot be charged with a 'persistent failure to enforce', and is insulated from the reach of sanctions if it asserts that it made a reasonable allocation of resources to another area believed to have a higher priority.

May I initiate a complaint directly if my rights are violated?

If you're a businessman:

YES: As a business person with intellectual property, you are a 'rights holder' and may initiate a complaint under the Agreement. Associations and federations with a business interest in intellectual property rights can also be recognized as rights holders. Rights holders can seek redress against violators under another country's judicial and administration procedures that must be made to conform to the requirements specified by NAFTA.

If you're a worker:

YES, BUT: Although individuals and unions can file complaints with their own 'National Administrative Office' (NAO) (government agencies established under NAFTA) those complaints cannot be against a company or individual. They can only be against a government's 'persistent failure to enforce' certain limited specified aspects of its own law. It is up to the NAO to decide whether or not to proceed with a complaint.

Do I have the right to bring legal action in the country where the violation occurred?

If you're a businessman:

YES: As a businessman you have standing both to file a civil suit and to demand a criminal investigation in the other country. Under the NAFTA Agreement, other governments must 'make available effective enforcement procedures' to protect intellectual property.

If you're a worker:

NO

If the violations continue and go unpunished by the other country, may I seek remedies at a higher level?

If you're a businessman:

YES: You may take your case to the NAFTA Free Trade Commission.

If you're a worker:

NO: Neither individual workers nor their unions have standing to seek remedies at a higher level. Only government agencies can pursue complaints related to labour. Even they must demonstrate that the other *government* has engaged in a *persistent pattern* of failure to enforce *its own laws* in the limited areas of minimum wage, child labour and health and safety standards, and *only* if the persistent violations relate to *exported* goods or services.

If the other government refuses to abide by the decision, are trade sanctions imposed?

If you're a businessman:

YES: Tariff benefits may be suspended and duties imposed on the entire industrial sector if the other government refuses to provide effective remedies to protect your intellectual property.

If you're a worker:

UNLIKELY: NAFTA benefits can be suspended only if the offending government fails to pay a fine 180 days after it is imposed. The value of the suspended benefits can be no greater than the value of the fine. There are no minimum fines. The arbitral panel setting the fine is required to take into account a government's 'resource constraints' for enforcement activities, when it sets the amount of the fine. When a fine is paid, it goes into a fund that is recycled back to that government to help it enforce its laws. There are no provisions for auditing how those funds are actually spent.

Thus the provisions of NAFTA do not treat workers (who own little intellectual property) and businesses (which own a lot of intellectual property) even-handedly.

To summarize, although there were some attempts by the US government to comply with non-discrimination obligations through conducting an impact assessment study, introducing compensation measures for low-income workers (among whom racial/ethnic minorities and women are over-represented) and introducing a side agreement on labour rights, these have been grossly inadequate.

Obligation of result We first consider job gains and losses. It is not easy to assess the impact of any particular policy measure on job gains and losses because many other things happen at the same time as the policy. Some mainstream economists have offered estimates of job losses and gains linked to NAFTA. For instance, those at the Office of the United States Trade Representative (USTR) claim that NAFTA is linked to an increase in US employment, noting that US employment rose from 110.8 million people in 1993 to 137.6 million in 2007, an increase of 24 per cent. The average unemployment rate was 5.1 per cent in the period 1994–2007 while it was 7.1 per cent during the period 1980–93 (USTR 2008). However, these increases reflect a variety of changes in the economy and cannot all be directly attributed to NAFTA. More sophisticated estimates of job gains/losses have been produced by G. C. Hufbauer and J. J. Schott at the Institute for International Economics. In their 2005 study, after acknowledging the difficulties in making estimates of the employment effect of NAFTA, they concluded that over 100,000 jobs per year were created linked to NAFTA. They estimated that 8,500 manufacturing jobs are supported by every $1 billion of US exports; and on this basis, they calculated the number of jobs created by the annual average expansion in US exports over the period of 1993–2003. To calculate job losses, they use the number of workers certified eligible for the NAFTA-TAA programme and find that 58,000 jobs were lost per year (Hufbauer and Schott 2005).[14] Thus, overall they suggest a net gain in terms of jobs.

This estimate has been criticized by other economists, such as Robert Scott from the Economic Policy Institute, on a number of methodological grounds. He notes that Hufbauer and Schott (ibid.) erroneously include re-exports of goods imported from other countries, despite the fact that such goods normally do not support manufacturing employment in the USA; they also argue that eligibility under the NAFTA-TAA programme grossly understates job losses. Scott et al. (2006) provide alternative estimates which exclude re-exports. According to these estimates, the USA experienced an overall loss of 1,015,290 jobs between 1993 and 2004 owing to changes related to NAFTA. While 941,459 US jobs were maintained or created as a result of the growth in exports to Mexico and Canada, the growth in imports from those two countries resulted in the displacement of 1,956,750 jobs. The greater part of the net job displacement took place in the manufacturing sector (658,930 manufacturing jobs displaced corresponding to 64.9 per cent of the total job losses). The remaining 356,361 jobs that were displaced over this period include various service-sector support jobs, such as accounting, computer programming and legal and financial services. Although these numbers are small relative to the size of the labour market as a whole, they are more significant relative to the manufacturing sector, where trade had the largest impact (Blecker 2003).

Scott et al. (2006) also estimate job displacement by social group (see Table 8.1). Workers with a high school degree or less were particularly hit by job losses. Workers of Hispanic origin and other minority groups were displaced proportionately more than white and black workers. Men have been disproportionately affected as compared to women: 63.9 per cent of workers displaced were male, while they made up only 55.2 per cent of the total labour force. Female workers comprised 36.1 per cent of displaced workers though they made up 47.8 per cent of the labour force. Scott's estimates of job loss and gain have been criticized, mainly because his method examines the employment effects of changes in actual trade flows but does not account for the underlying causes of the changes in trade flows, which might be changes in trade regulations, but also fluctuations in exchange rates, or differences in economic growth (Blecker 2003).

It might be argued that job displacement does not matter; many of those displaced quickly find other comparable jobs. However, Kletzer (2001), in his analysis of the Dislocated Worker Survey, finds that only two-thirds of dislocated workers from high-import-competing industries find a new job within one to three years, and 40–50 per cent of those re-employed experience a loss in earnings. A study of re-employment of workers whose job loss was specifically related to NAFTA was conducted by Beneria and Santiago (2001). In their study of two factories in upstate New York that were relocated to Mexico, they found that displaced male workers were more successful in finding jobs than displaced female workers, although more women had received retraining and benefited from Trade Adjustment Assistance (TAA) funds. Women had difficulties in translating the retraining into jobs because the training was designed based on gender stereotypes. The type of courses taken by men and women were different, channelling women towards care work, such as courses on human services and childcare, and men towards other types of activities normally viewed as more appropriate for them, such as sales and computer courses. The overall relocation of workers led to a deterioration and polarization in their labour market status, with only about one fourth of them being able to find jobs that required higher skills and paid higher wages. Women disproportionally suffered during the transition process (ibid.). So even if overall men were disproportionately subject to job loss compared to women, they may have found it easier to get re-employed than women. Similarly, workers of colour may be less likely to be easily re-employed when they lose their jobs

TABLE 8.1 NAFTA trade-related job displacement, 1993–2004: analysis by social group, changes due to growth in:

| | Labour force share (%) | Net exports | | Difference for labour force shares |
		Jobs displaced	Share of total (%)	Net exports (%)
Education				
	11.1	-147,232	14.5	3.4
Less than high school	31.8	-376,073	37.0	5.2
Some college	29.6	-268,312	26.4	-3.1
College +	27.5	-223,675	22.0	-5.5
TOTAL		-1,015,291	100.0	
Sex				
male	55.2	-649,048	63.9	8.7
female	47.8	-366,242	36.1	-11.7
TOTAL		-1,015,291	100.0	
Wage category				
less than $7.23 per hour	16.4	-126,185	12.4	-4.0
$7.23 to $11.99 per hour	30.6	-322,714	31.8	1.2
$12.00 to $17.81 per hour	25.1	-262,395	25.8	0.8
$17.81 to $30.84 per hour	20.8	-224,602	22.1	1.3
more than $30.84 per hour	7.2	-79,393	7.8	0.7
TOTAL		-1,015,290	100.0	
Race				
Non-Hispanic white	70.9	-703,003	69.2	-1.7
Black	11.5	-111,908	11.0	-0.5
Hispanic	12.3	-139,520	13.7	1.4
Other	5.2	-60,853	6.0	0.8
TOTAL		-1,015,285	100.0	

Source: Scott et al. (2006: 16, Table 1.5), based on data from the Bureau of Labour Statistics and Census Bureau

than white workers, and if they do get a new job, it is more likely to be a lower-wage and lower-benefit job (Ranney 2003). Indeed, the jobs that were displaced the most were generally the better-paying jobs. Scott et al. (2006) estimated that there was a nationwide loss of $7.6 billion in wage premiums. Imports displaced more jobs in higher-paying industries than exports created in those industries; and the demand for labour in traded-goods industries declined owing to the increase in trade deficit, shifting these workers to other industries where wages were lower compared to traded-goods industries.

However, a focus only on how much US workers lose or gain jobs as a result of NAFTA is conducive to the view that workers in one NAFTA country are losing/gaining at the expense of workers in the other NAFTA countries, and steers attention away from the job losses experienced since 2000, by manufacturing workers, especially lower-skilled workers, in all three NAFTA countries; and the weakening of labour rights in all three countries, particularly for low-income workers, among whom women and people of colour are over-represented. The rights of large-scale owners of property have been strengthened, to the advantage of big business, with a particularly adverse impact on rural Mexicans, as discussed in Chapter 7. One of the results has been an increase in the flow of migrants (including many undocumented migrants) from Mexico, swelling the ranks of Hispanic workers in the USA. Here we give just one example to illustrate how NAFTA operates to strengthen the rights of those who own large-scale property, and weaken the rights of those who have no property, based on the story of Pedro Martin, as told by Carlsen (2008).

Pedro Martin used to work on a chicken farm just outside the village of Pegueros in Jalisco. Although many of Pedro's friends and relatives had already left Pegueros because of joblessness and poverty in their home town, Pedro said he was 'determined to stick it out in Mexico'. But he is not sure he'll have a job any more after the removal of all protective tariff barriers to US poultry imports. As Lorenzo Martin, president of the neighbouring Tepatitlan Poultry Farmers Association and the head of a large, well-established poultry farm in the area, said, 'If the United States starts selling things extra cheap outside the United States, then it won't just be small farmers and individuals who will be leaving. It will be people like me.' Some of the displaced farmers could end up migrating to the USA and working in substandard conditions in poultry processing plants. For example, Tyson – the world's largest poultry producer – has been sued twice for operating an illegal immigrant smuggling operation that included recruiting in Mexico, providing false documents, and employing undocumented workers. It is estimated that this enabled the company to drive down wages by 10–30 per cent. As Carlsen (ibid.: 2) puts it:

NAFTA promised win-win economic integration throughout the continent. These two chicken stories do add up to a win-win – but only for the likes of Tyson. Tyson wins when it takes over the Mexican market share and drives Pedro's company out of business. It wins again when it hires Pedro, now unemployed, as an undocumented worker in a US plant. Meanwhile, for its workers – migrants and native, documented and undocumented – corporate mobility coupled with repressive immigration laws means lower wages, fewer benefits, and less power in the employer–employee relationship both abroad and at home. If we add in US government corn and soybean subsidies that have delivered an estimated $1.25 billion a year in feedstock savings to Tyson and its three closest competitors, things could hardly be better for the food giant.

Mexican migrant workers face discrimination and unequal treatment in the USA. Those who work on US farms are particularly vulnerable, as documented by Farm Worker Justice (2006). Despite the increasing mechanization of agriculture, nearly all fruits and vegetables must still be tended and picked by hand. This makes the labour of migrant and seasonal farm workers critical for the US farms. In 2002, farm workers earned on average just $10,000 to $12,500 per year (nearly 20 per cent below the federal poverty line). Farm workers mostly work ten to twelve hours a day and six to seven days a week in frequently unsanitary and unsafe conditions. Children often join their parents in the fields to supplement the family income. In most cases, employers provide no benefits, whether health coverage, sick leave or disability insurance. They rarely provide education on health hazards or equipment for workers' protection in pesticide-saturated fields. Housing provided to workers is often in overcrowded and substandard trailers, sheds and garages. Despite all these bad conditions, farm workers often cannot speak out owing to language barriers, ignorance and most importantly fear of repercussions such as loss of wages and deportation. The US National Labour Relations Act explicitly excludes undocumented farm workers from protection.

We conclude that while it is problematic to quantify overall job gains and losses attributable to NAFTA, there is evidence to suggest that NAFTA has not resulted in an equal enjoyment of rights at work, with the most vulnerable being the hardest hit. This is not consistent with the obligation to fulfil economic and social rights in a non-discriminatory way.

Minimum core obligations (with respect to the right to food in Mexico)

Trade policy needs to be in compliance with the minimum core obligation of governments to ensure that no significant number of people is deprived of minimum essential levels of economic and social rights. Here, we illustrate this principle with respect to the right to food. The International Covenant on Economic, Social and Cultural Rights (ICESCR) includes the right to food as part of the right to an adequate standard of living (Article 11).

The Special Rapporteur on the right to food further clarified its meaning:

> The right to food is the right to have regular, permanent and unrestricted access, either directly or by means of financial purchases, to quantitatively and qualitatively adequate and sufficient food corresponding to the cultural traditions of the people to which the consumer belongs, and which ensures physical and mental, individual and collective, fulfilling and dignified life free of fear. (Ziegler 2006: 4)

Governments are bound to respect, protect and fulfil the right to food. The obligation to respect means that the government should not arbitrarily reduce existing access to food without providing adequate alternatives. The obligation to protect means that government has a duty to prevent non-state actors from violating the right to food. The obligation to fulfil means that the government must take positive actions to identify vulnerable groups and to implement policies that ensure the access of these groups to adequate food.

States have obligations not only to their own citizens but also to those of other countries. Extraterritorial obligation means that states should ensure that their policies and practices do not lead to deprivation of the right to food for people living in other countries. This does not necessarily require states to provide any resources but does require that they do no harm. In addition, states should ensure that third parties subject to their jurisdiction (such as business corporations) do not violate the right to food of people living in other countries (ibid.).

The human rights responsibilities of corporations have been spelled out in the report on the Norms on the Responsibilities of Transnational Corporations and Other Business Enterprises with Regard to Human Rights, adopted by the Sub-Commission on the Promotion and Protection of Human Rights on 26 August 2003. This document states that corporations have the obligation to promote, secure the fulfilment of, respect, ensure respect for and protect human, economic, social and cultural rights, as well as civil and political rights, recognized in international as well as national law.[15] The Committee on Economic, Social and Cultural Rights has noted the responsibilities of business with respect to the right to food in General Comment 12: 'While only States are parties to the Covenant and are thus ultimately accountable for compliance with it, all members of society – individuals, families, local communities, non-governmental organizations, civil society organizations, as well as the private business sector – have responsibilities in the realization of the right to adequate food ...' (para. 20).

Obligation of conduct Trade agreements must not jeopardize access to minimum essential levels of food (in terms of both quantity and quality), for people in any of the countries whose governments are party to the agreement. How do the provisions for agricultural goods in NAFTA match up to this? In relation to agricultural trade between the United States and Mexico, NAFTA required Mexico to phase out restrictions on imports over a ten-year period, with the exception of corn, dry beans and milk powder, which were to be phased out over a fifteen-year period.[16] But the significance of NAFTA lies not only in its trade provisions. Even more important were NAFTA investor rules that allowed transnational agribusinesses to acquire land for farming and to set up processing plants (Public Citizen 2004b). In addition, NAFTA does not rule out de facto export subsidies, and this has benefited large corn[17] producers in the USA, as explained by Fanjul and Fraser (2003). Corn is the largest recipient of US government support and dominated by a few agribusiness firms such as Cargill, and Archer Daniels Midland (ADM). Support to US corn production is no longer provided through guaranteeing minimum prices (this would contravene NAFTA and other trade liberalization agreements) but works through a system of direct payments based on land area and past output, providing a cushion against risk in the market and providing additional capital for investments. Fanjul and Fraser (ibid.) calculated the de facto export subsidy implied by these payments and found that there is an annual subsidy to US exports to the Mexican market of between $105 and $145 million, which exceeded the total household income of the 250,000 corn farmers in the state of Chiapas. There appears to have been no study of the potential impact of NAFTA provisions on the right to food in Mexico before the agreement was signed.

Obligation of result NAFTA's rule empowering US investors to buy land in Mexico and guaranteeing grain traders access rights to Mexican markets led to the substantial degree of concentration of agribusiness after NAFTA went into effect. Corporations like ADM, Cargill and ConAgra have intensified their control over the production process (Public Citizen 2004a). Only three firms, namely Cargill, ADM and Zen Noh, export over 80 per cent of US corn. While the four largest chicken firms controlled half of the US processing and production market, the top four US beef packers controlled 81 per cent of the US market. The merger of Tyson Foods with meat packer IBP created the world's largest marketer of beef, pork and chicken products. From 1993 to 2000, the profits of agribusiness giants increased enormously (ConAgra's profits grew by 189 per cent between 1993 and 2000, and its net income increased from $437 million in 2000 to $774 million in 2000. Archer Daniels Midland's profits nearly tripled during the 1993–2000 period, while it posted strong net earnings of $511.1 million in 2000; Woodall et al. 2001).

In addition many US corporations bought corn-processing or tortilla-making factories in Mexico, and NAFTA led to the destruction of 28,000 small to medium-sized Mexican businesses through the investment and service sector rules that gave guaranteed access for Wal-Mart and other mega-retailers. Retail prices for basic food products increased sharply (for example, the cost of tortillas rose by 50 per cent) while the prices paid to Mexican farmers fell (Gerson et al. 2004).

As discussed in Chapter 7, the right to a minimum essential level of food (in terms of quality and quantity) was undermined in Mexico by these processes.

Accountability, transparency and participation

Governments have an obligation to conduct trade policy, like all other policy, in ways that are accountable, transparent and participatory. Here we examine the dispute settlement mechanism of NAFTA. Formal dispute settlement mechanisms have been established in six areas under NAFTA (Hufbauer and Schott 2005). Chapter 11 is formulated for investor-state disputes over property rights; Chapter 14 introduced special provisions for handling disputes in the financial sector via the dispute settlement process outlined in Chapter 20; Chapter 19 establishes a review mechanism to decide on whether final anti-dumping and countervailing duty decisions made in domestic tribunals are consistent with national laws; Chapter 20 designs a government-to-government consultation, at the ministerial level, to deal with high-level disputes. These mechanisms allow corporations to challenge laws and policies determined by legislatures in the three NAFTA countries.

We concentrate on Chapter 11, which was established to provide equal treatment among corporate investors from each country. Certain articles in Chapter 11 have been more contentious than others in terms of the protection of investor rights versus the scope of state intervention to regulate private investment. Hufbauer and Schott (ibid.) list the key ones as follows: investment liberalization rights for foreign investors (Article 1101); guarantees to protect existing investments established under conditions that are more favourable than the current reservations held by individual states (Article 1108); national treatment rights (Article 1102); most-favoured-nations rights (Article 1103); minimum international standards of treatment (Article 1105); performance requirements (Article 1106); and provisions for compensation in the event of expropriation.[18] Article 1110 states that a host country cannot expropriate from a foreign investor (either directly or indirectly) unless the following criteria are met: the expropriation is done for a public policy aim; on a non-discriminatory basis, according to due process of law; and with fair compensation.[19]

NAFTA is unique in giving rights to private foreign investors to take legal action against states parties; this right is granted not only to investors who are NAFTA nationals but also to any company incorporated in one of the NAFTA countries. The WTO does not grant private parties access to the dispute settlement mechanism in the way that is done by NAFTA. The WTO mechanism focuses on disputes between states and limits the participation of non-parties such as private firms or NGOs to at most submitting *amicus curiae* (i.e. friend of the court) briefs in panel hearings (ibid.).[20]

NAFTA investor-state disputes can be heard in two international arbitration bodies: the International Centre for the Settlement of Investment Disputes (ICSID), which operates under the auspices of the World Bank, and the United Nations Commission on International Trade Law (UNCITRAL). As noted by Yannaca-Small (2005), the proceedings for the first ten years of NAFTA were far from fully transparent. First, while ISCID applies a policy of publicly registering all cases, under UNCITRAL rules ad hoc (non-institutional) arbitration may take place anywhere without any requirement for registration. Secondly, access to the proceedings and submissions by non-disputant parties has been limited. While NAFTA Articles 1128 and 1129 provide for access to documents and submissions to the US, Mexican and Canadian governments, and for posting the submissions on the Web, NAFTA articles do not make the proceedings accessible to non-disputant private parties unless there is permission from the parties to open the proceedings, or the tribunal opens up the proceedings to *amici curiae*. Thirdly, there is not a general binding rule on publishing awards. These awards usually remain confidential unless the parties to the dispute agree to disclose them (ibid.).

NAFTA's Annex 1137.4 does provide for the possibility of publishing awards. However, the ICSID convention states that an award can be published only when both parties give their consent. In about 50 per cent of the cases, ICSID has obtained the consent of the parties to publish the award. Similarly, according to the UNCITRAL rules, an award may be made public only with the consent of the parties. However, unlike ISCD, UNCITRAL does not have professional staff to provide any administrative oversight for arbitration proceedings and does not collect or compile final decisions in arbitration cases, and therefore cannot make them available to the public, although they are sometimes made public by the plaintiffs. Thus, a UNCITRAL case was able to proceed for years without the public being aware of it. This shows that under UNCITRAL rules, there is even less transparency than under the ICSID rules. Some reforms were proposed by ICSID, such as providing a mechanism for injunctive relief, greater public access to awards, *amici curiae* participation, disclosure rules for panellists and an appeals procedure. However, these changes can be made only if all 140 contracting states ratify the amendment, thus it is not clear how long such a process may take (Bottari and Wallach 2005).

The governments that agreed NAFTA have taken some steps in response to the criticisms about the transparency of the system. In July 2001, the NAFTA parties stated that there is not a general duty of confidentiality imposed by NAFTA and agreed that they would make all documents submitted to or issued by Chapter 11 tribunals publicly available in a timely manner (being subject to certain exceptions for confidential or privileged information). In October 2003, the governments of Canada and the United States, and in July 2004 the government of Mexico, stated that they would consent, and request disputing investors and tribunals to consent, to holding open-to-public hearings (being subject to measures to protect confidential business information). A statement was issued that outlines the procedures for non-disputing party participation in Chapter 11 proceedings (Gantz 2009). As a result, virtually all Chapter 11 hearings have become open to the public. However, because of the technicality of the proceedings, in reality very few people attend these hearings (Kinnear 2005).

Although these small steps have been taken towards increased transparency, the accountability of the process is still open to question. Gantz (2009) argues that none of the subsequent reassessment of NAFTA Chapter 11 provisions has significantly affected the Chapter 11 language or the NAFTA tribunal process, although it is an improvement that public concerns about NAFTA investor rights and transparency issues have been taken into account.

In the fifteen-year history of NAFTA, at least fifty notices of arbitration, including those that are dormant or abandoned, have been filed by foreign investors against NAFTA governments. Two cases against Canada and four cases against Mexico have resulted in award of monetary damages, while no monetary damages have been awarded against the USA, as of early 2009. Each NAFTA government has been a respondent in sixteen or more cases (all being Canadian investors in the case of the USA) (ibid.).

A variety of legislation and policies have been challenged by corporate investors, as discussed by Bottari and Wallach (2005). For example, US waste management company Metalclad Corp challenged decisions by Mexican local government to deny a permit to operate a hazardous waste landfill in La Pedrera, San Luis Potosi; and by the state government to create an ecological preserve in the area; and claimed $90 million in compensation. A NAFTA tribunal ruled that Mexico violated NAFTA Articles 1105 (minimum standards of treatment) and 1110 (expropriation and compensation), and ordered Mexico to pay $16.7 million (Sinclair 2008).[21] The value of the award is large relative to Mexico's environmental protection budget.

There are also cases in which governments' policies on protection against toxic substances have been challenged. Sinclair (ibid.) gives the full list and details of various investor-state disputes as of 1 January 2008. Among them, US chemical company Ethyl Corporation challenged a Canadian ban on the import and inter-provincial trade of the gasoline additive MMT, claiming $250 million in compensation. The Canadian government repealed the ban and settled 'out of court' with Ethyl for $13 million. In a case against the state government of California, the Canadian chemical company Methanex Corp. challenged California's phase-out of MTBE, a gasoline additive which has contaminated ground and surface water throughout California, and claimed $970 million in compensation. However, the investor's claims were dismissed by the tribunal in August 2005 on the ground that the link between California's MTBE ban and Methanex operations was not legally significant (Gantz 2009).

A US agribusiness and a US subsidiary of a British multinational company – Archer Daniels Midland – challenged the Mexican government on a number of regulations, including a tax on sales of soft drinks sweetened with high-fructose corn syrup, claiming that it discouraged the import, production and sale of high-fructose corn syrup. The tribunal issued an award in favour of the agribusiness and against Mexico in November 2007.

As these examples demonstrate, NAFTA Chapter 11 has enabled corporations to sue governments and secure orders for governments to pay huge amounts of compensation. Cases have challenged environmental and health laws as well as zoning and permit policies; and have undermined accountability and participation by overruling standards and regulations agreed by democratically elected bodies, including Congress, state legislatures or city councils (Public Citizen 2004b). Chapter 11 of the NAFTA dispute settlement mechanism does not uphold standards of accountability, transparency and participation.

Conclusion

This chapter has examined NAFTA in the light of human rights standards, considering both the obligations of the US government to those living in the USA, and its extraterritorial obligations to those living in Mexico. Although there were some attempts by the US government to comply with non-discrimination obligations through conducting an impact assessment study, introducing compensation measures for low-income workers (among whom racial/ethnic minorities and women are over-represented) and introducing a side agreement on labour rights, these have been grossly inadequate. NAFTA strengthened the rights of wealthy corporations, and helped them to become wealthier; while it weakened the rights of low-income workers, among whom racial and ethnic minorities and women are over-represented. While it is not possible to be completely definitive about overall job gains and losses attributable to NAFTA, there is evidence to suggest that NAFTA has not resulted in an equal enjoyment of rights at work, with the low-income workers being the hardest hit. Men disproportionately lost jobs, as compared to women; but women who had lost their jobs found it harder to get new comparable jobs than men who had lost their jobs. Workers of Hispanic origin were harder hit in terms of job loss than other racial/ethnic groups. All workers of colour who lost their jobs found it harder to secure new comparable jobs than did white workers. Neither conduct nor result appears to be consistent with the principle of non-discrimination and equality.

No thought appears to have been given by the US state to its extraterritorial obligations regarding NAFTA. For instance, there appears to have been no study of the potential impact of NAFTA provisions on the right to food in Mexico before the agreement was signed. Following imports for the USA and the increased influence of US corporations, retail prices for basic food products increased sharply, while the prices paid to Mexican farmers fell (Gerson et al. 2004). The right to a minimum level of nutritious food has been undermined in Mexico, in part owing to the actions of US corporations. The government of the USA is complicit in this deterioration, in the subsidies it provides to US agribusiness (especially for corn syrup) and its failure to adequately regulate corporations involved in the supply of food in Mexico.

NAFTA is unique among trade agreements in granting foreign investors the right to sue governments for introducing measures that are found to impede the investor's freedom to make profits. There is a lack of adequate provision for accountability, transparency and participation in the operation of the NAFTA dispute settlement mechanism. Overall, the evidence discussed here suggests that the US state has negotiated and operated a trade agreement that does not comply fully with its human rights obligations.

Notes

1 Committee on Economic, Social and Cultural Rights, Statement entitled 'Globalization and economic, social and cultural rights', 18th session, May 1998.

2 Ibid.

3 As defined in the General Agreement on Trade and Tariffs, Article 1, most-favoured-nation treatment requires that 'any advantage, favour, privilege or immunity granted by any contracting party to any product originating in or destined for any other country shall be accorded immediately and unconditionally to the like product originating in or destined for the territories of all other contracting parties'.

4 The principle of giving others the same treatment as one's own nationals. GATT Article 3 requires that imports be treated no less favourably than the same or similar domestically produced goods once they have passed customs.

5 MacNaughton (2009) points out that the Universal Declaration of Human Rights (UDHR), Article 2, prohibits discrimination on grounds of 'property'; and that this is widely regarded as referring to economic status. She notes that the official Spanish version of the UDHR uses the term *posición económica* for 'property', rather than *propiedad* or *patrimonio*.

6 TAA consists of the Trade Adjustment Assistance for Workers, Alternative Trade Adjustment Assistance (ATAA), and Reemployment Trade Adjustment Assistance (RTAA) programmes. For an overview of the programme and a discussion of its problems, see Rosen (2008).

7 Yearly appropriations at first increased but then declined. The total amounts appropriated were (in 2000 dollars) $0.91 billion in 2003; $1.21 billion in 2004; $0.93 billion in 2005; $0.82 billion in 2006; $0.71 in 2007; and $0.75 billion in 2008. Calculated from US Department of Labour, TAA statistics, www.doleta.gov/tradeact/pdf/5YearApprop.pdf. Constant prices are calculated by the author using CPI-All Urban Index taken from Bureau of Labour Statistics.

8 www.doleta.gov/tradeact/taa_reports/petitions.cfm (accessed 3 September 2010).

9 They base their calculation on the estimated number of workers covered by certifications in the NAFTA-TAA programme and the estimated number of workers who lost their jobs; R. E. Scott, 'The high price of "free trade": NAFTA's failure has cost the United States jobs across the nation', Economic Policy Institute, November 2003.

10 www.doleta.gov/tradeact/taa_reports/performance_reports.cfm (accessed 5 September 2009).

11 www.doleta.gov/tradeact/docs/ParticipationNum.pdf.

12 A wage subsidy is provided to older workers as an alternative to benefits that help eligible workers to get back to work. Accordingly, '... eligible workers age 50 or older who obtain new, full-time employment at wages of less than $50,000 within 26 weeks of their separation may receive a wage subsidy of 50 per cent of the difference between the old and new wages, with a maximum of $10,000 paid over a period of up to two years' (ETA 2010).

13 All the information regarding the changes to the TAA programme are taken from the Department of Labour's FY2010 Congressional Budget Justification document, www.dol.gov/dol/budget/2010/PDF/CBJ-2010-V1-06.pdf.

14 They acknowledge that using the NAFTA-TAA programme understates the figures because not all workers who are displaced owing to NAFTA apply for this assistance programme.

15 Other important intergovernmental instruments that apply to TNCs are the OECD Guidelines, under which all partners are bound to establish national contact points to deal with complaints of violations by a TNC; the ILO Tripartite Declaration of Principles Concerning Multinational Enterprises and Social Policy, the International Code of Marketing of Breastmilk Substitutes adopted by the World Health Organization and UNICEF, and the Code of Ethics for International Trade in Food adopted by the Codex Alimentarius Commission; and the UN Secretary-General's Global Compact initiative, by which TNCs can commit themselves to respect the protection of human rights within their sphere of influence and make sure that they are not complicit in activities that violate human rights.

16 www.cbp.gov/xp/cgov/trade/trade_programs/international_agreements/free_trade/nafta/customs_procedures/prov_specific_sectors/agricultural_products.xml.

17 The term 'corn' is used in the USA. In Mexico the same crop is termed 'maize'.

18 According to Articles 1102 and 1103, a host country must treat foreign investment and investors 'no less favourably than domestic investors or investors from any other country in like circumstances'. Since this issue of fair and equitable treatment is not clearly defined, it is open to misinterpretation and case-by-case treatment. Article 1105 requires governments to meet minimum standards of international law, and Article 1106 prohibits governments from imposing performance requirements on investors, such as requiring firms to use domestic inputs (Hufbauer and Schott 2005).

19 Fair compensation implies compensating foreign investors for profits lost owing to regulation for domestic social policies (environment, human health, safety).

20 See Hufbauer and Schott (2005) for a further discussion on other differences between the WTO and NAFTA dispute settlement mechanisms.

21 Mexico applied for statutory review of the tribunal award in the BC Supreme Court; however, most of the award was allowed to stand and Mexico paid an undisclosed amount to the US company.

References

Beneria, L. and L. E. Santiago (2001) 'The impact of industrial relocation on displaced workers: a case study of Cortland, New York', *Economic Development Quarterly*, 15(1): 78–89.

Blecker, R. (2003) 'The North American economies after NAFTA: a critical appraisal', *International Journal of Political Economy*, 33(3): 5–27.

Bottari, M. and L. Wallach (2005) 'NAFTA Chapter 11 investor-state cases: lessons for the Central America Free Trade Agreement', Public Citizen's Global Trade Watch.

Carlsen, L. (2008) 'Two chicken stories: NAFTA's real winner and losers', America's Program, Centre for International Policy (CIP), 17 April, www.ilw.com/articles/2008,0514-carlsen.shtm.

CESCR (Committee on Economic, Social and Cultural Rights) Fact Sheet no. 16 (Rev. 1), Geneva.

— (2009) General Comment 20, 'Non-Discrimination in Economic, Social and Cultural Rights' (Article 2, para. 2), E/C.12/GC/20.

CTC (Citizen's Trade Campaign) (2001) 'NAFTA's double standard: what can you do if your rights are violated?', Citizen's Trade Campaign fact sheet.

De Schutter, O. (2007) 'Reconciling trade and human rights: lessons from the battlefield', Keynote speaker address, in *Reconciling Trade and Human Rights: The New Development Agenda*, ed. A. Simpson, conference report.

Delp, L., M. Arriaga, G. Palma, H. Urita and A. Valenzula (2004) 'NAFTA's Labour Side Agreement: fading into oblivion? An assessment of workplace health & safety cases', UCLA Center for Labour Research and Education.

ETA (Employment and Training Administration) (2010) 'Trade adjustment assistance – services and benefits', Washington, DC: US Department of Labor, http://www.doleta.gov/tradeact/pdf/Benefits_Services_Factsheet.pdf.

Fanjul, G. and A. Fraser (2003) 'Dumping without borders: how US agricultural policies are destroying the livelihoods of Mexican corn farmers', Oxfam Briefing Paper no. 50.

Farmworker Justice (2006) 25th Anniversary Report, Washington, DC, http://www.fwjustice.org/files/reports/25thAnnivbooklet.pdf.

Gantz, D. A. (2009) 'The United States and NAFTA dispute settlement: ambivalence, frustration and occasional defiance', Arizona Legal Studies Discussion Paper no. 06-26, James E. Rogers College of Law, University of Arizona.

GAO (Government Accountability Office) (2006) *Trade Adjustment Assistance: Most Workers in Five Layoffs Received Services, but Better Outreach Needed on New Benefits*, GAO-06-43, Washington, DC.

Gerson, T., R. Islas, F. Wright, A. Zelada, K. M. Hernandez and A. Ayao (2004) 'The impact of NAFTA on the US Latino community and lessons for future trade agreements', Joint report by Labour Council for Latin American Advancement and Public Citizen's Global Trade Watch.

Hufbauer, G. C. and J. J. Schott (2005) *NAFTA Revisited: Achievements and Challenges*, Washington, DC: Institute for International Economics.

Khor, M. (2007) Keynote speaker address, in

Reconciling Trade and Human Rights: The New Development Agenda, ed. A. Simpson, conference report.

Kinnear, M. (2005) 'Transparency and third party participation in investor-state dispute settlement', Paper presented at the Symposium 'Making the Most of International Investment Agreements: A Common Agenda', co-organized by ISCID, OECD and UNCTAD, Paris, 2 December.

Kletzer, L. G. (2001) *Job Loss from Imports: Measuring the Costs*, Washington, DC: Institute for International Economics.

Kunnemann, R. (2007) 'The extraterritorial scope of the International Covenant on Economic, Social and Cultural Rights', Document D18e, Food First Information and Action Network (FIAN).

MacNaughton, G. (2009) 'Untangling equality and non-discrimination to promote the right to health care for all', *Health and Human Rights*, 11(2): 47–62.

McCombie, J. and A. Thirlwall (1994) *Economic Growth and the Balance-of-Payments Constraint*, London: Palgrave Macmillan.

Milberg, W. (1994) 'Is absolute advantage passé?: towards a post Keynesian/Marxian theory of international trade', in M. Glick (ed.), *Competition, Technology and Money: Classical and Post-Keynesian Perspectives*, Cheltenham: Edward Elgar.

Prove, P. (2007) 'Becoming acquainted? International trade and human rights', Speaker address, in *Reconciling Trade and Human Rights: The New Development Agenda*, ed. A. Simpson, conference report.

Public Citizen (2004a) 'The ten year track record of the North American Free Trade Agreement: US, Mexican and Canadian farmers and agriculture', NAFTA at Ten Series.

— (2004b) 'The ten year track record of the North American Free Trade Agreement: undermining sovereignty and democracy', NAFTA at Ten Series.

Ranney, D. (2003) 'NAFTA in the United States: an assessment', in Hemispheric Social Alliance, *Lessons from NAFTA: The High Cost of Free Trade*, Hemispheric Social Alliance's Monitoring and Alternatives Committee from Mexico, the United States and Canada, June.

Rosen, H. F. (2008) 'Strengthening trade adjustment assistance', Peterson Institute for International Economics Policy Brief no. PB08-2.

Scott, R. E., C. Salas and B. Campbell (2006) 'Revisiting NAFTA: still not working for North America's workers', Economic Policy Institute Briefing Paper no. 173.

Shaikh, A. (2007) 'Globalization and the myth of free trade', in A. Shaikh (ed.), *Globalization and the Myths of Free Trade: History, Theory, and Empirical Evidence*, Routledge Frontiers of Political Economy, New York: Routledge.

Sinclair, S. (2008) 'NAFTA Chapter 11 investor-state disputes (to 1 January 2008)', Canadian Center for Policy Alternatives.

Solomon, J. (2001) 'Trading away rights: the unfilled promises of NAFTA's Labour Side Agreement', *Human Rights Watch*, 13(2(B)), April.

Tucker, T., B. Wu and A. Prorok (2005) *Trade Wars – Revenge of the Myth: Deals for Trade Votes Gone Bad*, Public Citizen's Global Trade Watch.

USDA (United States Department of Agriculture) (2008) 'North American Free Trade Agreement (NAFTA)', US Department of Agriculture – Foreign Agricultural Service fact sheet, January.

USITC (1991) *The Likely Impact on the United States of a Free Trade Agreement with Mexico*, Washington, DC: US International Trade Commission.

USTR (Office of the United States Trade Representative) (2008) 'NAFTA – myth vs. facts', USTR Fact Sheet, Washington, DC, www.ustr.gov/sites/default/files/NAFTA-Myth-versus-Fact.pdf.

Woodall, P., L. Wallach, J. Roach and D. Patel (2001) 'Down on the farm: NAFTA's seven-years war on farmers and ranchers in the US, Canada, and Mexico', Public Citizen's Global Trade Watch Research Report.

Yannaca-Small, C. (2005) 'Transparency and third party participation in investor-state dispute settlement procedures', Working Papers on International Investment no. 2005/1, OECD Investment Division, April.

Ziegler, J. (2006) 'Economic, Social and Cultural Rights: the right to food', Report of the Special Rapporteur on the right to food, 16 March.

9 | REGULATION: PENSION REFORM AND HUMAN RIGHTS IN MEXICO

Gabriel Lara Salazar

Mexico's retirement security system

The social security system in Mexico is primarily public and is regulated by an array of bills. The system has always been a complex one, but this feature has particularly increased since the reform of the Instituto Mexicano del Seguro Social (IMSS) – the largest public pension provider – in 1995[1] and the 2007 reform of the State Employees' Social Security and Social Services Institute (ISSSTE). In practice, those reforms have led to a transition from a defined benefit system to a defined contribution system.

The current system covers only people employed in the formal labour market. It includes people working for private firms or businesses, and people working for all branches of the federal government.

The first, and by far largest, group of labourers fall under the IMSS system, based on tripartite contributions by employer, employee and federal government, as a proportion of the worker's salary. Each worker chooses a private fund administrator, called an AFORE (Administradora de Fondos para el Retiro), to administer the money collected through contributions. In turn, the AFORE charges a fee and invests the worker's money through a diversified portfolio of financial assets using a dedicated entity known as SIEFORE (Sociedad de Inversión Especializada en Fondos para el Retiro). Although the system was privatized, contributions are still collected by IMSS and then handed over to AFOREs. Most of the AFOREs are run by banks (although IMSS has its own AFORE, called Siglo XXI).

The second group of employees, who are part of the formal economy – namely those employed by the federal government – are covered by ISSSTE. Their pension is based on contributions by each employee and the federal government, as a proportion of the worker's salary. Until recently, the ISSSTE pensions were withdrawn from and paid for through a collective fund composed of contributions from the government and its workers, as administered by ISSSTE. Nevertheless, a new law has been enacted allowing for this system to become privatized, following IMSS and the 1995 reforms.

While this might appear a standard pension system, it actually entailed important changes in terms of the responsibility of different players in the provision of social security. The pension system in Mexico formally started when the IMSS Law was enacted in 1943, followed by the ISSSTE Law in 1959. To pay pensions, IMSS collected a weekly contribution by employers and the federal government, based on the worker's or employee's salary. Under that original scheme, the worker did not contribute into his/her own pension fund.

With the transition to a privatized system, the employers' and the federal government's shares decreased, being absorbed by the employees themselves to compensate for this reduction.

As a result, the year 1997 displayed a turning point in the rules of social security and the provision of pensions, at least in terms of employees' salary. Workers started to contribute from their own earnings to their own retirement. The contribution is compulsory, and has replaced almost entirely the government's obligations to contribute to the pensions of privately employed workers.

Progressive realization and non-retrogression

Obligation of conduct Neither the IMSS reform (1995) nor the ISSSTE reform (2007) was geared towards providing universal access to social security in Mexico. The modifications pushed by the government blatantly ignored ILO's Convention 102, a commitment undertaken by the Mexican government in 1982, which established the obligation to advance towards universal access to social security, regardless of employment conditions. In blatant contravention of this commitment, the Mexican government has not made any effort to progressively realize universal coverage. In effect, access to a retirement pension continues to operate under the same limited scheme which has been operational since the 1940s. As such, these pensions are understood as a benefit that belongs to those who contribute to the system – not as a human right that belongs to every person and which has to be fulfilled at a certain age.

According to the XII Census of Population and Housing (*XII Censo General de Población y Vivienda*), in the year 2000 the economically inactive population aged sixty and older included 5,764,175 persons. Of that population, only 1,177,029 people were effectively receiving a pension through IMSS or ISSSTE in 2001. More than 4.5 million people aged sixty and older had no support at all in terms of receiving a pension in Mexico.

Table 9.1 illustrates that this situation has seen no substantive change throughout the intervening years. Given the overall ageing trend of the Mexican population, the gap between those who should be receiving a pension and the number of pensions that are effectively granted has not diminished, regardless of the reforms.

The IMSS and the ISSSTE reforms implied a transition from the collective fund or defined benefit pensions system (also called pay-as-you-go) to individual funds, or defined contribution pensions. The collective fund system used to work in the following way: employers, the government and employees contributed an amount equivalent to a proportion of the labourer's salary into a collective fund from which pensions were paid once a worker retired.

TABLE 9.1 Total number of pensions granted by IMSS and ISSSTE

	2001	2002	2003	2004	2005	2006	2007
IMSS[a]	765,949	824,008	874,630	935,943	992,502	1,047,210	1,051,341
ISSSTE[b]	411,080	441,970	476,072	510,138	547,318	578,392	612,205[c]
TOTAL	1,177,029	1,265,978	1,350,702	1,446,081	1,539,820	1,625,602	1,663,546

Notes: a. Figures include early retirement   b. Figures include retirement by worked time and by age   c. Estimated through December 2007.

Source: Author's elaboration based on IMSS (2007), and for ISSSTE *Primer Informe de Gobierno 2007, Anexo Estadístico*

The amount of the pension was calculated by taking into account the average salary, the number of years the employee worked, the age of retirement and life expectancy. It is called a defined benefit pension because it is possible to estimate its amount before the moment of retirement is reached.

The defined contribution system accumulates, during a pre-established time period, the employee's or tripartite contributions. It is not possible to know the amount of the pension beforehand because it depends not only on the years worked and the amount paid into an individual account, but also on interest rates and fees charged for the management of the account. The only certainty in this system is that the labourer will contribute money regularly into the private account.

As a result of going from a collective fund to an individual fund system workers were pressured to increase the number of years they worked, and this triggered uncertainty regarding the amount of the pension a worker would receive upon retirement. Furthermore, the Mexican government's arguments for reforming the system began to focus on the better operation of a private system.

Before the reform, IMSS pensions were granted to workers aged sixty-five who had fulfilled at least 500 weeks of contributions to the system. The 1995 law more than doubled the required contribution time, scaling it up to 1,250 weeks (see Table 9.2). Under the new IMSS Law, employees and workers

TABLE 9.2 The changing qualification conditions for an IMSS pension

	1973 law	1995 law
Age	65 years for full pension	65 years for full pension
Number of weeks	Last 500 weeks (almost 10 years)	1,250 weeks (24 years)

Source: Author's elaboration based on IMSS 1973 and 1995 laws

would have to amass twenty-four years of paid work in the formal economy to qualify for a pension.

Obligation of result According to data from the Department of Social Development,[2] there were 3.7 million poor people aged seventy and older in Mexico in 2007. To address this situation, the federal government has designed a programme targeting elderly people in rural areas. This programme offers 500 Mexican pesos every month to persons who can demonstrate that they are aged seventy or older and that they reside in a community of up to 20,000 people. The programme reached 1,201,808 persons during the first quarter of 2008.[3]

This effort to provide some kind of financial support to the impoverished elderly is not to be compared with the benefits of having a pension. First and foremost, the amount of money they receive is one third of the minimum pension. Secondly, the programme can be accessed only from the age of seventy, not sixty. Thirdly, residence in a rural area has to be proven – tacitly discriminating against the poor living in urban areas. Fourthly, persons with a pension also have access to a network of IMSS clinics and hospitals; this is not the case for those who did not contribute to the system.

This is a meagre effort on the part of a government that is not willing to realize its obligations in terms of providing pensions to all elderly persons. The Mexican government transformed the Mexican people from rights bearers – regardless of formal employment status, social condition and geographic location – into passive beneficiaries of government support.

Non-discrimination and equality

Obligation of conduct It is relevant to point out the opportunity the federal government had when faced with the option to expand the social security coverage through legal reforms, although finally opting to keep coverage as it was. This particular decision contravenes the 'no discrimination' provision enshrined in human rights principles: the Mexican federal government is discriminating according to the labour conditions of its population. Additionally, the programme for elderly people is designated exclusively for rural people and, again, the federal government takes actions that discriminate on the basis of geographical conditions. Since the introduction of the defined contribution system there has been a repeated pattern of discrimination.

Although there is scarce comparable official information on pensions coverage disaggregated by different groups, age and gender, it is possible to use the data from the active labour force and their access to social security in order to establish some tendencies to future pension coverage and some comparisons (see Table 9.3).

First of all, the data show that regardless of age, education or gender, 63 per cent of the active labour force does not have access to social security. According to age distribution,[4] there are two important findings: men have

TABLE 9.3 Active labour force and social security access, disaggregated by age, education and gender

	Men			Women		
	With	Without	Not specified	With	Without	Not specified
14 to 19 years old	417,022	2,191,990	8,518	236,590	1,034,479	4,467
20 to 29 years old	2,627,190	3,579,581	33,865	1,844,514	2,206,782	24,351
30 to 39 years old	2,794,607	3,742,062	42,723	1,750,190	2,464,948	17,752
40 to 49 years old	2,161,452	3,219,919	36,529	1,431,201	2,169,605	16,801
50 to 59 years old	1,202,594	2,350,806	31,255	539,161	1,319,893	19,294
60 years old and beyond	369,605	2,009,382	11,257	118,490	858,165	4,733
Not specified	1,952	8,218	87	2,335	2,291	0
TOTAL	9,574,422	17,101,958	164,234	5,922,481	10,056,163	87,398
No formal education	139,036	1,368,306	2,002	39,623	905,926	1,225
Pre-school	3,226	15,098	0	93	3,543	0
Primary	1,768,211	7,092,813	35,333	685,083	3,880,857	21,041
Secondary	2,747,067	4,701,316	46,240	1,222,212	2,642,189	22,764
High school	1,927,405	2,063,716	38,951	1,006,428	1,109,113	15,969
Teacher training school	163,122	36,681	1,122	298,116	53,613	878
Technical studies	464,813	357,118	5,773	851,380	676,043	5,260
Undergraduated	2,137,284	1,596,846	33,487	1,672,410	850,773	16,680
Graduated	192,723	90,360	987	131,227	41,950	1,280
PhD	29,050	14,922	339	12,172	5,711	415
Not specified	3,343	10,514	0	3,920	6,178	1,886
TOTAL	9,575,280	17,347,690	164,234	5,922,664	10,175,896	87,398

Source: Elaborated using data from Instituto Nacional de Estadística, Geografía e Informatica, *Encuesta Nacional de Ocupación y Empleo, 2° Trimestre 2007*

more jobs with social security than women in all age groups; but also men (without access to social security) have more jobs than women without access to social security. Nevertheless, because both men and women are facing a scarcity of jobs giving them access to social security and qualifying them to receive a pension (after 1,250 weeks of paying contributions to social security) they face equal odds. This is true for the age groups 20 to 29 years old and 30 to 39 years old, who constitute nearly half of the 63 per cent of the active labour force that does not have access to social security.

According to Table 9.3, an even worse situation prevails with regard to education. Again from the latter percentage, the active labour force with no formal education, pre-school, primary and secondary education reaches 47 per cent of that 63 per cent of the population. The market economy demands unskilled jobs (usually low-wage-paying jobs), and many of those are temporary or are located in the informal sector. Given this panorama, the odds are limited for a worker with only primary education and between 20 and 59 years old to accumulate 1,250 weeks of contributions to the social security system, as is required to receive a retirement pension.

The privatization of the social security system means that, for a large majority of people in their early and mid-work life terms and with low levels of education, the system chosen by the federal government is almost certainly denying them a future pension. It remains to be seen whether some new or modified policies for all elderly people will be implemented to close the gap that privatization was never meant to address.

Obligation of result The challenge posed to these private systems by age and education level is particularly severe when one looks at the disproportionate effects on women in the workforce in most developing countries. Women tend to work more often in the informal sector (Sinha 2002: 32).

Studies have shown that women spend a significant part of their life without working in the formal labour market; whether they work at home or they stop working owing to maternity or because of the nature of the jobs women do, such as laundering other people's clothes or preparing and selling home-made food. These reasons explain why women spend less time in jobs within the formal labour market.

Again, the increase in the number of weeks in which a worker must contribute to social security to access a retirement pension have a disproportionate effect on women as compared to men owing to the conditions described previously. Nevertheless, women were supposed to benefit in the privatized system: the money they could accumulate in their individual accounts could be claimed at age sixty, even though they might not have met the pension prerequisites. Previous pension systems denied them this. But the issue remains the same: women do not participate in the formal labour market as consistently as men. The legal reforms did not take this into consideration and subsequently there have not been any efforts to solve this condition, within the social security system or outside it. This lack of action from the federal government is in clear violation of its equity obligation in an issue that is so crucial to women.

Transparency and accountability

Obligation of conduct The process to reform IMSS and ISSSTE laws and privatizing its pensions systems were undertaken in a time of limited transparency and accountability. Nevertheless, those are changes impacting today's workers' future pensions. Thus, there should be mechanisms to inform individual accounts holders about their assets and let them make decisions on the type of investments they would like to be made.

The mechanism in the hands of individual account holders to enhance their pension is to select the optimal financial portfolio combination. In other words, this means having a balance between high-risk/high-interest and low-risk/lower-interest financial assets; a young account holder can bear a bulkier high-risk portfolio and use his or her youth as a safety net in the event of financial losses, meaning there is time to correct the combination. A mid to senior account holder would not want to compromise a large proportion of his or her money by placing it in high-risk financial assets; rather, he or she would want to invest in financial assets with a guaranteed interest rate – although the interest rate will be lower by definition. This is a basic principle of investing future pension resources.

However, this is a highly specialized area, meaning that in real life the maths necessary to maintain a balanced portfolio are complex and demand time and knowledge of the financial world. This does not accord with the reality that most Mexican workers face: they work forty-eight hours a week, they have almost no technical school education and they earn no more than US$458 a month.[5]

Given this scenario, the private system needs a regulatory body to enforce provision of information for account holders by AFOREs and to oversee the latter. This regulatory body in Mexico is the Comisión Nacional del Sistema de Ahorro para el Retiro Inicio (CONSAR), and the information produced for account holders regarding the different options they have in terms of investing their money has been simplified by CONSAR, supposedly for protective reasons. Since 28 March 2008, there have been five different portfolio options[6] for specific investments by a Sociedad de Inversión Especializada en Fondos para el Retiro (SIEFORE); each one balances the type of financial assets it has and the age of the account holder. This means that the older the account holder, the safer the portfolio is, but at the same time the interest will be lower and vice versa.

The names and age ranges of the five portfolios are:

- Basic 5: 26 years old and less;
- Basic 4: between 27 and 36 years old;

- Basic 3: between 37 and 45 years old;
- Basic 2: between 46 and 55 years old;
- Basic 1: 56 years old and more.

The system moves account holders between portfolios based on their age and gives them the option to move only to a safer portfolio, for example if an account holder is 50 years old, he or she will be in portfolio Basic 2, but will be given the option to move to Basic 1. If the holder does not choose an option, CONSAR will tell AFORE to invest the holder's money in the portfolio corresponding to his or her age. This is the actual option workers – as account holders – have to maximize the future amount of their pension, and it is important to note that the worker can only choose a combination of financial assets, not the specific instruments SIEFORE is going to invest in. This is a limited mechanism for the account holder to maximize her investments, since control of her portfolio is in the hands of an unknown functionary at SIEFORE, so one can be forgiven for wondering for whom SIEFOREs are really working. Besides, it is highly probable that low-income workers would not benefit from it for the reason discussed earlier (amount and number of contributions).

In effect, the government is accountable for this situation because the government decided to move to a system in which difficulties are addressed by individual workers. The solution mechanisms for this situation are against the interest of the majority of workers; and the government's responsibility to protect their human rights is brought into question.

The current legislation[7] obliges AFOREs to send to each account holder a note of the balance of his or her money at least once a year. This must inform the holder of the amount of contributions, the amount charged[8] by AFORE in fees, and the overall profit from the portfolio. This information should enable the account holder to assess whether the chosen AFORE is doing a good job, especially in terms of fees and profit performance. So based on this information and charts comparing all AFOREs – also contained in the notification – account holders can change AFOREs as many times as they want. This option has led to an 'advertisement war' between AFOREs to keep account holders and/or persuade others to join. This makes it hard for workers to choose between the eighteen AFOREs, mainly because of the complexity of the fees scheme.

Based on this, the Federal Congress changed the law in April 2007 so that by March 2008 all AFOREs will provide details of net 'profit' to the workers. This will be calculated by subtracting the commission charged from the gross profit. This legislative change will enable workers to better choose an AFORE and their investment portfolio. Workers will also assume the losses when SIEFORE invests in risky assets (remember that the worker can choose only a combination of financial assets, not the specific instruments SIEFORE is going to invest in). So, no matter how simplified the information is, the worker always assumes the losses (and the benefits). But clear information will not change the fact that there is more risk placed on workers' shoulders than on the private companies running the system because of the simple fact that what is at stake is the future livelihoods of workers. There is not enough transparency in this private pension system to pronounce it in compliance with the human rights provision that the government is supposed to meet.

Obligation of result As a result of going from a collective fund to an individual fund system workers were pressured to increase the number of years they work. Meanwhile it triggered uncertainty regarding the amount of the pension a worker is to receive upon retirement. The Mexican government's arguments for reforming the system were based on an assumption that the private sector would run the sector more efficiently. There has been no significant improvement in terms of the amounts paid through the new pension scheme.

The management companies of retirement funds (AFOREs) have gained a great deal owing to the fees that they charge for the management of every single individual account. According to CONSAR, at the end of May 2008 eighteen AFOREs were operating in Mexico. The resources these eighteen companies were managing[9] amounted to 867.924 billion pesos – 8.2 per cent of Mexico's GDP[10] and almost 34 per cent of the federal budget in 2008.[11]

Despite the 38,888,922[12] individual accounts that currently exist, IMSS had only 14,390 workers registered in May 2008.[13] This means that almost two-thirds of the existing accounts are inactive, i.e. without account movement and without contributions from the account holder or the government. This is due to the increase in informal employment, temporary employment, self-employment and unemployment. These 24 million persons embracing different forms of earning a living have one thing in common: they were once part of the formal economy, and thus have an individual retirement account, to which they have ceased to contribute.

Article 37 of the Retirement Savings System Law (Ley de los Sistemas de Ahorro para el Retiro), which addresses the fees an AFORE can charge, does not specify what will happen to an inactive account. As such, it is possible that, at a certain moment, the fees will be bigger than the interest generated, 'eating up' the funds in the account. In such a perspective, the account could end up being cancelled,[14] based on Chapter XI of the CONSAR 22-13[15] memo. AFOREs are businesses; they will continue charging fees on individual accounts, even if they are inactive. AFOREs will have no remorse in consuming the scant savings of workers who, because of an unstable economic environment, have no formal employment. By rule, private entities do not absorb social costs, unless clear limits are imposed on them.

National enterprises should hypothetically generate new employment opportunities owing to the reduction from 95 per cent to 70 per cent in the share of their contributions into the system. Even though we lack estimates of the amount of money that enterprises stopped contributing to the system after the reform, it is possible to affirm that the promise to generate formal employment has not materialized. Furthermore, the percentage of temporary and informal employment continues to rise. This implies that while enterprises gained from the fact of contributing less to the social security system, they failed to contribute to a better economic environment.

Based on CONSAR data, during June 2008 SIEFOREs[16] invested 16.7 per cent of the workers' assets in resourcing private debt in Mexico, which in essence means making financial loans to national enterprises, and this has been growing. Ironically, the workers are the ones who finance national enterprises, given that they cannot access the money in their individual accounts in the short term. It seems that national enterprises gained much more than the savings from no longer having to contribute their original share to the workers' pension scheme; when the system was reformed they also gained access to a steady source of money for their private ventures.

The federal government's role must be examined because part of SIEFOREs' portfolio and financial instruments are composed of government debt. This proportion represented 97 per cent of the total instruments of SIEFOREs at a given moment (Rodríguez 2005). Since 2000, this proportion has been decreasing, in favour of national enterprises. Nevertheless, government debt still comprises 61.3 per cent of SIEFOREs' portfolio today. Foreign governments have also benefited, given that since 2002 investment by SIEFOREs in foreign financial instruments was approved.[17] In June 2008, foreign instruments represented 6.5 per cent of the SIEFOREs' portfolio.

The natural 'losers' of the pension system's privatization are the labourers. First, their required work time more than doubled. Secondly, the amount of their pension did not increase significantly, especially for the largest portion of the labour force, who earn between one and two minimum wages. Thirdly, they are underwriting all the risks involved in having their retirement funds invested in financial instruments with variable returns. There are no clear provisions regarding what would happen if an AFORE declared itself bankrupt. But what is most likely to happen is that the government would have to absorb the costs – as in the recent bailout of banks in the USA – which means public money could be used to avert the bankruptcy of private corporations. In the end, these costs would be paid by Mexican society.

To sum up, the AFOREs are the big winners of the privatization of the pension system. They earn fees for managing accounts of a sector that is compelled to give them their savings, without a choice. Furthermore, the money that the AFOREs invest is not their own; as such, if their investments fail, they go out of business – but none of the employees will lose their own retirement benefits.

It is the workers who absorb the costs and the risks of the system, a situation exacerbated by the fact that employment is not growing. The privatization violated the obligations of the Mexican state to respect and protect rights that had already been gained by the labourers. It is the state which has the obligation to rectify the asymmetries in the risks it created, based on a limited vision of how to solve the drying up of the common pension fund.

Conclusions

Fulfilling human rights obligations implies the expansion of the social security model beyond employment conditions and/or the creation of another option for the rest of the population. Those changes did not take place; on the contrary, the decisions taken by federal government stripped away certainty of income (a pay-as-you-go system) and brought uncertainty to many workers by more than doubling the time required to be granted a pension. And these reforms keep denying the necessary conditions for the rest of the population to gain access to an equitable system of social security by targeting only a limited programme at them.

What justified this decision? Improvements in well-being for most workers and the population at large were not the primary driving force; rather, financial strengthening and new business options were the priorities driving the pension privatization. Moreover, the amount of resources (8.2 per cent of GDP and growing) controlled by private investors from the pension system for at least the next fifteen years speaks for itself.

The costs of reversing the privatization of the system are high both financially and politically, so transitioning from a private to a public system is unfortunately not an option for the government.

Nevertheless, there are immediate interventions that need to be made to address equality for women; and to start a second system to progressively offer the rest of the population the option of gaining a pension.

Finally, it should be noted that privatizing social provisions – such as pensions – has no clear benefit for workers and the population; the loss of benefits and the risks assumed by the workers are not something a government committed to fulfilling human rights and the right to social security in old age should allow.

Notes

1 The IMSS Law was changed in 1995. The reformed Bill began to take effect in July 1997.

2 Secretaría de Desarrollo Social (2008), *Programa de Atención a los Adultos Mayores de 70 años y más en Zonas Rurales*, www.sedesol. gob.mx/index/index.php?sec=3003&len=1.

3 Secretaría de Desarrollo Social (2008), *Primer informe trimestral 2008 del Programa de Atención a los Adultos Mayores de 70 años y más en Zonas Rurales*, www.sedesol.gob.mx/

archivos/8015/File/1ertrim08/penccg/02_Adul-tos_Mayores_de_70_anos.pdf.

4 Starting at fourteen years old because that is the age at which labour is first considered in statistical data.

5 The principle of economic efficiency would lead you to question whether there was really any economic incentive to invest time and effort in designing a portfolio if the expected return/gain – because of the amount

and number of contributions – is almost the same no matter how much risk you take.

6 www.consar.gob.mx/rendimiento_neto/rendimiento_neto.shtml.

7 Ley de los Sistemas de Ahorro para el Retiro.

8 There are two main types of commission: one for each weekly mandatory deposit made by employers, employees and federal government. The other commission is a monthly proportional charge based on the worker's fund balance.

9 The figure includes only the accumulated money from early retirement and retirement sub-accounts and not the money coming from voluntary and housing contributions; www.consar.gob.mx/boletin_estadistico/recursos.shtml.

10 Secretaría de Hacienda y Crédito Público, *Criterios Generales de Política Económica 2008*. GDP for this year is estimated to be 10,524.3 billion pesos. www. apartados.hacienda.gob.mx/finanzas_publicas/documentos/criterios_generales/criterios_politica_2008.pdf.

11 *Decreto de Presupuesto de Egresos de la Federación 2008*, www.diputados.gob.mx.

12 Figure taken from www.consar.gob.mx/boletin_estadistico/cuentas.shtml.

13 *Comunicado No. 267 de la Coordinación de Comunicación Social del IMSS*, 10 July 2008.

14 According to Mendez (2008), in December 2007 CONSAR cancelled 1 million inactive accounts with a zero balance owing to many weeks of commission fees being charged with no contributions.

15 www.consar.gob.mx/normatividad/pdf/normatividad_emitida/circulares/Circular_CONSAR_22-13.pdf.

16 Remember that SIEFORE is an entity dedicated to investing the worker's money in a diversified portfolio of financial assets.

17 *Reforma al artículo 48, fracción XI de la Ley de los Sistemas de Ahorro para el Retiro del 10 de diciembre de 2002.*

References

Decreto de Presupuesto de Egresos de la Federación (2008) www.diputados.gob.mx.

Instituto Mexicano del Seguro Social (1973, 1995) *Ley del Instituto Mexicano del Seguro Social.*

— (2006) *Informe al Ejecutivo Federal y al Congreso de la Unión sobre la situación financiera y los riesgos del Instituto Mexicano del Seguro Social, 2005–2006.*

— (2007) *Memoria Estadística 2007.*

Instituto Nacional de Estadística, Geografía e Informática (2000), *XII Censo General de Población y Vivienda 2000.*

— (2005) *Encuesta Nacional de Empleo y Seguridad Social 2004.*

— (2007) *Encuesta Nacional de Ocupación y Empleo, 2° Trimestre 2007.*

Ley de los Sistemas de Ahorro para el Retiro (1996) May, www.diputados.gob.mx/Leyes-Biblio/pdf/52.pdf.

Mendez, E. (2008) 'Consumed by the AFORE, one million inactive accounts cancelled by CONSAR', *La Jornada*, 12 January.

Presidencia de la República (2007) *Primer Informe de Gobierno 2007.*

Rodríguez, F. T. (2005) *Evolución del Sistema de Pensiones Mexicano*, Presentation by the Director de Inversiones de AFORE XXI, during the 11th Technical Meeting of the American Committee on Organization and Administrative Systems, April.

Secretaría de Desarrollo Social (2008) *Primer Informe Trimestral 2008 del Programa de Atención a los Adultos Mayores de 70 años y más en Zonas Rurales.*

Secretaría de Hacienda y Crédito Público (2008) *Criterios Generales de Política Económica 2008.*

Sinha, T. (2002) *Can the Latin American Experience Teach Us Something about Privatized Pensions with Individual Accounts?*, Research Report 1, International Centre for Pension Research.

10 | REGULATION: PENSION REFORM AND HUMAN RIGHTS IN THE USA

Radhika Balakrishnan

Ageing populations and pension reform

Pension and Social Security in the United States have been and will continue to be critical issues in public policy debates. This is largely due to the fact that the population reaching retirement age is projected to increase significantly while the working-age population who pay into the public and private pension systems is projected to decline. This chapter examines pension reform in terms of its human rights implications within the context of the shift in responsibility from the public to the private sector in the USA. More specifically, the focus is on regulatory changes that allowed pensions to move from a system that is guaranteed by government to one that is, to varying degrees, managed by the private sector. We pay particular attention to the obligations of the state to protect in cases where changing regulation shifts the burden of responsibility to the private sector. Therefore, this chapter looks at the impact of changes in regulation that take responsibility to provide for old-age security away from government and leave the livelihoods of people who are no longer working to the vagaries of the market.

Pension reform and human rights obligations and instruments The right to social security is framed under Article 9 of the International Covenant on Economic, Social and Cultural Rights (ICESCR), and is elaborated as General Comment 19 by the Committee on Economic, Social and Cultural Rights. General Comment 19 defines the right to social security in terms of access and maintenance of benefits to secure protection and to provide adequate income security in times of economic distress (Darooka 2008: 4).

General Comment 19 also recognizes that in addition to contribution-based social insurance, there is a need for non-contribution-based social security provisions to ensure that everyone is 'adequately' covered (ibid.: 5). Other international human rights instruments also ensure the right to social security; e.g., under Article 5(e)(iv) of the International Convention on the Elimination of All Forms of Racial Discrimination, states parties are obligated to guarantee the right to social security and social services to everyone without any distinction (UN 1969). Article 6(1) of the Convention on the Rights of the Child states that states parties are under an obligation to recognize for every child the right to benefit from social security (UN 1989: 3). This Convention also reaffirms the right of every child to a standard of living adequate for the child's physical, mental, spiritual, moral and social development. The Convention on the Elimination of All Forms of Discrimination Against Women (CEDAW) obligates states parties to take appropriate measures to foster the right to social security for women, while the ILO Convention on Social Security (Minimum Standards), Convention 195, elaborates nine different types of social security and covers corresponding contingencies, including medical care, sickness, unemployment, old-age, employment injury, family, maternity, invalid and survivor's benefits (Darooka 2008: 5).

The obligation to protect General Comment 19 (UN 2007: 14) has specific language on the obligation of government to protect and provides language on the regulatory oversight necessary to ensure adequate access.

> The obligation to protect requires that State Parties prevent third parties from interfering in any way with the enjoyment of the right to social security. Third parties include individuals, groups, corporations and other entities, as well as agents acting under their authority. The obligation includes, inter alia, adopting the necessary and effective legislative and other measures, for example, to restrain third parties from denying equal access to social security schemes operated by them or by others and imposing unreasonable eligibility conditions; arbitrarily or unreasonably interfering with self-help or customary or traditional arrangements for social security that are consistent with the right to social security; and failing to pay legally required contributions for employees or other beneficiaries into the social security system.
>
> Where social security schemes, whether contributory or non-contributory, are operated or controlled by third parties, State Parties retain the responsibility of administering the national social security system and ensuring that private actors do not compromise equal, adequate, affordable, and accessible social security. To prevent such abuses an effective regulatory system must be established which includes framework legislation, independent monitoring, genuine public participation and imposition of penalties for non-compliance.

In this chapter we focus primarily on the states' obligation to protect within the context of other human rights obligations, such as progressive realization; non-retrogression; non-discrimination and equality; and participation, transparency and accountability. The ICESCR specifies that states parties have the obligation to 'achiev[e] progressively the full realization of the rights recognized in the present Covenant [...] to the maximum of available resources' (UN 1976). Just as states must affirm that they are taking solid steps towards realization of these rights, there is a specific duty on the part of states parties to avoid retrogressive measures that would endanger economic, social and cultural rights. The fundamental principle of non-discrimination and equality states that 'Everyone is entitled to all the rights and freedoms set forth in this Declaration without distinction of any kind, such as race, colour, sex, language, religion, political or other opinion, national or social origin, property, birth or other status' (UN 1948).

Lastly, regarding the principles of participation, transparency and accountability, human rights cannot be effectively realized unless the right of participation of the affected populations in seeking redress for violations is respected. These principles are once again brought up in General Comment 19 in respect to the right to social security.

The United States' retirement security system

In the United States, pension and Social Security will continue to be critical issues in public policy debates owing to the convergence of demographic pressures and the current financial crisis. The US Census Bureau projects the number of elderly to increase from its 2002 level of 12.5 per cent to 16.3 per cent by 2020, while the working-age population (20–64) is projected to decline from its current level of 59 per cent to 57.2 per cent in 2020 (Karczmar 2005). It is important, therefore, to examine the ways in which public and private pensions currently function and intersect, especially with regard to the Social Security system.[1] Most salient are the changes that the Social Security and pension systems have undergone, and to understand these changes in relation to regulatory policy measures and human rights obligations.

In the United States there are essentially two types of pension plans: (i) defined benefit (DB); and (ii) defined contribution (DC). A defined benefit plan is sponsored by an employer and pays a stated amount upon retirement based on length of service and final average salary. A DB plan is both permanent and guaranteed by the government. A DC plan is determined by contributions made by the employee and the employer, plus investment returns on those contributions. There are various forms of DC plans, including Individual Retirement Accounts (IRAs), 401(k)s and profit-sharing plans. In these types of plans, individual participants, not employers, are responsible for selecting the type of investment to which their assets are allocated (Balakrishnan et al. 2009: 58). A significant distinction between the two plans is that in a DB plan the *employer* bears the risk, whereas in a DC plan the *employee* bears the risk (ibid.: 58). Another important difference relates to the precariousness of both plans. The precariousness of DC plans is threefold: (i) investment returns are unknown; (ii) the participant's rate of spending in retirement is unknown; and (iii) the lifespan of the participant is unknown.

Social Security does not fall into either of the aforementioned categories, as it is a form of state-sponsored retirement benefit not provided by employers, but funded by payroll taxes levied against both the employee and employer. This public provision of pension is not linked to a particular occupation and is based on the number of years worked and contribution to the payroll tax.

The important part of this system is that it has a minimum floor and goes up based on contribution to the system, and in some ways, like a DB plan, offers a known amount that the recipient will receive at retirement.

Retirement in the United States: a brief history In response to the devastation wrought by the Great Depression, Franklin D. Roosevelt enacted the Social Security Act on 14 August 1935, thus laying the basis for a national retirement pension scheme. The rise of private pensions in the 1920s played havoc with numerous life savings during the Great Depression; this opened the door for Congress to introduce a federal-administered retirement plan under the terms of the 1935 Act.

This law established two social insurance programmes to help with old age and unemployment: (i) a federal system of old-age benefits for retired workers who had been employed in industry and commerce; and (ii) a federal–state system of unemployment insurance. No further major changes were made in the programme until the 1950s, when it was broadened to cover more types of jobs, such as farming (OASDI 2003: Section 1, p. 2).

The Supplemental Security Income (SSI) was established in 1972[2] with benefits first paid in 1974. It was created as a basic national income maintenance system for the aged, blind and disabled; this system differed from the ones it replaced by being administered by the Social Security Administration (SSA), with an approach similar to the way benefits were administered under the Social Security programme (SSA 2007b: 4).[3] The next important revision came when President Ford signed legislation in 1974 establishing the Employee's Retirement Income Security Act (ERISA). The ERISA authorized a study of salary reduction plans that influenced the 1978 legislation creating 401(k) plans (EBRI 2005).

An important aspect of these legislative changes is that they promoted the defined benefit concept and gave rise to a whole new class of investment products to service this new market. For instance, ERISA provoked a major upsurge in commercial management of pension funds, establishing the Pension Benefit Guaranty Corporation (PBGC). The PBGC was instrumental in guaranteeing workers' benefits for defined benefit plans by insuring the basic benefits in all schemes in return for a compulsory insurance premium. The law also required that pension plan assets must cover liabilities. The PBGC insures defined benefit plan benefits up to certain limits to protect plan participants in the event of a termination (Kinneen and Purcell 2008: 2). The legislation in the ERISA is seemingly advantageous, since its very name suggests advocating for better retirement security. However, the legislation that enacted ERISA is the leading factor in how retirement security has become progressively more *insecure* over the past few decades.

The shift from defined benefit to defined contribution Once the legislation was enacted there was a dramatic shift from defined benefit to defined contribution plans, beginning in the late 1970s. Though defined benefit and contribution plans fall into a separate category to the state-provided Social Security programme, the retirement systems are interrelated. In their report 'The changing impact of Social Security on retirement income in the United States', Butrica et al. (2004: 2) turn their attention to the implications of such interconnectedness:

> Because the essence of defined contribution plans is to increase an individual's responsibility for his or her own retirement saving and to shift investment risk from employers to employees, the trend away from defined benefit plans and toward defined contribution plans may affect the relative importance of government programs such as Social Security and SSI.

The shift was not an unconscious move; it resulted from enacted regulatory changes emerging from ERISA and the creation of the PBGC. Furthermore, this legislation reflected shifting economic ideologies occurring at a global level that advocated market-based, private sector solutions to pension planning. Implicit in the thinking was the assumption that the market could not fail. The end result was the marked reduction in the state's role in guaranteeing basic rights. Although the shift from DB plans began in the late 1970s, it was in the 1990s that these measures made their full impact. In addition, international financial institutions, such as the World Bank and the IMF, have released reports encouraging privatization. Lawrence Summers, an advocate for pension privatization, commissioned the World Bank's report 'Averting old age crisis' in the early 1990s. This report concluded that the flawed part of the system was in the public sector, thus creating a need to privatize pension schemes as much as possible to deal with and avert this flaw.[4] President Bush's proposals to privatize social security in 2007 were the first explicit move towards the privatization of this system.

Progressive realization and non-retrogression

Obligation of conduct On the whole, coverage of Social Security in the United States has increased. Two years after the programme began, in 1937, approximately 33 million persons worked in jobs covered by the Social Security system, constituting roughly 58 per cent of the labour force. In 2002, out of a total workforce of approximately 159.3 million workers, about 152.8 million (96 per cent) of all jobs were covered under Social Security (OASDI 2003: 1). It is clear that Social Security and SSI have played a vital role in the improved economic security of the nation's people. Though it is difficult to claim a causal impact, it is important to note that in 1935 a person who had reached the age of 65 was expected to live another 12½ years; today it is 17½ years. A report by Virginia P. Reno (2007) for the Economic Policy Institute (EPI) articulates the importance of such a system: 'Social Security has long

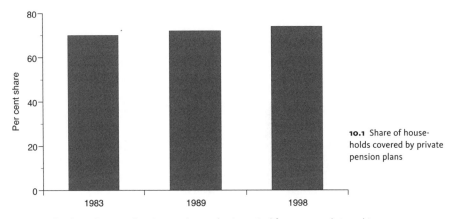

10.1 Share of house-
holds covered by private
pension plans

Source: Weller (2002a), www.epi.org/economic-snapshot/entry/webfeatures-snapshots-archive-05152002

been a source of bedrock security for retirees. Almost all elders receive it. It lifts 13 million elders out of poverty. [...] While it is an important anti-poverty program, Social Security is a critical source of income for middle-income and upper-middle-income seniors as well as for low-income retirees.'

Since Social Security's beginning, many policy changes have occurred to expand coverage. For example, in 1960 the age fifty requirement for disabled worker benefits was removed. The 1967 amendments provided disability benefits for widows and widowers aged fifty or older. The 1972 amendments made available automatic cost-of-living increases in benefits tied to increases in the Consumer Price Index (CPI) and created the delayed retirement credit, which increased benefits for workers who retire after the full retirement age (then age sixty-five), though during the present crisis this obligation is once again being debated (OASDI 2003: 3).

Because of the increase in defined contribution plans, Social Security has in many cases become a source of supplemental income to private pensions. In the statement that people eligible for Social Security receive it is clearly stated that this benefit is only part of what one should expect to live on in old age. In addition, since workers have become more and more reliant on private plans, the changes in private pension and the impact of these changes have become increasingly important. However, the number of households that was covered by at least one of these pension plans has remained essentially flat since 1983 (see Figure 10.1)

Defined contribution is now the predominant form of pension plan in the United States. In 1980 there were approximately 250,000 qualified DB pension plans covered by the PBGC. By 2005, there were fewer than 80,000 qualified plans. Concomitantly, the number of defined contribution plans has dramatically increased. This is significant because the worker's retirement income depends on his or her success in investing these funds, and the employee rather than the employer bears the investment risks. Therefore, the shift from

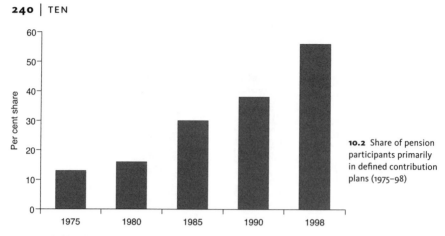

10.2 Share of pension participants primarily in defined contribution plans (1975–98)

Source: Mishel (1998), www.epi.org/economic_snapshots/entry/webfeatures_snapshots_archive_08302000/

traditional DB plans to DC plans represents erosion in pension quality. The increase in the DC plans is illustrated in the graph below.

There is a definitive inverse relationship occurring over time between the two types of plans: DB is declining while DC is increasing. This inverse relationship between the two plans is illustrated in Figure 10.3. Because of this trend, only one in five working Americans enjoy *guaranteed* pension benefits, about half the share as of 1980. Furthermore, nearly 25 per cent of the workforce currently lacks any form of an employer-based plan. Again, the implication of such a trend is the increased precariousness of the financial circumstances that retirees will face as a result of these trends in non-coverage and the dominance of DC plans. The financial crisis of 2008 led to steep declines in the value of the stock market and household wealth and laid bare the volatility of these markets, the impact of which was fully experienced by all workers covered by

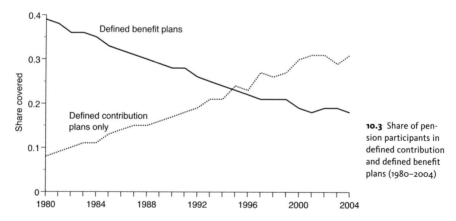

10.3 Share of pension participants in defined contribution and defined benefit plans (1980–2004)

Source: M. Lawrence, J. Bernstein and S. Allegretto, *The State of Working America 2006/2007*, An Economic Policy Institute Book, ILR Press, Ithaca, NY, ch. 3, Fig. 3J, www.stateofworkingamerica.org/tabfig/2008/03/ SWA08_Chapter3_Wages_r2_Fig-3J.jpg

a DC plan. The debate on DB and DC plans has once again taken centre stage as government, in particular state governments, which are required to balance their budgets, is now trying to eliminate and/or weaken the DB plans that many government employees still have. Relevant to this discussion are two vital conclusions drawn from Weller's study 'Retirement out of reach': (i) relying on financial markets to generate adequate retirement savings within the existing institutional framework will most likely not work; and (ii) retirement savings should be insulated from financial market volatility as much as possible by reducing the risks in defined contribution plans (Weller 2002b: 8).

As Robin Blackburn notes in his book *Banking on Death*, the rise of DC plans in the USA since the 1980s was dramatically influenced by the rise in 401(k) plans, a specific type of DC plan (Blackburn 2002: 106). Such an increase was not unplanned; there was legislation that allowed for such a plan to be possible via the Revenue Act of 1978. This Act included a provision that became Internal Revenue Code (IRC) Sec. 401(k) (for which the plans are named), which added permanent provisions to the IRC, authorizing the use of salary reductions as a source of plan contributions. The ERISA was the Act that truly opened the door for such legislation. Within four years of this Act, many major companies, e.g. Johnson & Johnson, PepsiCo and JC Penney, had developed and began operating under 401(k) plans (EBRI 2005).

Therefore, the movement of plans from defined benefit to defined contribution is retrogressive, since vulnerability to investment risk is increasing and the stability of employees' pensions is being eroded. In addition, regulatory measures are not in place to address these effects; rather, the regulatory apparatus is facilitating instability and consequently the vulnerability of workers. These regulatory changes also indicate a failure of the obligation to protect.

Obligation of result The poverty rate among the elderly has decreased since Social Security began. According to the Social Security Administration's Accountability Report for fiscal year 2004, poverty among the elderly was reduced by 37 per cent over the previous thirty years: decreasing from 16.3 per cent in 1973 to 10.2 per cent in 2003; in 2006 it was 9.4 per cent. For example, in 1959 the US Census Bureau estimated that more than 35 per cent of elderly Americans were poor; by 2003, in large part because of changes in the Social Security and Medicare systems, the poverty rate among senior citizens was 10.2 per cent. The following graph illustrates this decrease in poverty.

However, it is important to note that though poverty rates have declined since 1959, they have clearly levelled off since 2000. According to the US Census Bureau's report *Poverty in the United States: 2002*, the number of elderly Americans living in poverty increased from 3.4 million in 2001 to 3.6 million in 2002, though the poverty rate remained unchanged at 10.4 per cent (Proctor and Dalaker 2003: 1).

It is also important to note that the official definition of poverty is an

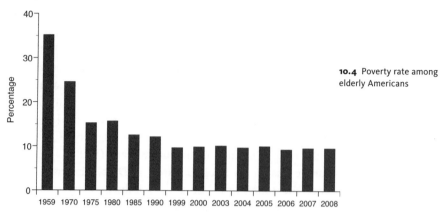

10.4 Poverty rate among elderly Americans

Source: US Census Bureau, *Historical Poverty: People*, Table 12, 'People 65 Years and Over with Incomes Below 125 per cent of the Poverty Threshold, and the Near Poor', www.census.gov/hhes/www/poverty/data/historical/people.html

arbitrary construct that is very low and does not effectively measure a baseline income necessary for a household to maintain food, clothing and shelter. Currently, 3.4 million seniors aged sixty-five and older live below the poverty line, having annual incomes of less than $9,699 for an individual or $12,186 for a two-person household; the 2008 threshold for poverty for those over sixty-five is $10,326 for an individual and $13,030 for two people. Millions more are barely making ends meet just above the poverty line, with nearly a quarter of older Americans (22.4 per cent) having family incomes below 150 per cent of the poverty threshold ($14,503 for an individual and $18,279 for a couple). These poverty levels suggest that retirement policies and regulation are not progressive but are regressing. *Age Shock* notes that 'in the US and UK the proportion of the elderly who are poor is at least double the rate in most other advanced countries' (Blackburn 2006: 41). The United States' high level of poverty rates is thus demonstrative of the fact that, while Social Security coverage has gone up, it is still not enough.

Non-discrimination and equality

Obligation of conduct While coverage is compulsory for most types of employment, approximately 6.5 million workers did not have coverage under Social Security in 2002 (OASDI 2003: 1). As stated earlier, the extent and adequacy of that coverage is good, but not sufficient. This is especially true for specific groups of the nation's population, namely women, racial minorities and informal workers. Surprisingly, even though Social Security has steadily increased since its inception, its roots were inherently discriminatory. There were millions of people not covered by the 1935 Act, including farmers, women in domestic service and rural workers, especially Southern blacks and itinerant whites. True, universal coverage wasn't established until amendments adopted in 1950 and 1954 (ibid.: 85–6). However, even fifty years later, there is still evidence to suggest that there is discriminatory policy inherent in the USA's retirement system. The reliance on contributory retirement plans to supplement Social Security discriminates against women who have not been part of the paid labour force in a type of job that provided those benefits and against those who have precarious employment that provides little or no contributory system. The other problem is that many employers will not contribute to a DC plan if the employee does not contribute a certain amount, leaving people who are poor and do not have the resources necessary to put away a part of their pay for the future without the benefit of either a pension or the employer contribution.

The issue of retirement security is vital for women, owing in part to their lower wages, interrupted work histories, role as caregivers, and longer life expectancy. Although the female labour force participation rates have increased dramatically and are now approaching those of men, women earn less than men, are more likely to work part time, and often have interrupted careers (Munnell and Jivan 2005: 2). In the USA, the retirement systems are rooted in a model that assumed that men are the breadwinners (Balakrishnan et al. 2009: 61). Yet it does not properly accommodate those who do not work, such as housewives, in its eligibility requirements. If one is born after 1928, one must work for at least ten years (to gain forty credits, not necessarily continuous)[5] to be eligible for Social Security retirement benefits (SSA 2007a: 2). Those who have not worked, or who have worked only part time (and thus have not achieved the minimum credit), are not eligible to receive Social Security. Also, no account is taken of women's unpaid work in the current system, nor of all the women and men who work in the informal sector.

Obligation of result An accountability report issued by the SSA concluded that the average monthly benefit for a retired woman in 2002 was $740, compared to $983 for a man (SSA 2003). In 2001, 60 per cent of single women (never married, divorced or widowed women) aged 47–64 anticipated retirement incomes below twice the poverty threshold, compared to 33 per cent for single men and 16 per cent for married couples in that age range (Weller and Wolff 2005: 12).

Weller and Wolff (ibid.: 13) report on the level of inequality present in the US retirement system:

> The retirement income that whites could expect in 2001 was almost three times as large as that of African Americans or Hispanics; single males could expect, on average, to have retirement income that was almost twice as large as that of single females; and homeowners could expect to have retirement income that was more than four times as large as that of renters. Not surprisingly, then, 57 per cent of African Americans or Hispanics, 60 per cent of single women,

and 71 per cent of renters could expect to have retirement income that was below a threshold of twice the poverty line. This compares to 23 per cent of whites, 33 per cent of single men, and 20 per cent of homeowners.

In terms of the general well-being of elderly groups, Wolff et al. (2006) found that, since 1989, although the general well-being for black populations increased in 2001, it decreased for Hispanic and single-female populations, and these numbers have most likely worsened since the economic crisis.

The switch from DB plans to DC has serious implications for discrimination and equality; not only is there widespread inequity in retirement wealth, the overall level of retirement security has decreased, even during the booming stock market of the 1990s. Thus there is also inherent class discrimination present in the current pension system, which is in turn connected to race. In 2000, 73 per cent of high earners (the 20 per cent with the highest incomes) had pension coverage, compared with 18 per cent of low earners (the 20 per cent with the lowest incomes). Hispanic workers are covered at a startlingly low rate of 29 per cent, compared with 43 per cent and 55 per cent for their African-American and white counterparts, respectively (Mishel et al. 2003).

Transparency and accountability

Obligation of conduct Although current regulatory mechanisms exist, such as PBGC, their reach is limited, biased and insufficient. The PBGC's creation was inherently biased towards privatization as it was created under the ERISA, which simultaneously opened doors for the creation of the 401(k) plans. Further, PBGC is insufficient and limited owing to the fact that it does not insure DC plans, only DB plans. Though in DB plans some regulatory measures of insurance exist, such as PBGC, the state has no obligation when it comes to people's retirement accounts being wiped out by the downturn in the stock market or when pensions are provided in terms of stocks, as in the case of Enron, where the employees had no recourse when their entire savings disappeared overnight. Congress planned for PBGC to be a last resort for pension coverage. However, since Congress passed the ERISA in 1974, more than 160,000 companies have voluntarily ceased honouring their pensions (Blackburn 2002: 71). Pension coverage has thus been a major issue surrounding labour strikes in the United States in recent decades, and at the heart of the debate in state-level budget discussions.

The PBGC's role in regulating pensions or lack thereof raises a number of important questions that the government must consider, beyond the critical social security debates that have taken place. Questions such as: Why is there no regulation to insure defined contribution plans (which now constitute the majority of private pension plans)? How is it that terminations have increased, thus endangering the employee? Why does the PBGC not prevent the employee from bearing all risks, not just some? Answers to these questions will serve to enrich the discussion as we search for policy changes to further maintain the economic security of the American population.

The other important issue in terms of transparency is that of the regulation of the sectors that manage the investments of the pension funds. The changes in the regulatory framework that made markets more volatile and precarious did not take into account the state's obligation to protect from third parties when there is an impact on the right to social security in old age.

Obligation of result Many arguments in favour of defined contribution assert that DC plans have higher returns and thus are more optimal than DB plans. However, if one closely examines the rate of returns for the two different plans, the opposite is actually true. In a study conducted by Munnell et al. (2006), it was found that DB plans provide a higher return than the 401(k) plans. They attributed the unexpectedly lower return rate to investment fees, which account for 75 to 90 per cent of total expenses associated with managing 401(k) plans.

Although most of Bush's plan to privatize Social Security was met with great opposition, the question has once again risen in the context of the US debt and budget deficit after the financial crisis. There is plenty of research to suggest that if the taxation cap ($106,800 for 2010) were raised for Social Security, the problem of coverage could be virtually fixed. According to Doug Henwood, a heterodox American economist, lifting the cap and taxing higher incomes would keep the system solvent indefinitely (Gaal 2007).

Moreover, beyond the needed measures for Social Security reform, proper private pension regulation is needed. These reforms go hand in hand with reforms necessary for the entire financial sector, but when the right to social security is tied to how the financial markets operate, the obligation to protect requires that there is some guarantee of a return that will take care of minimum core needs in old age. The regulatory measures taken must be examined in order to reveal their biases so it is clearer who are the winners and losers from such measures. Though seldom mentioned in comparison to Bush's privatization push, another Bush initiative which exemplifies how closely regulatory measures should be examined is the Pension Security Act of 2003. In a brief for the Economic Policy Institute, Harding and Weller (2003) examined this Act and drew the following conclusions:

> According to supporters of the Pension Security Act, the bill is designed to protect worker pensions. [...] But in reality, the House bill and the Treasury Department's proposed regulatory changes are a step backward for pension security. The Pension Security Act will weaken current protections and won't curb the kinds of corporate abuse that left Enron and WorldCom workers with empty pension accounts. The House bill would not prevent over-concentration of employer stock in worker 401(k)s, it would not ensure that employees

receive unbiased financial advice, it would not prevent insider trading, it would not allow employees to sue executives for criminal activity, and it would not enhance the transparency of pension fund management.

Such regulation is indicative of the challenges that must be faced so that human rights obligations are not neglected. The debate in the USA in 2010 about the crisis is being cast in terms that will most likely lead to a further erosion of the reliable income supports the elderly require. Many argue that the retirement age needs to be raised instead of merely increasing the income level that can be taxed for social security.

Obligation to protect The obligation to protect has been violated in two ways: in the failure to enact proper regulatory mechanisms to cover the losses borne by employees when investing funds privately; and enacting legislation that not only allowed for, but encouraged, privatization of the pension system. If the operating assumption in the US retirement system is that it is comprised of three parts – Social Security, pension and private savings – the government has three separate areas of responsibility: (i) banking regulations; (ii) defined pensions; and (iii) social security.

Thus, there is a threefold aspect to the obligation to protect. As stated earlier, the PBGC's limited role in covering only DB plans is the first part. Secondly, since the ERISA's inception in the 1970s the state has encouraged the proliferation of private pensions, particularly the increase of DC. This increase has been accompanied by increased overall vulnerability, which is linked to the failure to protect. Lastly, the state's inability to regulate and protect private savings is the final way in which it failed to enact legislation to: (a) promote rights; and (b) create additional regulatory mechanisms. These are all demonstrative of how the United States government has failed to adequately protect the rights of its elderly citizens. This failure to protect is resulting in a violation of the right to an adequate standard of living, a right that is explicitly included in the ICESCR.

Conclusion

The changes in the regulatory structure that have occurred over the last few decades have made the right to social security in old age less broadly experienced. Over 2.3 million women over the age of sixty-five (11.5 per cent) live at or below the poverty line, while slightly over one million – 6.6 per cent – of senior men live in poverty. Nearly one in five – 19 per cent – single, divorced or widowed women over the age of sixty-five are poor, and the risk of poverty for older women only increases as they age. Women aged seventy-five and over are over three times as likely to be living in poverty as men in the same age range. Only 416,000 men in this age range live at or below the poverty line, while over 1.3 million women aged seventy-five and over are poor. Among married women, longer female life expectancy makes it likely that they will outlive their spouses, and be left without any additional sources of income (Cawthorne 2008: 2).

Given this stark reality, it is critical to examine the impact of regulatory changes on human rights outcomes. The case of pension reform is just one instance where human rights norms provide a powerful tool with which to examine the impact of regulation not just of the pensions system but of the financial sector in general on the lives of the elderly, and to use the right to social security as a way to ensure that the most vulnerable in our society are provided for.

Notes

1 The term Social Security in the United States is used to describe the US government programme that provides the elderly with income; the right to social security encompasses much more than that.

2 See Public Law 92-603, approved 30 October 1972 (86 Stat. 1329), in Compilation of the Social Security Laws, vol. II.

3 *Supplemental Security Income (SSI)*, SSA Publication no. 05-11000, ICN 48020, issued by the Social Security Administration, June 2007, p. 4.

4 It is important to note that Lawrence Summers was also the person who helped change the regulatory framework that caused the financial crisis in 2008.

5 The amount of annual earnings needed for a credit is increased each year in proportion to increases in average wages in the economy. In 2004 the amount of earnings needed for a credit was $900. In 2007, one credit was awarded for each $1,000 of earnings, up to the maximum of four credits per year.

References

Balakrishnan, R., D. Elson and R. Patel (2009) *Rethinking Macroeconomic Policies from a Human Rights Perspective*, Policy Innovations, Carnegie Council.

Blackburn, R. (2002) *Banking on Death, Or, Investing in Life: The History and Future of Pensions*, London and New York: Verso, under New Left Books.

— (2006) *Age Shock: How Finance Is Failing Us*, London and New York: Verso, under New Left Books.

Butrica, B. A., H. M. Iams and K. E. Smith (2004) 'The changing impact of Social Security on retirement income in the United States', *Social Security Bulletin*, 65(2).

Cawthorne, A. (2008) 'Elderly poverty: the challenge before us', Center for American Progress, Issues/Domestic, July, www.americanprogress.org/issues/2008/07/elderly_poverty.html.

Darooka, P. (2008) 'Social Security: a woman's human right', PWESCR Discussion Paper no. 2.

EBRI (2005) 'History of 401(k) plans: an update', *Facts from EBRI*, Employee Benefit Research Institute (EBRI).

Gaal, C. (2007) 'A tale of fear and greed: the push to privatize Social Security', *ZMagazine*, 1 September.

Harding, S. and C. E. Weller (2003) 'Retirement made riskier: House pension bill, Treasury proposal ignore the real problems', Economic Policy Institute Issue Brief no. 189, 9 April.

Karczmar, M. (2005) 'Reform of the US pension system: political controversies defeat demographic and financial realities', *Current Issues: Demography Special*, Deutsche Bank Research, 19 July.

Kinneen, K. and P. Purcell (2008) 'Investment policy: issues for Congress', *CRS Report for Congress*, September.

Mishel, L. (1998) 'Not your father's pension plan', *Snapshot*, 30 August 2006 (based on EPI analysis of *Share of Pension Participants in Defined-Contribution Plans*, Employment Benefit Research Institute.

Mishel, L., J. Bernstein and H. Boushey (2003) *The State of Working America 2002–2003*, Ithaca, NY: Cornell University Press.

Mishel, L., J. Bernstein and S. Allegretto (2007) *The State of Working America 2006/2007*, An Economic Policy Institute Book, Ithaca, NY: ILR Press.

Munnell, A. H. and N. Jivan (2005) 'What makes older women work?', *Work Opportunities for Older Americans Series 1*, Center for Retirement Research, Boston College, September.

Munnell, A., M. Soto, J. Libby and J. Prinzivalli (2006) 'Investment returns: Defined Benefit vs. 401(k) plans', Issue Brief no. 52, Center for Retirement Research, Boston College, September.

OASDI (2003) 'Old Age, Survivors, and Disability Insurance (OASDI) public-use microdata file', 2001 data, Social Security Administration, October.

Proctor, B. D. and J. Dalaker (2003) *Poverty in the United States: 2002*, Current Population Reports, US Census Bureau, September.

Public Law 92-603 (1972) 86 Stat. 1329, approved 30 October, in *Compilation of the Social Security Laws*, vol. II.

Reno, V. P. (2007) 'Building on Social Security's success', Economic Policy Institute Briefing Paper no. 208, 20 November.

SSA (2003) 'Fast facts and figures about Social Security', Office of Policy, US Social Security Administration, www.ssa.gov/policy/docs/chartbooks/fast_facts/2003/fast_facts03.html.

— (2007a) 'Retirement benefits', SSA Publication no. 05-10035, Social Security Administration, January.

— (2007b) 'Supplemental Security Income (SSI)', SSA Publication no. 05-11000, ICN 48020, Social Security Administration, June.

— (2007c) 'Fact sheet' on Social Security, Social Security Administration, www.lb5.uscourts.gov/resources/archive-durls/05-10648(1).pdf.

UN (1948) Universal Declaration of Human Rights, G.A. res. 217A (III), UN Doc. A/810 at 71 (1948), Department of Public Information, United Nations, New York.

— (1969) International Convention on the Elimination of All Forms of Racial Discrimination, G.A. res. 2106 (XX), entered into force 4 January 1969, in accordance with Article 19.

— (1976) International Covenant on Economic, Social and Cultural Rights, G.A. res. 2200A (XXI), 21 U.N.GAOR Supp. (no. 16) at 49, UN Doc. A/6316 (1966), 993 U.N.T.S. 3, entered into force 3 January.

— (1989) Convention on the Rights of the Child, *Treaty Series*, vol. 1577, United Nations.

— (2007) General Comment 19, 'The Right to Social Security (Art. 9)', Social and Economic Council, United Nations, www.unhcr.org/refworld/docid/47b17b5b39c.html.

US Census Bureau (n.d.) *Historical Poverty Tables – People*, www.census.gov/hhes/www/poverty/data/historical/people.html.

Weller, C. E. (2002a) 'Slow growth for pension coverage', *Snapshot*, 22 May, Economic Policy Institute.

— (2002b) 'Retirement out of reach: financial markets will not generate adequate retirement income for average household', Economic Policy Institute Briefing Paper, August.

Weller, C. E. and E. N. Wolff (2005) *Retirement Income: The Crucial Role of Social Security*, Washington, DC: Economic Policy Institute.

Wolff, E. N., A. Zacharias and H. Kum (2006) 'Net government expenditures and the economic well-being of the elderly in the United States, 1989–2001', Levy Economics Institute of Bard College Working Paper no. 466, August, www.iariw.org/papers/2006/WolffZacharias.pdf.

ABOUT THE CONTRIBUTORS

Nursel Aydiner-Avsar completed the BS programme in management engineering at Istanbul Technical University (ITU) in 2002. She obtained her master's degree in economics at ITU in 2005. During 2002–05, she worked as a research and teaching assistant in the Economics Branch of the Management Engineering Department at ITU. She then moved to the USA to attend the doctorate programme in economics at the University of Utah. She received her PhD in economics at the University of Utah in 2011. She worked at the University of Utah as a research assistant in the 2005/06 academic year and as an instructor from 2006 to 2010. Her main areas of research are labour economics, development economics and applied econometrics, and she worked on trade and wage structure in Turkey for her dissertation. Besides her studies on trade and wages, she has also written papers on issues such as employment and educational gender inequality in Turkey. She worked as a research assistant for Radhika Balakrishnan and Diane Elson, and at the same time contributed to two chapters on the USA in *Economic Policy and Human Rights*. She is currently an assistant professor of economics at Gediz University in Izmir, Turkey.

Lourdes Colinas is an economist working as a researcher at the UN Economic Commission for Latin America and the Caribbean in the Social Development Unit. She obtained her master's degree in the sociology of development at the University of Essex. Her research interests include gender issues, social protection, indigenous peoples, poverty and human rights. She is currently studying for her PhD in sociology.

Roberto Constantino is an economist from the Universidad Autónoma Metropolitana (Mexico; UAM-X). He has specialized in public policy (Mexico); science and environmental technology (South Korea) and environmental economics (Siena, Italy). He is a professor at the Department of Economics of the UAM-X. Currently he is chairman of the Research Unit on Economic Policy and Development in the Economics Department of the UAM-X. His most recent book is entitled *The Chimera of the Mexican Development*, co-edited with Carlos Rozo (UAM, Mexico, November 2010).

Sarah Gammage is an economist working with the International Labour Organization in Chile on social protection and development. She has a PhD in development economics from the Institute of Social Studies in The

Hague and a master's degree in economics from the London School of Economics and Political Science. She has worked with and for a number of international and multilateral organizations, including the International Centre for Research on Women, the International Institute for Environment and Development, the Economic Commission for Latin America and the Caribbean, and the United Nations Development Programme. She has written academic and policy research articles on gender and trade, poverty, labour markets, migration and the environment.

James Heintz is Associate Research Professor and Associate Director of the Political Economy Research Institute at the University of Massachusetts, Amherst. His recent publications include: 'Financial regulation, capabilities and human rights in the US financial crisis: the case of housing', co-authored with Radhika Balakrishnan and Diane Elson (*Journal of Human Development and Capabilities*, 12(1): 153–68, 2011).

Gabriel Lara Salazar was the Capacity Building Coordinator in FUNDAR Centro de Análisis e Investigación in Mexico. In this position he worked to 'translate' FUNDAR's experience and knowledge in budget analysis, budget advocacy, access to information and human rights into capacity-building materials and processes. He has facilitated budget analysis and advocacy training in fourteen countries across Africa, Asia and Latin America, with the training programme of the International Budget Partnership. He also worked doing budget analysis during a key National Health Law reform in Mexico. Lara Salazar worked for FUNDAR for ten years. Prior to that he was on the advisory staff of the director of the Mexican Social Security Institute for five years. Lara Salazar studied political science at the Instituto Tecnológico Autónomo de México (ITAM). He is currently working as a consultant on budget analysis, advocacy and capacity-building around the world.

Kristina Pirker has a PhD in Latin American studies from the Universidad Nacional Autónoma de México (UNAM) and an MA in sociology and political sciences from the University of Vienna, Austria. Her research topics are Social Movements, Political Parties and the State in Central America and Mexico and Transparency, Accountability and Citizen Participation in Public Policies. She is assistant professor at the Department of Latin American Studies and working in the Department of Sociology in the Faculty of Political and Social Science (UNAM). She has published articles about different issues related to Central America and Mexico in Mexican and international academic journals. Between 2005 and 2010 she worked as Academic Coordinator and Researcher in the Mexican NGO FUNDAR Centro de Análisis e Investigación, undertaking research on social policy, transparency and freedom of information policies.

Daniela Ramírez Camacho is a researcher at FUNDAR Centro de Análisis e Investigación in the capacity-building area. She has participated in capacity-building processes with civil society organizations demanding rights for indigenous people, women and people with disabilities. She designs and facilitates workshops, learning materials and follow-up processes to incorporate the right to know and budget analysis into different rights agendas. In FUNDAR she also participated in the Health, Citizenship and Human Rights Project. She studied on the master's programme in political science at El Colegio de México and Latin American studies and anthropology at Maclester College, Minnesota.

Carlos Salas is a Mexican labour economist at the Institute of Labour Studies and El Colegio de Tlaxcala. He is the author of *The State of Working Mexico*.

Alberto Serdan-Rosales holds an MA in social policy and administration from the University of London, UK, granted by the British Council Chevening programme. He has worked in several civil society organizations: as a full-time researcher at FUNDAR and GESOC, and as a director at Propuesta Cívica and Coalición Ciudadana por la Educación. His work has focused on public policy and budget design and implementation from a human rights perspective, on monitoring public expenditure and social welfare programmes, on monitoring budget transparency, and on education reform, political reform and civic participation. In these subjects, he has attended conferences and given lectures to a wide range of audiences: international organizations such as UNDP, UNDESA, the Inter-American Development Bank, the International Budget Project, the International Association for Feminist Economics; the Mexican government and Mexican Congress; universities such as El Colegio de México and FLACSO; the Federal District Human Rights Commission; as well as several CSOs through community workshops. He has been a volunteer for eighteen years in institutions focused on children and young people.

INDEX

About Zed Books

Zed Books is a critical and dynamic publisher, committed to increasing awareness of important international issues and to promoting diversity, alternative voices and progressive social change. We publish on politics, development, gender, the environment and economics for a global audience of students, academics, activists and general readers. Run as a co-operative, Zed Books aims to operate in an ethical and environmentally sustainable way.

Find out more at:

www.zedbooks.co.uk

For up-to-date news, articles, reviews and events information visit:

http://zed-books.blogspot.com

To subscribe to the monthly Zed Books e-newsletter, send an email headed 'subscribe' to:

marketing@zedbooks.net

We can also be found on **Facebook**, **ZNet**, **Twitter** and **Library Thing**.